SAM SMOLIK

THE
DAILY PURSUIT
OF
EXCELLENCE

THE **4** LEADERSHIP KEYS TO
ACHIEVING SUPERIOR PERFORMANCE

2ND EDITION

Endorsements

"So much of business literature is theoretical and untested. When you invest 50 years of your life into something with the passion and skill of Sam Smolik, amazing things happen. Businesses have been improved and transformed, people have been changed, and most importantly, through his focus on safety, lives have been saved. I am grateful that he took the time to document this for the rest of us, allowing his impact to continue. Very well done!"
– Kevin Garland, Chief Executive Officer, Mountaire Farms

"By collecting decades of experiences in his book, *The Daily Pursuit of Excellence,* Sam Smolik created the definitive blueprint for manufacturing excellence. It simplifies the complexities of operating discipline into a step-by-step instruction manual that both the newest and most seasoned professionals can immediately use. Sam's fun stories, simple wisdoms, and insightful perspective will change the way you think, improve your organization's performance, and is a book that every new person should read on day one of his/her career."
– Dustin Olson, Chief Executive Officer, PureCycle Technologies

"To read this book is to know Sam Smolik—honest, open, straightforward, and sincere who cares for and enjoys people. As a close friend for over 60 years, I believe I'm qualified to offer this insight on the man. Sam has always been a leader, but a leader that made others feel like they were. His story telling technique is backed by hard guidance and real examples to cover complex topics in a way that the reader can enjoy and perhaps absorb. For many readers, this is an opportunity to benefit from an industry executive that you never had the chance to interview."
–David Zimmerman, PE and Former Group President, KBR, Inc.

"I wish *The Daily Pursuit of Excellence* had been available and part of the required reading list when I was in business school. It doesn't matter if you are just starting your career or if you are a CEO, Sam Smolik's book is a must read. It clearly illustrates how to achieve Operational Excellence, which should be the ultimate goal of any business or organization."
–Rogers Hoyt, Jr., Chairman of the Board, Ducks Unlimited, Inc.

"Having the privilege of knowing Sam for over forty years, not only working for him early in our careers but later having him serve on one of my public company boards, I can attest to the power of his design and execution in improving business performance. His book accomplishes what hundreds of other publications have attempted to do, which is to simplify and clearly state how to achieve step change in an organization. This is an excellent read for not only senior leaders in an organization but also for mid and entry level personnel looking for ways to affect change with positive results."
–Charlie Shaver, Chairman and Chief Executive Officer, Nouryon Chemicals (Carlyle Private Equity)

"Having spent a couple decades behind the curtain at the enterprise-level with some of the world's most advanced Operational Excellence-driven companies (e.g., Chevron, ExxonMobil, LyondellBasell, etc.), I am comfortable concluding that Sam's book is the most comprehensive on the topic—from the tactics and anecdotes for leaders to the strategies and philosophies behind the best Operational Excellence Management Systems in industry today."
– Joe Stough, Founder and Former Chief Executive Officer of Syntex

"Sam Smolik is the ideal author of this definitive book on achieving excellence. He combines senior leadership experience at three global energy/chemical companies with a clear, concise writing style. His book is destined to be a best seller on this topic. I highly recommend our clients use Sam's wisdom in how they lead."
–George Pilko, Founder and Chairman, Pilko & Associates

"In his humble, unique way, Sam has turned a lifetime of learning into a must-read book on the essence of common sense in leadership. He has taken a subject many take for granted

and provided a clear roadmap for current and future leaders to achieve Operational Excellence. His passion for leading people leaps off the page and is a powerful, contagious lesson. Thanks Sam, for reminding us that Goal ZERO is achievable through motivating people to perform at their best."
–Chet Thompson, President & Chief Executive Officer, American Fuel & Petrochemical Manufacturers (AFPM)

"Sam's passion for safety really comes through in this book. Safety performance is about leadership, culture, processes, and discipline. This book is a very practical guide for achieving excellence in performance."
– Bob Patel, Chief Executive Officer, W. R. Grace, and former Chief Executive Officer, LyondellBasell

"Built on his experience as a successful senior operations executive and influential board member, Sam Smolik's practical advice on leadership and driving outstanding business performance is an invaluable guide for executives of all levels and industries. This book is a must read for anyone seeking to take his/her organization to the next level of performance and competitive differentiation!"
–Robert W. Bryant, Former Chief Executive Officer, Axalta Coating Systems

"*The Daily Pursuit of Excellence* challenges all organizations to raise operational performance expectations and provides a roadmap/framework to meet these high-performance aspirations—no injuries, no defects, no missed opportunities. The book is a "toolbox" of ideas (drawn from Sam's personal experiences) on how to fully support and bring out the best in team members. Leaders at all levels can benefit from Sam's experiences and suggestions here."
– Phil Hawk, former Chairman and Chief Executive Officer, TEAM, Inc.

"Sam Smolik was my very first management new hire at LyondellBasell after I was brought in to help the company recover and emerge from bankruptcy. Our employees led the way with best-in-class operational performance, cost structure and most importantly, industry leading safety results. "
– James Gallogly, Former Chief Executive Officer, LyondellBasell

"Sam Smolik is a true industry leader with a lot of proven success. His companies have prospered by achieving Excellence. *The Daily Pursuit of Excellence* is strong because it is real event driven with truthful outcomes."
– **Jon Hodges, Founder and Chief Executive Officer, Evergreen North America**

"Sam Smolik's decades of experience in high hazard industries and his passion for safety led him to write this book about achieving excellence. Safety is about culture, people, and a focus on embedding it as a core value. Sam's approach is to make this book a must read for anyone who wants a roadmap for achieving excellence."
– **Katie Mehnert, Chief Executive Officer, ALLY Energy**

"As Sam vividly demonstrates, this book is an indispensable guide for any organization, or individual, considering a move to a culture of excellence. His work is grounded in a robust intellectual framework that leaders can recognize and engage in as a hands-on approach that will interest all shareholders, stakeholders, and leadership teams. I found this book very practical in developing both a company's and an individual's value creation strategy that benefits all stakeholders regardless of market considerations."
– **Tyrone Michael Jordan (TJ), Corporate Board Member and former President & Chief Operating Officer of Dura Automotive Systems**

"Sam Smolik has had a distinguished career and has always been a champion of Operational Excellence. Sam has done an outstanding job of capturing the lessons learned as well as best practices, not only from his own experience, but also from others in the industry. The principles can be applied to improve business performance in any area. A must read for today's managers."
– **Jeet Bindra, Retired President, Chevron Global Manufacturing**

"It was a privilege for me to work with Sam and contribute to the step change in LyondellBasell's safety performance. He brought leadership and drive to LyondellBasell and changed our safety culture and mindset. Goal ZERO is part of our daily vocabulary and ZERO will be reached in occupational safety, process safety and environment thanks to what Sam brought

to LyondellBasell. His book will help you discover your journey to Goal ZERO. Enjoy!"
– Jean Gadbois, Senior Vice President Manufacturing Europe, Asia, and International, LyondellBasell

"*The Daily Pursuit of Excellence* is a must-read for any leader seeking a shift change in his/her company performance. It guides readers step by step through the delicate journey to Excellence. It reads like a novel and speaks to safety practitioners in very clear and straightforward terms. This Opus demonstrates Smolik's lifetime commitment to the industry and unveils an inspiring legacy to the young generation of Leaders for Excellence. Hats off, Sam. Job well done!"
– William Garcia, Executive Director, Cefic, The European Chemicals Industry Council

"*The Power of Goal ZERO,* Sam's first book, inspired me with safety ideas. I used it as one of the textbooks in my Construction Safety courses to introduce safety culture. The book delivers safety ideas from real cases enabling me to explain safety concepts from different perspectives."
– Dr. Chien-Ho Ko, Director of the Craig and Diane Martin National Center for Construction Safety; Department of Civil, Environmental & Architectural Engineering; University of Kansas

The Daily Pursuit of Excellence will help you gain an edge on your competition, grow your brand, and most importantly, develop a more loyal, engaged workforce. Sam's book offers valuable lessons for business majors who want to launch, manage, or work in successful companies; therefore, I believe it should be required reading in business schools around the country."
– Marianne Gooch, President, DynaComm

Thinking outside the box, challenging the routine, striving to continuously improve, and leading from the front are hallmarks of Sam Smolik. Add to this a unique ability to motivate thousands of staff across all continents and a perfect team player—that is the Sam I knew. Sam has bridged the gap between academic's style of teaching and industry requirements. A must read for all managers who want to achieve lasting success in their operations."
– Ashok Kulkarni, Former Road Safety Manager—Asia, Africa, Middle East & Oceania, Shell International

"This book should be required reading for anyone in operations or EH&S roles, as it will accelerate their understanding of both the systems and the behaviors required to drive improvement. Not only does *The Daily Pursuit of Excellence* clearly describe the mindset required and the justification for setting a goal of zero for undesirable events, but the book also provides a road map to take the necessary steps to get there."
– **Mike McCandless, Managing Director—Operational Excellence/Risk Management, Pilko & Associates**

"Sam knows his stuff. Through his leadership at some of the safest companies in the world, he has reduced risk, saved lives, and driven Operational Excellence. This book describes how to apply the highly successful Goal ZERO approach to both safety and Operational Excellence, all wrapped up in a management system. A must read for leaders committed to world-class performance!"
– **Laurence Pearlman, Managing Director, JMJ Associates**

"Informed by an almost 50-year career of leadership experience with some of the world's most recognized and admired manufacturing companies, Sam has captured the essence of how strong and empathetic leadership can drive sustainable business performance to the highest levels. Sam's blend of strategic intent with real world examples of successes and failures makes for a compelling and inspiring read. Sam gets it!"
– **Don A. Young, Executive Vice President of Environment, Safety, Health & Sustainability, J.M. Huber Corporation**

"Sam's Goal ZERO approach enables teams and organizations to translate their business aspirations into individual and collective actions which very quickly bring tangible improvements. On a personal level, Sam's leadership was second to none and he had the rare ability to take you on a journey with him—you were determined to play your part in making a positive contribution. I highly recommend his Goal ZERO strategy and related actions for making a step-change in any company's organizational effectiveness."
– **Tim Wotton, Head of Communications, Peninsula Petroleum, London**

"I witnessed first-hand the power of Goal ZERO when I went to work for Sam. Goal ZERO is about a complete culture shift in the beliefs workers have regarding how to take the best and safest actions to become excellent in everything they do. The change was remarkable; over time an observable culture shift had taken place. The transformation was one of the most exciting and rewarding experiences of my career."
– **Cynthia Childs, CSP/CIH (retired), Former Americas HSE Director, LyondellBasell**

"Sam Smolik has taken a lifetime of experiences and crafted a toolbox for leaders and aspiring leaders who have the courage to grab the tools, follow the blueprint, and transform the effectiveness and efficiency of their organizations. This book will charm you with its style, capture you with its numerous examples and guide you on a pathway to a better tomorrow. Take a well-deserved break, sit down, and enjoy a challenging read. You'll be glad you did."
– **Alex Pollock, Equipping You, LLC**

SAM SMOLIK

THE
DAILY PURSUIT
OF
EXCELLENCE

THE **4** LEADERSHIP KEYS TO
ACHIEVING SUPERIOR PERFORMANCE

2ND EDITION

Names: Smolik, Sam, author

Title: *The Daily Pursuit of Excellence*:
The 4 Leadership Keys to Achieving Superior Performance
(Second edition of *The Power of Goal ZERO*)

Author: Sam Smolik

Library of Congress Control Number: 2022908201

ISBN: 978-1-7364585-7-0 Hardcover
               978-1-7364585-8-7 Paperback
               978-1-7364585-9-4 eBook

Quality First Publishing
Houston, TX 77056

Book design by Brett Carr, Kodiack Studios.

CONTENTS

Acknowledgments

This book is dedicated to the thousands of people that I worked with throughout my career. My career spanned through three highly reputable companies and with inspirational people all around the world. I worked with many fine people in industry associations for the betterment of the industry as a whole. Extensive global travel was the norm, meeting new people everywhere I ventured to. My approach was to provide collaborative leadership and encouragement while marveling at how well people responded, came together as a team, and came up with creative ideas.

As I was approaching retirement from LyondellBasell, I commissioned a global team to help me build out a comprehensive vision for taking Operational Excellence to the next level. We called the program Technology and Knowledge Management (TKM) and focused on a balanced and integrated approach to Leadership, People, Systems, and Culture. I want to acknowledge the team members for their terrific work: Giorgio Bagni, Rick Beleutz, Shane Fandry, Jean Gadbois, Jim Hillier, Eric Mesle, Tom Myers, Dustin Olson, Patricia Shieh-Lance, and Edwin Stotefalk.

Thanks also go to my many colleagues and friends that read the drafts of my book and provided invaluable feedback for improvement: Ellen Bitterman, Mark Cluff, Bill Cook, Brian Cook, Rebecca Corbin, John Evans, Jean Gadbois, William Garcia, Marianne Gooch, Brett Hafer, Phil Hawk, Jon Hodges, Gary Jones, Tyrone Michael Jordan (TJ), Julie Lautens, Mike McCandless, Mike McGinnis, Katie Mehnert, Tom Myers, Dustin Olson, Laurence Pearlman, Bruce Piasecki, George Pilko, Jan Pilko, Alex Pollock, Emily Boykin Poole, Gerry Scott, Joe Stough, Lara Swett, Bert Visser, Peter Webb, and

David Zimmerman. Writing the book provided us with unique opportunities to share thoughts and ideas. Each of you helped to make the book better, I learned from you, and I am extremely grateful.

Finally, this book couldn't have been written without the support of my terrific wife Stephanie. We've been married for 48 years, and she has been my rock. We've had many terrific experiences traveling the world and are now at the stage of enjoying our grandchildren. Stephanie has been supportive and patient with my many hours of writing, just as she has been throughout my entire career. I am a lucky guy. We are a true partnership.

Foreword

by Bruce Piasecki, AHC Group President and Founder and
New York Times bestselling author

Summary: Sam Smolik has offered a book of significant corporate and social impact. Thirty years from now, in returning to your shelves at office or home, you might say: "I am glad I came across this life summary in 2022." The hashtags of this book include leadership, operational excellence, global firms, competition, and I'd add "compassionate management styles."

Background: I have benefited from knowing Sam since he first worked as a top executive at Dow, when my firm was young. More than thirty years later, Sam Smolik's advice has crystalized in this book. Back about a decade, I knew Sam when he was major senior executive at Shell, where we'd visit him at One Shell Plaza, in the skyrise. He was kind and compassionate and giving then, too. He has always been generous with his time, a fine mentor. And when it came to writing a book, he reached out to me, so the roles switched for a bit. And now we have this fine book before us.

Timing of This Book: This gifted articulate former executive has taught us how to protect the wealth of a global firm with wit, focus, and discipline. After the tragedies at so many failed enterprises—from Volkswagen's emissions scandals to the fraudulent claims of bribery and wrongdoing in other firms—it pays to invest the time to read up and reflect on this life of positive lessons in management. Risk enterprise systems, and the power of gaining leverage over Goal ZERO protocols, are the name of the game today, from Walmart and Unilever to the many smaller firms supplying a world of giants.

In this readable book, Sam gives you a game plan worth delivering on.

Why This Book is Consequential in Business and Society Today: As more and more firms go global, with complex risk enterprise systems, the executives running these firms encounter, every day, new and lasting forms of competitive advantage and significant risk. I've called this management decision-making "in a swift and severe world."

In fact, I am certain that many social ills can only be improved through better corporate management of risks—from poverty to pandemics to social unrest. This is what I called "social response capitalism" in my book, World Inc. Sam has taken the concept and operationalized it, internalized all this into how a global firm must operate.

Ignoring Sam's advice comes at a cost, coast to coast. You can run into a wall faster than ever before or begin an ascent of magnifying consequences. Everything is faster and more furious in a sense, but getting the systems right in the first place matters more than ever. In between these two goal posts of prevention and performance, you will find survival, failure, and the accumulation of great wealth. Sam Smolik's career and work is about finding that exact middle, the sweet spot of Operational Excellence.

In this book before you—a smart book—Sam has written an available, well-researched, and important summary of how to enhance your performance and the performance of your organization. You can think of this as a sustained tutorial you will never forget. He even starts from his early Boy Scout experiences and those as a quarterback on his high football team. There is a down-home sportiveness to his earnest portrayal of what works. This is not a dry book; instead, it is full of nutrition for the aspiring manager and executive.

Academic thinkers called the transformation to these higher performance standards "good to great" (Jim Collins), or "re-engineering" your firm. Those frames only take you so far into the realm of the aspirational. Smolik takes you over the goal line. The voice in this book is valid, authentic, and of consequence. It does not surprise me to learn that Sam Smolik—after Dow, Shell, and LyondellBasell—serves on corporate boards. We are all lucky he has now taken the time to write this book based on so much experience doing.

How He Learned to Make the Complex Simple Again:
Sam learned his lessons from being a Vice President of
Environment, Health, and Safety at Dow, then Shell, and
finally at LyondellBasell. Each stage of his career becomes a
springboard for intelligent narratives about what works and
what does not in managing complex organizations. It is fun to
collect these asides and tales, along with the larger argument.

The Daily Pursuit of Excellence is a master's guidebook on
how to achieve superior performance in every sense of the
phrase "achieving results." What do you think about when
you think of mastery? I can see Sam passing efficient spirals,
making the right moves for short-yard gains and the long-term
wins. Mastery is about achieving results even in the thorny and
the rough and the tumble. He thinks on his feet in this book
but always with sound principles and steady footing in fact and
management experience. He will teach you how to be adept in
the short run and adaptive in the long.

The key components of this book are available for your
reflection in the Table of Contents. View its intelligence as one
found in the best-designed menus. You have a feast of options
before you; but Sam makes the sequence of what to learn
digestible and actionable. Read this book from start to finish,
as I have in its early drafts to this complete formulation.

Preventing Something from Going Wrong: Sustainable
organizations require a great deal of effort. As Sam aptly notes,
this effort must be sustained with "a passion for leadership and
people." It is a happy day when a book like this comes out as it
helps us all have faith in the future and look around the corner
of our firms with wealth, result, and satisfaction before us.

While it is accurate to say the bulk of this book is about
preventing something from going wrong, it is much about what
is right. You get the feeling of this in a passage on balance,
where Sam talks about how he coached his son's baseball team
for nine years, despite all his other obligations.

You can see these values and principles in this life work of
Sam Smolik. I trust you will benefit from reading this book and
enjoy and cherish it as much as I have.

Introduction

The Daily Pursuit of Excellence is the second edition of my first book, *The Power of Goal ZERO*. In the first edition, the focus was primarily on improving an organization's performance and achieving Operational Excellence. In this second edition, I have increased the focus on *you*. This book will help you to increase your effectiveness, influence those around you, improve your opportunity for advancement, and contribute to the success of your company. The book will also help you to understand how successful companies operate and to connect the dots of why things are done a certain way.

I was fortunate to spend a career with three leading international companies: Dow Chemical, Shell, and LyondellBasell Industries. I served as Global Vice President for each of these companies in a variety of Manufacturing, Environment, Health, Safety, Security, Operational Excellence, and Sustainable Development roles. My job was to help drive Operational Excellence and performance improvement globally and reduce the risk of terrible reliability, quality, and safety incidents from occurring. I wrote this book to share the tips and techniques that we found to be most effective. If you are advanced in your career, these tips will help to reinforce your current efforts. For those of you beginning your careers, the learnings and techniques will provide an awesome jump start for you.

While reading, think in terms of your particular business. The principles and examples are universal and apply to good leadership in every context. If you work in a manufacturing or service company, a hotel, a restaurant, a department store, or any other kind of business, the concepts will help you and your company to improve. I use real life examples to provide context and help to illustrate key points.

My career offered the opportunity for me to interact with and learn from literally thousands of individuals around the world. I am still learning today from my board of director experiences. I've met excellent people on every continent and learned that good ideas come from a wide variety of places. My constant obsession was to capture all of these good ideas and best practices and leverage to others. I was fortunate to have a job in which my team and I were able to assemble these practices into a common, global way of doing work—a management system. I now feel uniquely qualified to share these learnings for your benefit.

There isn't a silver bullet to achieving excellence. Many people and organizations work hard, but don't have a focus on the right areas. We learned to simplify the approach by a daily pursuit of excellence in 4 key focus areas—leadership, people, systems, and culture. These four focus areas are interrelated and impact each other in powerful ways. You must have a good management system that contains the expectations for how work should be done, a strong culture that supports the system, people that deliver results, and of course, strong leadership.

In this book, I will help you to understand how the most successful companies operate. I'll describe the importance of the 4 key focus areas and provide numerous tips and suggestions under each area. This book will help you to understand how you can have influence in each area and improve the performance of both yourself and your organization. If everyone in the organization understands these concepts, demonstrates ownership, and works daily on each one, amazing results will come. The book can serve as an ongoing reference as you progress through your career.

Since the launch of the first book, I've continued to see organizations with poor results. I've seen devastating and tragic incidents impacting individuals and organizations across all industries. People have needlessly lost their lives or been severely injured due to lack of discipline, poor practices, a culture of sloppiness, and a variety of other reasons. Quality problems have created significant issues with customers and disrupted supply chains. Top tier football teams have won a major game one week and then fallen apart the next. The coaches and players don't seem like the same team week to week. It's obvious that some individuals and leaders don't "get it" and don't understand what it takes to achieve consistency in performance on a regular basis.

Each of the readers of this book will be at different stages in his or her careers and will be working in different industries.

Therefore, to help level set and get everyone on the same page, here are a few important terms and definitions that will be used throughout the book:

- **Operational Excellence**—This is an overarching term and strategic objective for an organization. Quality, service, reliability, customer satisfaction, safety, and cost control all fall under the umbrella of Operational Excellence. This singular term helps create alignment and a clear expectation of performance excellence for people and the organization.

- **Management System**—A *management system* defines how things "should be done." A good system is a standardized way of doing work and should be simplified as much as possible. The management system is an organized collection of the company vision, mission, strategy, code of conduct, technology, standards, requirements, procedures, tools, and many other items. The elements of a system build on best practices and provide clear expectations for people in the organization. A good management system should be an active component of everyday work and must be continually maintained and updated.

- **Culture**—The *culture* in an organization defines how things "are actually done." The way people behave, the way people treat each other, their sense of ownership, their focus on the customer, their performance, and their insistence on excellence are all indicators of the culture in an organization.

This book is designed to help you and your colleagues create a *culture of excellence*. A culture of excellence establishes the environment for achieving extraordinary results. You want a culture in which every person acts like an owner, meets the organization's expectations, conducts him or herself in the right manner, treats each other with respect, and exceeds customers' needs. If you get the culture right, everything else becomes much easier.

In many organizations, there is a disconnect between the expectations of the company and the culture. When the culture and norms do not match the strategy and expectations in an organization, success is difficult to achieve. When people's behaviors and work are aligned with the expectations of the organization's management system, you are on your way to achieving a *culture of excellence.*

I felt the sense of urgency to take this book to the next level and help get the key points across in a clearer manner. I want you to be the best you can be and to drive rapid progress and transformation with the people you work with. You can make an incredible impact as an individual and as an influential leader no matter what your position is in your organization. I've seen the power of individual leadership at all levels in driving and achieving excellence. You can make a positive difference with others, whether on or off the job. Further, if you develop a coalition of like-minded individuals, you can help your company create a culture that's fun to work in, achieves excellence at all times, and wins. The culture in some of the best departments I've worked in was driven from the bottom up.

My greatest pleasure from the first edition of my book was getting feedback from readers. One person, early in her career, said the book totally changed her way of thinking. She said the book helped her to understand the big picture and to see why matching the culture with the expectations of an organization is so important. Small business leaders said they began applying the principles immediately. Many leaders in companies bought the book for their employees and said they were using the book to create alignment on their approach to excellence.

An interesting approach in several companies has been to organize group discussions around a particular section of the book. The section in the book provides the basis for the discussion, but, more importantly, the people discuss what they are doing regarding the particular topic and ways they can improve. Some universities are beginning to use the book in their classes and listing the book as required leadership reading. The overall feedback has been overwhelming and extremely gratifying.

Instead of writing a new book, I decided to make this one better. In this second edition, many new stories and techniques have been added for establishing the system and culture necessary for individuals and organizations to truly achieve excellence. You will learn some new techniques and be reminded of concepts that you already know. Use this book as a reference and refer back to it often.

Simplicity is a key theme in the book. Simplified procedures, processes, programs, and systems are always better for improved understanding and comprehension. The four keys to successful organizations are summed up in my Operational Excellence Model formula:

Operational Excellence =
Leadership + People + Systems + Culture

It's vitally important to understand the importance each of these components plays in achieving excellence. This high-level concept is simple and easy to remember. Simply put, *the culture and systems help create an environment in which leadership and people work and deliver superior performance.*

I've organized the chapters in the book to provide tips and suggestions for how you can drive progress within each of these tenets of the Operational Excellence Model. Make no mistake, achieving excellence is hard work and requires a daily, relentless pursuit. Utilizing a proven framework helps your organization to maintain a balanced focus on the areas that will accelerate improvement and help you to achieve success.

The Daily Pursuit of Excellence is a condensed version of successful techniques learned in a 50+ year career of helping to drive improvement in multinational organizations. The book describes a practical way to be a results focused leader and drive safety, reliability, quality, and superior performance. I provide a lot of large company examples, but the principles apply in all sizes of organizations.

The topics covered in this book help drive behavior and culture change in a positive way. Important concepts include building on a common theme, utilizing consistent terminology, driving simplicity, listening, communicating, and remaining practical.

"Safety" is used as an example or metaphor throughout the book. You must never allow anyone to get seriously injured. A serious injury impacts everyone: the injured person, family, friends, and co-workers in the organization. "Nothing is more important than the safety of our employees, customers, and the public." You hear this quite often. Some people just say it, but I want you to live it every day.

Safety is a *value* in an organization. If you understand this concept, then you will understand the value that culture plays in an organization. Culture becomes the company, thereby helping to drive Operational Excellence and Goal ZERO performance.

A key message of the book is that the *pre-conditions for achieving excellence in safety are the same as for achieving excellence in everything else.* You need strong leadership, competent people operating flawlessly, a good management system of best practices, solid technology, well-maintained assets, and a winning culture.

When you have each of these, you will not only achieve superior safety performance, but you will also *reduce defects, increase reliability, improve quality, lower costs, enhance the customer experience, and drive value to the bottom line. It makes perfect sense to passionately lead with safety.* Leading with safety protects people and also helps to achieve the other objectives important to your organization. When you read the examples regarding safety, challenge yourself to also think in terms of the other performance areas that are important to you.

My approach in the book is to illustrate key concepts in short, practical sections. I could have gone into much more detail in each section, but the book would have been too long. I utilize personal stories and anecdotes to illustrate the context and provide examples of how you, too, can help create a culture of excellence at any level. Imagine yourself in a similar situation when you read the stories. Demonstrating leadership and providing a sense of ownership for individuals at all levels are important elements for success. You want everyone to act as if they were an owner.

The principles enable rapid transformation in any organization. In today's competitive environment, individuals and organizations must be best in class to compete and win.

This book is written with great humility. I certainly don't want to give the impression that I have all the answers or that these recommendations are the only way to conduct your business. My life lessons have come from the school of hard knocks. I made many mistakes along the way and learned from each one. You may not agree with some of the recommendations and that's okay; diversity of thought is good and an important part of achieving excellence.

My stories and experiences are openly shared in the spirit of learning and improving, especially for young people. I use "we" throughout the book to describe examples because our terrific teams developed the processes together and drove results.

I'll also admit that I learned a lot while writing this book as I researched deeper into various topics. Giving presentations to organizations for the first edition of the book and listening to feedback also provided learning experiences. Hopefully, you will use this book as one of your key references and as a virtual mentor throughout your career.

We've all read many books on leadership and organizational effectiveness throughout our careers. I always felt if I learned one or two tips, then buying and reading the book was worth my time. I guarantee you will take away more than one or two tips and best practices that you can begin implementing today.

CHAPTER 1

Leadership Begins With You

"The most powerful leadership tool you have is your own personal example."
– John Wooden

"Let go of who you think you're supposed to be; embrace who you are."
– Brene' Brown

I'm a strong believer in the power of leadership at all levels. Individuals in any position in an organization can show leadership and work with a sense of ownership. Never underestimate the impact *you* can have on establishing a culture of excellence in your workplace.

This chapter is about you and becoming effective in your personal life and contributing significant value to your organization. Don't wait for others; take initiative to make the right things happen. No matter what your position is, or the size of your organization, you can be a results focused leader. This chapter includes life examples that I'll share to help you, as an individual, improve the quality of your work, provide leadership, and influence others.

The third manufacturing unit that I managed at Dow Chemical was Unit 1 in the Oyster Creek Division of Dow's Texas Operations. Unit 1 produced vinyl chloride monomer, which is an intermediate chemical for the production of polyvinyl chloride (PVC) pipe and other applications. During previous assignments, we spent considerable time aligning the people in the department around a common vision, getting their attitudes and behaviors right, and generally working hard to improve the morale and performance. However, I quickly realized that Unit 1 was different and already had a culture of excellence, and the culture was being created and led from the bottom up.

The superb technicians in the unit such as Gene Roberts, Jim Talbert, Bert Robles, and many others personally led a strong culture of caring for and helping each other, on and off the job. These people were proactive in everything they did, always looking for what needed to be done to make the unit better. Their attitudes and behaviors were contagious. These technicians were experts at their jobs and had enormous pride in their workplace. Unit 1 was an incredible place to work because of the people. These folks made my job much easier to focus on the important, high-level objectives such as technology improvement that took our plant to the next level of performance. The people in Unit 1 demonstrated leadership at all levels in every sense.

You can have an incredible impact on those around you. Your qualities, characteristics, and values all matter. These all begin to develop in early childhood and it's never too late to improve. Character begins with you as a person. Are you trustworthy, honest, and truthful at all times? On the job, be honest with your boss and your customers about little things as well as big things. Regardless of the pressure or temptation to make yourself or your company look better, don't risk credibility by lying, exaggerating, or misleading. Tell the whole story.

There are many short phrases that impact our thoughts and behaviors. I was active in Boy Scouts and was fortunate to earn the rank of Eagle Scout. One of the lessons from my early Boy Scout days comes from the Scout Promise, *I promise that I will do my best*. This phrase seems simple and yet is so powerful. That's all that we can do and all that we can ask from others.

Another good lesson is from the Boy Scout motto, *Be Prepared*. Learn all that you can about your job or project that you are working on. Keep yourself physically and mentally prepared. Be aware of what might go wrong and take precautionary steps to reduce the risks. Make sure you are well prepared for any task or job that you undertake.

Quality performance as an individual is critical if you ever expect to be successful in your endeavors. My father always told me, "Sam, if you are going to do something, do it the right way." I learned this at an early age. Doing quality work builds self-confidence and others around you see it. I always used to tell my children, "Don't leave a trail." Do quality work and clean up after yourselves. Check your work, avoid misspelled words in documents and letters you write, and try to minimize mistakes.

I spent the first seven years of my career in Research and Development. We were taught to conduct an extensive literature search before working on any new technology development. Build on what is already known rather than reinventing the wheel. When I transferred to my first manufacturing assignment, I asked one of the most respected plant managers for any advice he could give me. His advice was simple: "Learn everything you can about the unit where you will be working. Learn the technology, every piece of equipment, every line, and every valve in the plant. Become an expert in whatever you do." That was some of the best advice I ever received, and it served me well throughout my career. This was easy for me because I've always been naturally curious and inquisitive.

Be a continual learner. Lifelong learners enjoy their work more. Be careful of the people that think they know it all. Be totally competent at what you are doing and don't fake it. Build a strong basis of competence that creates a foundation for driving excellence. This applies to all types of work. Learn everything you can about your business and your work.

Time flies, so never waste a day. No matter how much time you have wasted in the past, you still have a full tomorrow. Effective time management is essential. Develop a good understanding of your priorities and what you want to accomplish. Spend your time laser focused on your priorities and avoid distractions. Be organized and disciplined. Focus on what only you can do and be careful not to get too bogged down in low value activities.

In this chapter, I'll cover topics such as integrity, values, credibility, passion, courage, being bold, time management, life balance, being proactive, sense of urgency, modesty and being humble, and communication. There is so much wisdom to be shared about leadership, but remember that it all begins with you as a person. *What are your values? Do you have integrity? Can people depend on you? Do you do what you say you are going to do?*

The example you set for others is critical. Don't wait to be told what to do; look for what needs to be done. Be proactive and go the extra mile. Willingly take on ownership and responsibility. Hold others to a high standard. Whether you realize it or not, others see what you do and how you conduct yourself. Your actions influence others. Know where you are going and what you want to accomplish, and make sure your current actions and behaviors are aligned with your goals. Remember that you are either gaining or losing ground every day.

People rarely accomplish anything by themselves. Learn from others and don't worry about who gets the credit. Give credit to others; it's always better to give than to receive. Set a positive example and be helpful to others. Always treat people with respect. You will often hear that the top reason for people leaving a company is their supervisor.

If you are currently in a leadership role or aspire to be, always evaluate your own behaviors first. Leaders must be absolutely committed to excellence themselves and expect excellence from others in even the smallest of things. These principles apply whether you are a single contributor, simply doing your job, or leading others. Gain the respect of others, make a positive difference, and be a role model. A good leader can inspire everyone in an organization to achieve his or her very best

The lessons in this book will help you to understand how everything fits into the big picture. If you aren't in a supervisory role, be patient, do quality work, and continue to develop your skills. Be a leader at whatever you do, and others will notice. This book can serve as a reference guide as you grow and progress up the ladder. The quote from Jack Welch is a good one: "Before you are a leader, success is all about growing yourself. When you become a leader, success is about growing others." Eventually you may land the top job.

Personal Values

Continue to shape and live up to your values. My values were heavily shaped by my parents, my faith, the Boy Scouts, and my competitive spirit from playing sports. Values are embedded in each of us at a very early stage in our lives. I'm sure that the Ten Commandments kept me out of a lot of trouble growing up.

For those of you who are parents, the values that your children will develop are largely in place by the age of 12. Utilize every tool and resource that's available and don't waste a day.

I've always approached life with a goal to be honest and ethical, and to always do my best. The Boy Scout Law includes quality values for anyone, and we always tried to live up to each of them:

A Scout is trustworthy, loyal, helpful, friendly, courteous, kind, obedient, cheerful, thrifty, brave, clean, and reverent.

My Boy Scout experiences taught lessons which have remained throughout my life. One is simply to leave your campsite cleaner than when you found it. Don't make excuses if the campsite isn't clean when you show up. Just clean it up—just do it! This philosophy definitely applies to every workplace and in every environment. If something needs to be done, don't complain, just do it. People don't like to hear excuses.

As we progress through life, we face many challenges to our values. It's not easy at times and the choices we make have long lasting consequences. Our friends and people we work with face these same challenges, especially leaders of companies in responsible positions.

I'll tell you a story while working at Dow that was a turning point in my career. I was blessed to have many superb supervisors and leaders. These leaders were tough, challenging, and demanding, and we always performed our work in an ethical manner. We followed the Dow and legal requirements at all times. I was happy and proud at the time to be working for Dow.

After several years of operations management, I became the Environmental Manager for Dow's Texas Operations in Freeport, Texas in 1994. At the time, Texas Operations was one of the largest chemical manufacturing complexes in the world with over 5,000 employees and 90 operating units. My predecessor in the role told me that one of the most important aspects of the Environmental Manager job was to manage risk. One of those risks he was referring to was legal compliance. Previously, I only knew one way, and that was full legal compliance. Well, it didn't take me long to understand what he was talking about.

One of the facilities was the magnesium production unit. Magnesium is a lightweight metal used in aircraft and other applications. The plant had been constructed in six months during World War II for the war effort. I quickly learned that the unit had many areas of potential noncompliance with the relatively new Environmental Protection Agency (EPA) regulations. The magnesium plant had been constructed long before any of these new regulations were enacted. This potential legal noncompliance was contrary to everything I had been accustomed to. I was very uncomfortable with this situation.

At the time, the Texas Operations site was led by a four-member Texas Operating Board (TOB). After considerable thought, I went to the TOB that had placed me in the job. Being careful on how I addressed the issue, I reminded them that I was new in the job and asked their advice. I asked them, "What should be my approach if I were to find a unit with major legal noncompliance, requiring potentially millions of dollars to remedy and possibly put the unit out of business?"

To my pleasure, each member of the TOB didn't hesitate and adamantly said they expected full compliance with the law, no matter the cost or consequences. The TOB showed strong leadership, integrity, and tone at the top. My predecessor had mistakenly thought that he was doing good by "managing the risk" of noncompliance. This experience demonstrated how often disconnects exist between top leadership and people down in the organization. We began addressing each of the potential noncompliance issues resulting in the magnesium plant closure within the next two years.

The purpose of this story is to illustrate the power of good values and strong leadership. Throughout my many years of global leadership in major multinational companies, I came across many challenging issues. I always researched each issue heavily so that I was personally comfortable with the right position to take. I was never going to provide leadership for any products or operations that I felt would endanger our employees, the public, or the environment.

This stance took courage, perseverance, and considerable discussion on many significant issues. My values, constancy of purpose, and strong executive leaders above and around me always helped to prevail. I rest well at night knowing that we did things the right way, and you can too.

EXCELLENCE NUGGET:
*Establish, understand,
and be true to your values.*

Integrity and Credibility

This section discusses the importance of your individual integrity and credibility. It doesn't matter if you are an individual contributor or aspire to be in leadership roles; integrity and credibility impact your reputation and have a significant impact on your success or failure. Your reputation is precious, so work on it proactively. These definitions are very important:

- **Integrity.** The quality of being honest and having strong moral principles.
- **Credibility.** The quality of being trusted and believed in.

The Code of Conduct in most companies is well written. This document reflects the expectations of the company. Read the code carefully and comply with it.

Truthfulness and honesty are essential. Many people get themselves into trouble because they don't want to deliver bad news. They tell "little white lies" or don't tell the whole story, leaving out pertinent facts. Always remember that people get over bad news, but they never get over being lied to. You will have a very difficult time rebuilding your reputation once you become known for not telling the truth.

A good practice is to always look at a particular situation from the other person's point of view. What information would he or she like to have and know about? Holding back pertinent information is often considered as bad as lying. Provide the bad news and full story right away, and then get on with correcting the situation.

Do what you commit to do, such a simple statement that is often not followed. If you commit to a certain action with your boss, make the action a high priority to get it done. If he or she asks you several times if the task has been done, you are already in trouble.

Be competent at what you do. Too many people try to get by and fake their way. Most people can see right through this charade. Whatever your line of work, learn everything you can about your job and become an expert.

Be principle focused, especially when making decisions. People often make a short-term decision that they later regret. If you face a difficult decision, don't just take the easiest path. Consider the impact the decision will have on your reputation and ensure you will be comfortable with the decision. How will you feel later when you look at the decision in your rearview mirror?

Finally, as a leader, be as honest with people as you possibly can. Honesty makes your job easier because you never have the difficulty of remembering what you told someone the last time you were together. Sometimes, of course, you have confidential information that you can't divulge. In these situations, you simply say that you can't talk about it at the current time. Never lie to your people. Tell the truth, tell the whole story, be trustworthy, increase your competency, deliver on your commitments, and remain genuine. All of these qualities will serve you well.

EXCELLENCE NUGGET:
Your reputation depends on integrity and credibility.

Passion

I heard a story long ago that illustrates the importance of passion for your work. Oscar and George were maintenance workers for the railroad. One day while they were working on the railroad track, a car drove up and John, the CEO of the railroad, stepped out. John knew George very well, and they began talking about old times. After the CEO left, Oscar asked George in amazement, "How do you know the CEO of the company?" George told him, "John and I started working together in the maintenance department many years ago. However, there was one major difference—it was just a job for me; I was working for $2.50 an hour. John, on the other hand, was **working for the railroad.** John had passion for the work he was doing and did everything he could to help make the company better from the very beginning. He loved his work and did whatever it took."

John is the type of person you want in your organization. Find people that don't just approach their work as a job. Find and develop those that demonstrate a daily drive to take ownership and make the workplace better. People that you have to constantly push certainly don't have the passion you are seeking.

Passion for work is when you can't wait to get started every morning. Passion for your family is when you can't wait to go home at the end of the day to be with them. Develop passion in all aspects of your life. When people have passion for something, they will do whatever it takes with persistence and enthusiasm. They create a sense of "Flow," which I will describe later in Chapter 3. Whether you are performing a task, leading a project, running a department, or you are the CEO, do it with passion.

Every results focused leader I know has passion for what he or she is doing. These leaders have a vision, are decisive, and are willing to make tough decisions. Passion for achieving excellence is contagious and is an effective enabler. Passionate people drive culture and culture drives behavior. Passion leads to so many terrific results: pride in your work, self-satisfaction, self-esteem, and successful outcomes. People without passion don't do great things. Whatever you do, do it to the best of your ability, and always do it with passion.

EXCELLENCE NUGGET:
Be passionate with your life's activities.

Courage

Around three weeks after I became Vice President of Environment, Health, and Safety (EH&S) at Dow, our CEO scheduled a meeting to approve the purchase of a manufacturing unit from another company. The purpose of the meeting was to assure all details had been addressed and everyone was in alignment. In preparation for the meeting, I met with our EH&S due diligence team for an update on their review of the acquisition.

To my disappointment, the due diligence team stated that the plant had phosgene reactors, which had stress corrosion cracking. Phosgene is an intermediate chemical which is extremely toxic and potentially deadly if inhaled. Stress corrosion cracking can lead to sudden and unexpected equipment failure. At Dow, we would have never operated equipment in such a state. To complicate matters, the population surrounding the plant had been moving closer to the site over time.

The due diligence team said they had communicated this defect to the commercial team in charge of the acquisition, and the commercial team said they had committed money to replace the reactors. However, the timeline for replacement was over a year.

Prior to the executive leadership meeting, I met with the Vice President of the business who was in charge of the deal. In our discussion, I told him I couldn't support the acquisition and operate the plant with the reactors in the current state. He believed that adding money into the budget to repair the problems was good enough. He was extremely furious and said that we had come this far and couldn't stop now. Despite his pressure, I told him that I was going to voice my opinion in the upcoming meeting.

During the executive review meeting, I explained that I had just become aware of the proposed transaction and was informed about the stress corrosion cracking issue prior to the meeting. From my experience, I wouldn't operate the plant in such a manner and have the risk of catastrophic failure with potentially serious consequences to the safety of our employees and the public.

To my surprise, my comments were the first time the CEO and the Vice President of Manufacturing had heard about the issue. The Vice President of the business said that we were getting the plant for 50 cents on the dollar. I said that I wouldn't take the plant for free and that's probably why it was being sold so cheap. The selling company obviously understood the risks. In the end, we stopped the deal and didn't make the acquisition. Incidentally, the plant was never sold and was shut down by the owner and dismantled a short time later.

The important learnings from this experience were:

- You must have ***courage*** to speak up, even when you are the lone voice in the room on a particular issue. Never remain quiet if doing so threatens your integrity. These jobs are not a popularity contest.
- **Processes** should be in place to identify and manage risks. In the above example, issues such as the stress corrosion cracking should have been elevated to the appropriate decision makers much sooner in the process.
- **Scorecards** can sometimes drive the wrong behavior. Even though the Vice President of the business knew about the safety concerns, his scorecard was to grow the business. Checks and balances in an organization are important and powerful.

Modest and Humble

A year after I began my career with Dow, I was assigned a project to lead the design, construction, and operation of a small research pilot plant. Our research group in Dow's Texas Operations had a small number of in-house contractor craftsmen that performed work for various projects.

After completing the design, I worked with one of the contractors, Ted, as he built the pilot unit. I was naturally proud of the pilot plant, the first one in which I had primary responsibility. Several of us were talking in the control room about various projects and then it was my turn. I talked about "my" pilot plant that "I had built." Ted was there and started laughing and said, "Sam, I don't remember seeing any wrenches in your hands." He caught me off guard and I was a little embarrassed.

Ted was right. I hadn't physically built the unit or even designed it totally by myself. Ted had physically constructed the unit, and I had received considerable help and advice from my supervisors and others on the design.

I made it a point from that moment on to say "we" instead of "I" when talking about work activities, projects, and accomplishments. Most of the things we do involve some amount of contribution from others. Ted taught a valuable lesson to me that day which has remained with me ever since.

I still hear people overusing the words "I" and "my" in the work environment. Talking in this manner doesn't sound right or come across well to others. Think about how you speak and give credit to others as much as possible. Avoid arrogance.

EXCELLENCE NUGGET:
Be careful saying "I" and "my."

Be a Winner

Be a winner in everything that you do. This means striving for excellence at all times. Winning leaders instill winning attitudes in their people. Richard Denny, the author of Motivate to Win, listed 10 differences between winners and losers:

1. **A winner makes mistakes and says, "I was wrong."** A loser makes mistakes and says, "It wasn't my fault."
2. **A winner credits his good luck for winning even though it wasn't luck.** A loser credits his bad luck for losing, but it wasn't luck.
3. **A winner works harder and has more time.** A loser is always "too busy," too busy staying a failure.
4. **A winner goes through a problem.** A loser goes around it.
5. **A winner says he's sorry by making up for it.** A loser says he's sorry and does the same thing next time.

6. **A winner knows what to fight for and what to compromise on.** A loser compromises on what he should not and wastes time on trivial matters.
7. **A winner says, "I'm good but not as good as I ought to be."** A loser says, "Well, I'm not as bad as a lot of other people."
8. **A winner looks up to where he is going.** A loser looks down at those who have not yet achieved the position he has.
9. **A winner respects those that are superior to him and tries to learn from them.** A loser resents those that are superior to him and tries to find fault.
10. **A winner says, "There ought to be a better way of doing it."** A loser says, "Why change it? That's the way it's always been done."

Leadership at All Levels

Achieving excellence in any organization requires strong leadership. I'm talking about *leadership at all levels* setting the right example and driving change. No matter your position in the organization, you should act like an owner and provide leadership to steer the organization in the right direction.

Naturally, the person at the top of a company, department, and location has the position power and the best opportunity for influence. However, I've seen culture driven and changed by individuals down in the organization many times over the years. These individuals influence by their personal power as opposed to positional power.

There are major differences between management and leadership. The concept of *management* is about executing a system and "keeping the trains running on time." However, it takes *leadership* to improve the system and drive transformative improvement. "If the train derails several times during the year, it takes leadership to make the changes that will prevent recurrence." Be a leader and keep driving improvement.

I remember a discussion during my time working for Dow in Europe. My boss at the time was Peter Berner. Peter was terrific, extremely enthusiastic, and motivating. I loved working for Peter. This period was a time of global cost cutting and personnel reduction. Reducing headcount was necessary. Sadly, in some cases, the downsizing was handled poorly by some of the leaders in the company.

Peter said to me, "Sam, I think Dow has lost its heart with the way the company is treating people." I smiled and responded, "Peter, do you think you've lost your heart?" He looked back at me with a puzzled look. "No, I don't think so." From that response, I said, "You definitely haven't. You always treat people with respect." I continued, "Do you think I've lost my heart?" Peter responded, "Absolutely not, but Roger (name changed to protect the innocent) definitely has. Look how bad he's treating his people." I agreed and we continued to discuss individuals that had and had not lost their respect for people.

We concluded that it's not the company but, rather, the people at all levels that shape the culture of a company. The best leaders that I have known always took care of their people even in the most difficult of times. The key for each of us, with the right values and behaviors, is to exert leadership, do our best to influence others, take care of people, and drive the company in the preferred direction.

Don't wait for others to take the lead. You have the ability in your own position to set a high standard and influence others. Set an example for others, conduct yourself with integrity and credibility, and continually push the organization towards the right behaviors.

Listen and Learn from Others

"A wise man is a man who knows he knows not."
– Socrates

I had the privilege to work with, learn from, and influence my counterparts at other companies around the world. This included work with industry associations such as the American Chemistry Council (ACC), American Fuels and Petrochemical Manufacturers (AFPM), American Petroleum Institute (API), European Chemical Association (CEFIC), National Safety Council, and many others. These organizations provided a forum for collectively improving safety performance across the industry.

Interaction with government agencies is vital. We initiated, negotiated, and signed, on behalf of Dow, the first Occupational Safety and Health Administration (OSHA) Voluntary Protection Program (VPP) corporate national agreement in 2003. It's important to work with people in governmental positions from a position of strength—treat them with mutual respect, and don't be subservient. These people have an important job to do, just as you do.

I always began these encounters to learn, not to impress others with what I knew. One of the most recent and powerful industry work groups was the Process Safety Advisory Group, which was co-sponsored by API and AFPM. Jerry Wascom, President of Refining and Supply for ExxonMobil, did a fine job of leading the team. ExxonMobil is an industry leader in process safety management and Jerry understood that, no matter how good your company is, bad things can happen. You must remain diligent and continually work to improve.

We were a working group of executives from several top tier companies. Our focus was on helping to prevent process safety incidents across the industry. We applied our collective knowledge and drove considerable progress in areas such as developing industry standards, sharing best practices and lessons learned, hazard identification, site safety assessments, mechanical integrity, and human factors.

In all of these encounters, I was able to learn from others and help drive improvement—all with the spirit of protecting people. I continued to learn and helped develop our own approach to achieving Operational Excellence. We never wanted to "reinvent the wheel," but, rather, build on our experiences and the experiences of others. Why would you ever want to work hard to develop something that someone else has already done?

Take every opportunity to listen and learn from others. Everyone has something to contribute. Often the quietest people have the most to offer. Get involved in additional activities both within and external to your company. Never stop learning.

Don't Hesitate To Be Bold

"Try and fail, but don't fail to try."
– John Quincy Adams

As a young engineer in research at Dow, I was on a team focused on improving Toluene Diisocyanate (TDI) manufacturing technology. TDI is used in the production of polyurethanes, primarily for flexible foam applications including bedding, furniture, and carpet underlay. TDI is also utilized for coatings, sealants, adhesives, and in transportation applications to make automobile parts lighter. This product leads to improvements in vehicle fuel efficiency, energy conservation, and emission reduction.

Dow purchased the TDI technology and had just commissioned a new production plant. Our department was conducting research on improving yields in the reaction of toluene diamine and phosgene to produce TDI.

The reaction technology involved a large wiped-film mixer that was a huge energy consumer and a maintenance headache. While we were conducting pilot plant runs on various incremental improvements, we had an idea for a different approach to the reactor involving high pressure liquified phosgene. We believed this new technology could eliminate the need for the wiped-film mixer, prevent plugging, and lead to much higher yields. However, this technology entailed a major shift from the existing technology.

We conducted numerous technology reviews with senior management during those days. One frequent attendee was Levi Leathers, a member of the Dow Board of Directors. He was a much older gentleman that had retired from Dow as the Executive Vice President of Manufacturing. Levi had a huge reputation across the company as a tough, smart leader who was very demanding.

I presented a summary of our current research during one of the technology reviews and concluded with future plans. I described our "long-term" plan to evaluate the new liquid phosgene concept. Levi became very interested and asked if I thought it would work, and I answered that I thought it would. He growled as usual and said to move the project up on the priority list and work on it immediately. "Why wait?" he asked. Levi's direction was all it took for our top management to quickly get on board with their support.

To make a long story short, the new technology was a huge success. The wiped-film mixer was eliminated, and the yield increased significantly, generating millions of dollars in increased profit. This new technology was so different from the previous technology that I'm not sure we would have ever tried it if Levi hadn't pushed it through.

The point of this story is to think big, be bold, and take reasonable risks based on the data at hand. Many breakthrough ideas never get implemented because people are too conservative and reluctant to take risks. Another lesson is how much influence an executive leader can have on a young person in an organization. Be bold!

Time Management—Prioritize Your Activities

Time is the most precious commodity we have. We each have 24 hours per day, 7 days per week, and 52 weeks per year— no more, no less. Manage your time carefully and protect the time of others. Avoid distractions. If you haven't done so recently, refresh yourself from one of the many self-help books or classes on time management.

One tip is to constantly keep your goals, plans, and priorities in front of you and stay focused on doing the most important items that will have the most impact on results. Don't let other people fill your agenda with low priority items.

I remember a time management class when I was beginning my career in which the discussion turned into how often we called our mothers on the telephone. Many people said it was difficult to find the time to do so. The instructor said it's all about prioritization. He recommended to change how we described the situation. He said, "If you haven't called your mother for a long time, tell her you haven't called because **everything else is more important.**" He was right. I could never tell my mother she was less important, so I always made it a priority to call her regularly!

The key is to prioritize your activities, stay focused, and maintain a constancy of purpose. This philosophy applies to every aspect of your life.

Life Balance—The Seven Fs

You hear a lot of talk about "work-life balance." I prefer the term "life balance" since work is such a big part of your life. It's important to approach work in a positive manner and as an integral component of your life balance. Work is not just a job; it's a career and something you should look forward to as an everyday part of your life.

There is an essential need to maintain overall balance in your life. One of the models I have followed for many years is the Seven Fs. The Seven Fs come from a good book by Justin Belitz, *Success: Full Living.* The Seven Fs are:

1. Faith
2. Family
3. Friends
4. Finance

5. Future focus
6. Fitness
7. Fun

Faith, family, and friends are obvious and the most important in my opinion. Finance includes managing your money so you can provide for your basic needs. Finance includes the need to work since most of us weren't born rich. Future focus involves planning, goal setting, and constantly checking that you are on the right path and living your life as you want to.

Fitness includes exercise, proper nutrition, sleep, and your emotional state. Your health, energy level, and fitness are extremely important. It's difficult to be an effective contributor if you let your health decline. Take time to exercise, eat right, and get enough sleep. It's not one or the other, but all of the above to maintain peak performance. And fun, we all need it.

Colin Powell was an American politician, diplomat, and retired four-star general who served as the 65th United States Secretary of State. He summed the message up nicely: "Have fun in your command. Don't always run at breakneck speed. Take leave when you've earned it; spend time with your families. Corollary: surround yourself with people who take their work seriously, but not themselves, those who work hard and play hard."

I always worked very hard; no one ever challenged my work ethic. I worked many nights and weekends, but I also used all of my vacation each year. Spending time away from work in the other Seven F categories actually made me much more effective when back at work. My terrific wife, Stephanie, helped me to maintain the balance in our lives.

One story involves our son, Brandon, as he was turning five years old and beginning to play baseball (tee-ball at that age). I loved sports and spending as much time with Brandon as possible, and I was always planning to manage his baseball team. However, his age for beginning baseball came at a time when our manufacturing plant had considerable problems, and we were working late every day. I faced a huge dilemma since I had always planned on managing, but, at the same time, I was needed at work.

I had always promised myself to put our family before work. So, after a lot of deliberation, I went to my boss and explained the situation. I told him I had decided to manage the team which would require me to be at practice and the games on some days at 4:00. I also said I would do whatever it took for the plant which included coming back out to work after practice or games as needed.

To my pleasure, he agreed and said I was doing the right thing. I managed Brandon's teams for nine straight years and enjoyed every minute. And our production plants didn't suffer since I had such a strong sense of ownership and did whatever it took. Of course, I didn't sit around watching much television during those years. You have to prioritize what you do with your time.

I've used this baseball example many times throughout the years when young people told me they didn't have time for their children's activities. These young folks were always surprised and glad to hear my story. You have the time; we all have 24 hours a day. How you spend your time depends on your priorities and effective time management.

The philosophy is to not neglect any of the Seven Fs for very long. There will always be periods of time when any one of the seven dominates. Work may dominate for a while due to a special project or other considerations. Family may dominate at times for a number of reasons. The key is to maintain balance over the long term and make sure you are living up to the values and priorities you have for yourself.

EXCELLENCE NUGGET:
Maintain balance in your life.

Excellence Begins with You
A SUMMARY

- You can be a leader and influence others around you at any level in the organization. Do quality work and maintain an ownership mentality.

- Develop a strong set of values and be true to them at all times. Maintain your credibility and integrity. Be trustworthy and protect your reputation. Show modesty and give credit to others.

- Tell the truth at all times. Be honest and keep people informed, especially with bad news. People get over bad news but won't forget if you hid something from them or lied.

- Be competent in what you do and don't bluff. Never stop learning. Be inquisitive and listen to others.

- Have courage to take reasonable risks based on the information that you have. Think big. Speak up even though you may be the lone voice in the room.

- Manage your time wisely. You have 24 hours a day, just like everyone else. Spend your time on the activities that will make the most positive difference. Avoid distractions.

- Maintain balance in your life. Follow the Seven Fs— Faith, Family, Friends, Finance, Future Focus, Fitness, and Fun.

CHAPTER 2

An Expectation of Excellence

"It's a funny thing about life; if you refuse to accept anything but the best, you very often get it."
–W. Somerset Maugham

Excellence is defined as "the quality of being outstanding or extremely good." Synonyms for excellent and excellence are distinction, first rate, superb, blue chip, choice, first class, five-star, top notch, top shelf, and numero uno. Excellence is inspiring. I love to watch any type of sporting event and see teams and individuals perform to perfection. I enjoy live music and truly appreciate bands in which every performer is doing his or her part superbly. I'm inspired when I see companies or organizations operate with quality performance. Excellence is obvious—you know it when you see it.

People want their company to be excellent, but most companies are good at best. You have to work just as hard to be good as to be excellent. If you have a mediocre organization and have frequent incidents, defects, and problems, you actually work harder dealing with the problems and constantly playing catchup.

If you are going to do something, do it the right way. Excellence begins with you as an individual. *What are your goals in life? What do you really want to achieve? How do you conduct yourself on a daily basis? Do you do what you say you are going to do? Do you deliver quality work at all times? Do you double-check your work to avoid errors? What kind of example do you set for others? What do others see and what would they say about you?* If you address these questions and others in the right manner, and others around you do the same, you are well on your way.

In business, there are many obvious reasons why a drive for excellence is important. One good reason is offensive: excellence positions your organization in a superior manner relative to the competition. Your products and services are best in class and consistently exceed your customers' expectations, resulting in added value creating opportunities.

Another good reason is a defensive one: excellence in your product, services, or operations helps to preserve value in the organization by preventing major problems and defects from occurring. In the book, I'll give several examples of how companies have experienced fatal incidents with workers, significant reputation loss, or billions of dollars in property damage and business interruption from subpar operations. A drive for excellence at all times is the only way to succeed and win.

I have often been asked, "What is most important—safety, quality, productivity, or reliability?" Don't let anyone drag you into this discussion about choosing one or the other. Operational Excellence is the overarching umbrella which means **zero defects in all areas.**

If you don't manage your costs and make a profit, the company won't survive. Issues in quality and reliability will destroy customer satisfaction and customers will run to the competition. Environmental incidents are wrong ethically and will cause you to lose your license to operate. And safety—everyone knows protecting people is paramount, but too many companies get serious only *after* a serious incident occurs. The answer is that you must maintain an intense and sustained focus on achieving Operational Excellence in all areas of your company.

The principles of Operational Excellence work in any type of organization, no matter how large or small. These principles apply to manufacturing, construction, service industries, sports, and nonprofit organizations. To win in business, you must be the best and strive for excellence in safety, profitability, reliability, quality, efficiency, consistency, cost management, and customer satisfaction as well as environmental, social, and governance (ESG) objectives—*all of these.* Excellence in performance for all areas of an organization may sound overwhelming, right? But it doesn't have to be; keep the approach well organized and clear for all.

Operational Excellence doesn't get the attention it deserves in many organizations *until performance declines or something goes extremely wrong.* It's similar in our homes. We take for granted a good supply of running water or electricity until we don't have it; then it becomes urgent.

Top leaders in companies like to focus on the items that create the most excitement—growth, innovation, technology development, mergers and acquisitions (M&A), and creating shareholder value—and so do I. Progress in Environmental, Social, and Governance (ESG) is critically important. Industry 4.0 is one of the new buzzwords focused on digital transformation of the industry and use of artificial intelligence. I contend, however, that you will never be successful in any of these areas and achieve superior performance if you don't have a solid foundation and constant daily pursuit of Operational Excellence in every aspect of your business.

The Operational Excellence Model

Let's turn now to the concept of Operational Excellence. It's important to look at the big picture and understand how everything fits together in developing a world-class, winning organization. I personally feel that a concept should be as intuitive as possible to help people fully endorse it. If you are going to have an impact on people, you need to explain things in a clear manner and check continually for understanding. A high-level framework helps to organize and frame your intentions and activities, which then allows you to go further into details as appropriate.

Achieving Operational Excellence is essential for accomplishing your ultimate objectives of reliability, customer satisfaction, profitability, and growth. An incredible number of factors are important for an organization to win. A disorganized, shotgun approach never works. It's helpful to break down the factors into reasonable and understandable components to ensure the path to excellence in performance becomes clear for all and to help with focus.

Profitability, shareholder value, customer satisfaction, Operational Excellence, safety, and winning are all the *results* of how well an organization performs. Many organizations set long-term goals for these objectives without specific plans of how to achieve them. Some leaders are very articulate and talk a good game, but don't deliver the results. You can't hope and wish your way to good performance, profitability, and winning. To achieve your desired results, it's vital to focus on the drivers that will most impact your ultimate objectives.

With this thought in mind, I created an *Operational Excellence Model,* which serves as a backbone for everything described in this book. The model works in any type of organization, large or small. To succeed, you must strive for excellence in *each* of these four components.

**Operational Excellence =
Leadership + People + Systems + Culture**

These four high level concepts are interrelated and are all critically important. The concepts may seem obvious, but it's incredible how often some get overlooked or don't receive consistent attention. Many leaders focus on some of the concepts, but few organizations have a disciplined approach to all four. Success is not built on one or the other, but all four. The chapters in the book are organized to help you understand how these concepts impact each other and also to provide you with tips and techniques under each of the categories. Let's provide a brief explanation for each element of the model.

> **Leadership**—The importance of leadership in any organization is well understood. Tone at the top is critically important, but you can provide leadership at any level. Just imagine how powerful an organization is when every person exerts individual leadership and acts like an owner. Leadership begins with you.
>
> **People**—The people in the organization do the work, provide the service, and produce the product. An organization is only as good as its people. Recruit and hire the right individuals. Provide them with the skills and competencies they need. Motivate and inspire them to do their best at all times. Recognize and reward desired behaviors and good performance often.
>
> **Systems**—A simplified system of strategy, processes, requirements, technology, and tools helps to build on past learnings and provides a foundation for driving performance to the next level. A management system

provides consistency for the way work is done in an organization. Leadership and people create the elements of the system, and then the system provides guidance for the organization. A good system helps eliminate frustration with individuals by providing them with easy to find tools and instructions they need to do their job. I can't emphasize simplicity enough when it comes to systems. Don't overdo it and create unnecessary bureaucracy. Each of you can contribute to improving your organization's system on a continual basis by giving feedback, providing suggestions, and building on learnings. A management system provides consistency for *how work should be done.*

Culture—Culture works both ways: leadership and people create the culture in the organization, and, alternatively, culture affects the way leaders and people in the organization conduct themselves, especially when no one is watching. You want a robust culture of performance that constantly inspires every individual to take ownership, excel at what he or she does, eliminate defects, and win. An organization doesn't stand a chance of being superior without the right culture. The culture defines *how work is actually done.*

Note the subtle but critically important difference between systems and culture. A system describes *how work should be done* and the culture describes *how work is actually done.* You can have the best strategy and system in the world, but it's useless if people aren't aligned as intended. The culture in the organization is a sign of how people perform on a daily basis. It's important to continually measure the quality of your culture.

You must understand the Operational Excellence Model clearly and be able to explain the model to others. Albert Einstein said, "If you can't explain it simply, then you don't understand it well enough." I'm not aware of many books that deal with these four topics in an integrated manner for achieving Operational Excellence. I saw a void and felt compelled to share the valuable lessons that we have learned in this space. Figure 1 helps to explain how the four elements of the model work together.

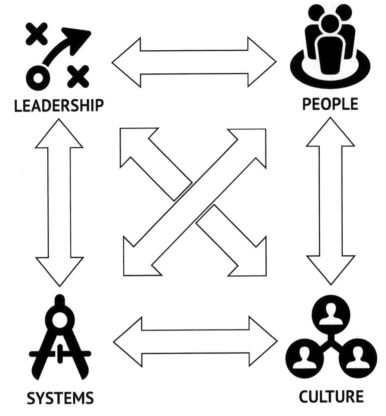

FIGURE 1: THE INTERDEPENDENCY OF LEADERSHIP, PEOPLE, SYSTEMS, AND CULTURE

I can't overemphasize that the elements in the model are totally interdependent. They yield significant results if improved together in an organized manner. Superior companies master all four. Here's an overview of how each of the elements in Figure 1 impact the other three.

- **Leadership**—Everyone understands that everything begins with good leadership. Good leaders begin by creating a strong vision and clear expectations for the organization. The details of the "what" and "how" of these expectations get anchored in the management *system*. Leaders clearly impact the *people* they work with and leaders work hard to create a *culture* of excellence.

- **Systems**—A good management system provides clarity and details for how work should be done. This guidance applies to both *leaders* and the *people* doing the work. If the documents in the management system are easy to understand and readily available, the information will help enable an aligned *culture.* Improvements in the system are continually needed to help drive the desired culture and behaviors of leaders and people.
- **Culture**—The culture in an organization represents the way work is actually done and if desired results are being achieved. When a culture is strong, it has a significant impact on the behavior of all *leaders* and *people* in the organization. New people quickly learn the culture that exists in an organization. If the culture and results in the organization are not matching expectations, *system* changes may be necessary.
- **People**—People do the work and deliver the products and services. In an organization with good transparency, people freely give input, information, and feedback to their *leaders.* Some people in the organization are responsible for developing and maintaining the management *system,* but everyone has a responsibility to provide input for continual improvement of the system. Finally, people's behaviors and actions help create the *culture* of the organization. People at all levels can have a major impact on the culture.

If you are mediocre in any of these four elements, you will *never* achieve world-class performance on a consistent basis. It's about the power of *AND:* leadership, people, systems, *AND* culture.

No matter what your position is in a company, you can make a difference and have a positive impact by applying these principles and influencing others. If you are a member of an organization, you are most likely already working on each of the categories listed above but may have not organized the focus in this way. The remainder of the book continues to discuss the four tenets of the model—leadership, people, systems, and culture—and how, together, they lead to excellence in performance.

Leadership and People

Companies, departments, and teams all consist of people. A collection of individuals from all walks of life come together for a common purpose. I've seen the full range of performance, from totally dysfunctional teams to others in which everyone is totally aligned, driving excellence in performance at all times. People will perform well if they are aligned on a vision of excellence, are excited about the future, understand the clear expectations of the organization, have the skills and competencies to do their job, and are recognized for their contributions.

Here's a story to illustrate the importance of people excellence in an organization. One day while writing this book, my wife, Stephanie, and I were on a trip and had car trouble. We had to spend the night in a hotel while our car was in the shop for repair. I selected a mid-ranged hotel from a leading hotel chain that I like to use. I decided to use hotel points that had been accumulated. That's where the quality problems began.

When I went to the website to reserve the room, the hotel chain's reservation website wasn't working. My next step was to call the hotel chain's 1-800 phone number. The recording said, "Your wait will be 10 minutes." After 20 minutes, I frustratedly hung up the phone and just paid for the hotel room. Once we got into the room, the television remote control didn't work, the hair conditioner dispenser in the shower was empty, the hair dryer was missing, and there was only a sheer, see-through curtain. The blackout curtain was missing for some strange reason and our room was exposed to the ground floor parking lot.

All of these defects by themselves were relatively minor, but the defects all added up to the antithesis of a culture of excellence. Corporate leadership and people didn't properly manage the website and 1-800 telephone number. The staff in the hotel were friendly people but definitely lacked a desire and sense of urgency for meeting the hotel chain's expectation of excellence. Leadership allowed the people and culture to be this way.

Don't allow leadership or people in your organization to operate like this. People make the difference. Leaders need to hire the right individuals, provide clear expectations, teach them about excellence in service, insist on quality performance, and provide continuous feedback and recognition. Chapters 1 to 4 are filled with leadership and people suggestions on how to improve your personal performance and how to motivate and inspire the people you work with.

The System Approach

I love all types of sports and have studied winning teams for many years. There are so many analogies between business and sports. Both have competitors. Both are committed to winning. Both take discipline, talented people, a game plan, and flawless execution.

Let's take football, for example. One of my favorite football coaches is Nick Saban at the University of Alabama. In 2021, he notched his seventh National Championship in college football. Saban is considered one of the greatest college football coaches of all time. Saban is one coach that gets it. If you listen to him speak, he always talks about "the system." He figured out and understood the power of a management system years ago. He continually updates and perfects his system on a regular basis.

He says that when he hires a new assistant coach, he wants the coach to come in and learn the Alabama system, not operate by his previous practices. Saban knows that if every new coach comes in and does things his own way, the team will never have consistency or achieve excellence in performance.

This doesn't mean the knowledge and processes the new coach brings are not valued. I'm sure that Nick Saban listens to ideas from new coaches and updates his "system" as appropriate to capture new and better concepts.

Saban's "system" includes processes for every aspect of his operation: how the organization identifies and accesses talent, how they recruit, how they onboard their new players and coaches, how they conduct practices, how they prepare for games, how they prepare their players mentally, how they conduct the game, how they call the plays, how they make sure every player executes every play flawlessly, how they analyze the game afterward, and how they make corrections as needed. Saban fine-tunes the processes on a continuous basis. Guess what? His team wins on a consistent basis.

If you watch Nick Saban on the sideline, it doesn't matter if his team is 30 points ahead (normally) or 30 points behind (almost never); he goes crazy if a player makes an unnecessary mistake. He's continually focused on flawless execution on every play no matter the score. He understands that in football, the only thing each player can do is to perform flawlessly on each play, one play at a time. If every player executes to perfection on every play throughout the game, the team has a good chance of winning. Saban never read my Operational Excellence model of leadership, people, systems, and culture; but he is a master of all four tenets.

Due to his focus and understanding of the importance of a system, it's obvious why the old saying is true: "He can take his team and beat you, and take your team and beat you!"

Saban has developed his system over the years which allows him to focus almost entirely on building a culture of excellence and on his players' execution. On the rare occasion that his team loses, you won't hear him say that he needs to figure out what went wrong and wonder about what needs to be done differently as you hear from so many mediocre coaches. Instead, he'll talk about going back and working on better execution of the system. Saban definitely understands the value of a good management system.

The principles for a company's management system are the same as they are in Nick Saban's football example. The Saban example for his team is similar to a small company or organization with only one location. A strong, robust system becomes increasingly important as your company grows with numerous departments and locations. Without a good system, the organization becomes entirely people dependent which leads to tremendous variation and inconsistent results. Create a good management system and then focus on flawless execution.

You often hear the saying, "The best defense is a good offense." I believe this saying directly applies to business.

I would much rather run a business proactively based on a system that has been thoroughly developed through the years and keeps getting better. This approach allows you to spend your time focusing on the people and flawless execution of your management system. Too many organizations wait for problems to occur and then spend countless hours investigating and figuring out how to prevent the problems from occurring again. This is a backwards, reactive approach.

A good *management system* is vitally important for any type of company. Systems describe how work should be done and can include items such as technology, best practices, requirements, procedures, and work processes. Many organizations have some type of management system, but the system is often out of date, too bureaucratic, impractical, and not always followed. Lack of a functioning system introduces unnecessary variation into the organization and creates conditions for undesired results.

The best leaders create a simplified system that builds on best practices of how work should be conducted, provides clear expectations, unleashes the power of people, drives change, and delivers continuous improvement. While leaders have many types of personal styles, all good leaders utilize a systems approach to help achieve their objectives.

Most young people entering the workforce don't understand management systems and the importance of compliance with standard requirements. Most of the requirements are built on past experience and help to achieve excellence in performance. Many requirements have been developed following significant incidents in the past resulting in loss of life, property damage, business interruption, or significant customer impacts.

New employees typically learn the importance of these requirements once they experience or witness a devasting incident themselves, but then it's too late. Reading this book will help you gain a clear understanding of the importance of a time-tested management system and develop a proactive sense of urgency for compliance and defect-free behavior.

Chapter 5 will provide a collection of work processes and practices that we've found to be most effective for achieving excellence and winning. These processes and practices are essential elements of a good management system, which will be described in Chapter 6. I'll discuss how to structure and simplify your system for maximum effectiveness.

ZERO Incident / ZERO Defect Culture

The fourth tenet of the Operational Excellence model is culture. Naturally, there are many soft factors in an organization's culture such as the attitudes of people—how people behave, how people treat each other, and how people work together.

Many cultures, however, lack an actionable component, one that helps drive intended behaviors at all times. We found that a ZERO incident or ZERO defect theme is extremely effective in shaping people's beliefs and behaviors. This particularly applies to manufacturing companies and in service industries such as hotels and restaurants.

In our company, we called the concept **Goal ZERO.** Goal ZERO is a foundational cultural tool that has an enormous impact across the entire organization. Goal ZERO helps to create a culture of discipline and is easy for people to understand. Here's a quick description to help you connect the dots throughout the book:

> *Goal ZERO serves as a foundation for a **culture** of doing things the right way, every day. Goal ZERO creates high level expectations for **leadership** and **people** as they drive towards and achieve **Operational Excellence.***

By the end of the book, you'll be able to answer the question, "What is Goal ZERO?" Goal ZERO is a strong, positive aspect for creating a winning culture. Goal ZERO is actionable and impacts every individual in an organization. Goal ZERO is a relentless focus on the basic building blocks of excellence: zero defects, zero rule breaking, zero unsafe acts, zero noncompliance, zero incidents, and zero missed value creating opportunities. Goal ZERO serves as a "north star" for your team in driving for excellence and perfection. It becomes a global code word for "doing the right thing at all times."

Vitally important, Goal ZERO is about compassion and caring for your people. Goal ZERO performance, Goal ZERO behavior, etc., are all terms you will hear from your people. It's a way to express your combined expectations and values in one term. A Goal ZERO mentality is powerful and provides simple clarity of expectations across the entire organization. Goal ZERO becomes a way of life for an everyday approach to safety, reliability, quality, and meeting customers' expectations. In Chapter 4, I'll describe the concepts for creating a ZERO defect culture.

Bad, Good, or Great

So now let's get back to the subject of excellence. We are all customers in our personal lives and business. At the highest level, we all want the same things: a good quality product or service, consistency, availability when we need it, and at a reasonable price. We also know how frustrating it can be when we pay good money and don't receive the expected product or service.

I've often told the story about how a restaurant can reside in one of three categories: **bad, good,** or **great.** We can all relate to this model whether it's a restaurant or any other type of establishment.

If you dine at a restaurant and the food or service is **bad,** you won't go back. The damage is already done. Even worse, you'll tell your friends about the experience. The result is a rippling effect for the reputation of the establishment and customers never forget. My earlier story regarding our hotel experience falls into the bad category. As a result, I am seriously considering changing our preferred hotel chain.

The second category, and most common, is that the food or service was **good,** but not anything special. People don't normally talk to others about these kinds of establishments to others because so many restaurants fall into this category. You may return, or you might go somewhere else the next time. It really doesn't matter because you have other choices.

The final category is the **great** restaurant. The food is outstanding and consistent every time. The service is impeccable. The restaurant is clean and has an inviting atmosphere. The staff is courteous, enthusiastic, and very welcoming. Everything seems perfect. You and your family or friends eagerly look forward to every visit. The food and drink prices may be higher, but the place is so popular that you have to make reservations way ahead of time. You brag about this kind of restaurant to others. People line up for a chance to dine there. The great reputation travels far and wide. This kind of establishment differentiates itself from the competition, and the results are enormous.

Why do so many owners of restaurants fail to make it to the great category? There are many factors for restaurants to be successful and great. The restaurant must have the right facilities and environment, superb food, motivated and enthusiastic people, consistent product and service delivery, marketing to get people in the door, and strict cost management. These items all fall within the four categories of leadership, people, systems, and culture. Many restaurants excel at one or more of these factors, but few are truly great in all four. The restaurant business is tough and has many challenges.

Your business has the same challenges. In our company, we always drove hard to be in the **great** category. Even a commodity business can differentiate itself from the competition by a constant focus on product consistency, on-time delivery, and mistake-free performance. Satisfied customers of good companies are not good enough because the customers might switch. Strive to be great and attract loyal customers who won't go anywhere else.

When your customers brag about your products and service, you are on your way to becoming great. It's relatively easy to differentiate your company because most of the competitors are good at best. In other words, achieve greatness through a focused approach of leadership, people, systems, and culture. Insist on Operational Excellence and a consistent Goal ZERO mindset at all times. Good isn't good enough anymore. Be great.

What Do You Really Want to Achieve? Are You Serious?

I've described the concepts of Operational Excellence and a ZERO defect culture. You must ask yourself if you are serious about taking your organization to the next level. It doesn't matter if you are the CEO of a large organization, the owner of a small business, a department manager, or a beginning employee. What level of intensity do you have for Operational Excellence and Goal ZERO performance? Does everyone around you see and feel the passion and expectations that you have?

Inherently, everyone agrees and fundamentally understands the importance of Operational Excellence, but where does leadership spend most of its time? In my experience, most of the time spent in corporate leadership teams and board of director meetings is on financial items—business strategy, earnings, cost management, customers, growth, and mergers and acquisitions (M&A). This allocation changes, however, *after* a major incident or operational problem occurs. The focus then changes to a reactive mode, but it's often too late; the damage has already been done.

Plenty of people monitor the financial results of a company. Wall Street has a laser focus on quarterly earnings. Countless investor calls and meetings take place throughout the year. The board of directors constantly focuses on earnings and the strategy going forward. This emphasis on cost management and profitability trickles down through the CEO, the leadership team, and the entire organization. Financial metrics are very clear and easy to track.

This financial focus is all perfectly understandable and, of course, very important. The smartest leaders, however, understand that financial results are *lagging indicators* of actions and performance. The key is a focus on the drivers of performance in a passionate and obvious manner. Every company has strategies and plans, but many companies fail in the execution of those plans. A manufacturing company will never achieve excellence in profitability if there is mediocre performance in operations, reliability, quality, and safety.

How much time is spent in your organization in a proactive way on Operational Excellence? Are you serious about Operational Excellence and do you demand and expect excellence at all times? Tone at the top and constancy of purpose lead the way in establishing a ZERO defect culture across the company.

An old Chinese proverb is pertinent when evaluating your approach to Goal ZERO performance and Operational

Excellence: "If you want to know your past, look into your present conditions. If you want to know your future, look into your present actions."

EXCELLENCE NUGGET:
Every company has strategies and plans but many companies fail to execute.

The Small Things Count

Have you heard the shoe tying story from the great college basketball coach, John Wooden? Wooden was the coach of the University of California (UCLA) basketball team from 1948 to 1975. His team dominated and won 10 national championships over 12 consecutive years.

At the first practice of each season, John Wooden would say, "Men, this is how you put your shoes and socks on." He would commence to show them the basic techniques of shoe tying. This technique was one of the processes in his management system. Some of the returning players had been through this before; however, it didn't matter. The players were going to review it again. The lesson began with choosing proper socks, putting the socks on without creases, sliding the shoe on carefully, and tying the shoe securely. Learning to tie shoes properly was vital to Wooden. It meant star players would never get a blister that would keep them from playing. A team can't be its best unless everyone's able to play.

I'm a firm believer that great results come from doing the little things right all of the time. Undoubtedly, one of the best ways to prevent incidents is to make sure everyone pays attention to detail at all times, task by task. I have participated in far more investigations than I care to remember where one of the causes of a major incident was typically the result of not following the process or inattention to detail. All of these incidents were preventable. That's why, long ago, I realized the power of a Goal ZERO approach on even the smallest of items.

Significant value destruction can occur to an organization when multiple, minor defects are allowed to occur. The danger of allowing minor defects to go untreated is that the defects become commonplace and habit, not even noticed by people in the organization. We call this "death by a thousand cuts."

An analogy is the story of the frog in hot water. If a frog jumps into hot water, he will immediately jump out. However, if the frog is in cool water and you begin to heat the water, he'll stay in until it's boiling and too late. He doesn't notice the gradual change of conditions.

The point of this section is that all of the small things matter if you truly want your company to excel. A Goal ZERO theme helps to make the concept clear for people. Embed this philosophy in your personal and organizational culture and mindset for everything, and you will stand a much better chance of avoiding not only small incidents but also significantly large ones.

EXCELLENCE NUGGET:
Every small detail is important.

Priorities are Constantly Changing

Following World War II, industrial capacity across the world was devastated and lacking. Since the battles had not been fought on its mainland, the United States was in an enviable position to supply the world's needs. This specific period ushered in global expansion for many American companies from the 1950s to the 1970s. The main priority at that time was producing products and getting them to the customers. The customers desperately needed the products.

Quality and cost were secondary considerations. Older Dow colleagues used to tell me about product quality during those years. The specification would call for a clear liquid and periodically the delivered product might be amber. The customer would complain, and the salesman would ask, "Do you want the product or not?" The customer begrudgingly took it since there was no other choice.

By the 1970s and 1980s, Germany, Japan, and a few other countries had rebuilt production capacity and become leaders in product quality. W. Edwards Deming had been sent by the United States to Japan following World War II, where he successfully taught statistical methods for improving quality and consistency. The Deming Prize is awarded annually in Japan for individuals and companies for their contributions to the field of Total Quality Management (TQM). W. Edwards Deming's book, *Out of the Crisis,* is a classic and a must-read.

Companies in the United States began to fall behind because of inferior quality in a wide variety of industries such as automotive and electronics. No longer did a company just need to produce a product; now consistent and superior quality was expected and demanded. Deming returned to the United States and the quality movement took center stage in the United States and around the world. Quality experts such as Joseph Juran, Philip Crosby, and others were in high demand. Conventional wisdom at the time implied the customer would pay a premium price for quality but that sentiment only lasted a short time. Premium quality simply opened the door for the sale.

In the early 1990s, several notable changes occurred that reshaped the industry landscape again. Global trade agreements further opened global markets. The internet began to emerge, improving global communication. Foreign companies accelerated their presence in the United States. Companies began to produce and ship products as global companies rather than country by country.

One example was Formosa Plastics, a Taiwanese company, which built a chemical manufacturing plant in Point Comfort, Texas, and provided low-cost competition we had not seen previously. Dow and most other American companies had high-cost structures, conducted considerable research and development, provided excellent employee benefits, and donated heavily to the communities in which the companies served. Formosa, on the other hand, came to the United States with a lean cost structure and few additional costs other than to make and ship the product. Companies like Formosa changed the competitive landscape.

Thus, the urgent focus on cost control began in the early 1990s. Companies had to tighten spending in order to compete. The same occurred in Europe and across the world. No longer was competition with other companies limited to the same country; competition was on a global scale. Shipping products around the world became easier, so a high-cost producer didn't survive very long.

Today's continuous advancements in information technology and artificial intelligence enhance our ability to communicate, transfer information, and monitor and control operations better than ever before. The tools and capability for enhanced quality control are constantly improving. Progress in Environmental, Social, and Governance (ESG) has become an expectation of every organization.

The point of this brief "history of the business world" is that the competitive environment is constantly changing. We have migrated from a focus on production, to a focus on production and quality, and, finally to a focus on **production** *and* **quality** *and* **cost.** All three elements are critical in today's world to compete and excel. Operational Excellence is the key differentiator with any organization. New technology development, of course, has always been a major factor in leapfrogging the competition.

Importance of Operational Excellence on Wall Street

Institutional investors on Wall Street understand the importance of Operational Excellence. Corbin Advisors is a leading research and advisory firm specializing in investor relations. Based on their 14 years of research, Corbin has identified the *Critical Five* investment factors most important to institutional investors beyond quantitative assessments when evaluating an investment. These include:

1. Leadership quality
2. Sound long-term strategy
3. Execution track record
4. Sustainable competitive advantages
5. Capital deployment

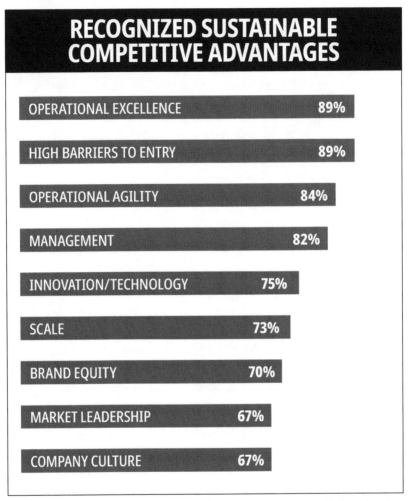

RECOGNIZED SUSTAINABLE COMPETITIVE ADVANTAGES

OPERATIONAL EXCELLENCE	89%
HIGH BARRIERS TO ENTRY	89%
OPERATIONAL AGILITY	84%
MANAGEMENT	82%
INNOVATION/TECHNOLOGY	75%
SCALE	73%
BRAND EQUITY	70%
MARKET LEADERSHIP	67%
COMPANY CULTURE	67%

FIGURE 2: CORBIN PROPRIETARY RESEARCH: INSIDE THE BUY-SIDE
SOURCE: CORBIN ADVISORS, 2020

Institutional investors identified Operational Excellence as the leading sustainable competitive advantage, in line with high barriers to entry (Figure 2).

There are many obvious measurements and indicators for Operational Excellence. A company's cost position may be a result of how efficient the company operates. Reliability of operation and quality of products and service are obvious indicators. Production outages, force majeure events, and significant quality incidents are all indicators for Operational

Excellence. Data for regulatory fines and penalties for safety and environmental performance are in the public domain.

Operation Excellence is the key to success for any organization. The remaining sections of the book continue to illustrate the importance of Operational Excellance and guidance for how to achieve it.

The Consequences of a Major Incident

This book is about achieving excellence in your personal life and in the organizations where you work. All of the tips and techniques add up to a formula for achieving a culture of excellence in everything that you do. However, there is an additional reason for writing this book. Very bad things can happen to good companies. The lessons learned in this book will greatly reduce the chances of a serious incident occurring. I will repeat myself several times—you can never allow a major unplanned event to occur.

Unfortunately, far too many terrible incidents and crisis situations have occurred and taken down companies throughout history. Bad things can happen to anyone, in any industry and in any company, regardless of size. And more disturbing, these incidents needlessly continue to occur, resulting in lives lost, billions of dollars in cost, business loss, and declining lack of trust in companies, industries, and government.

The worst incidents are when someone dies or gets critically injured. Such an event is a tragedy and is completely unacceptable. Every incident can be prevented. Every person has family members, co-workers, and friends. A serious injury or fatality impacts the entire community and is never forgotten.

Why do these incidents keep occurring? Generally, the incidents can be traced to a failure in execution. The causes are almost always a breakdown in one of the Operational Excellence Model tenets—leadership, people, systems, or culture. Organizations must maintain a healthy sense of urgency and culture to assure that correct protective measures and actions from previous incidents are always in place.

The following sections provide examples of things going badly wrong. Unfortunately, I could have given you a hundred examples. I'm always confounded by people in companies that gain an increased sense of urgency for Operational Excellence after a crisis or major incident. Why do these people wait? Terrible incidents can happen to even the best companies, but you can significantly reduce the odds with a proactive, disciplined focus on Operational Excellence.

These events that I will describe, sadly, were all preventable and didn't have to occur. If reading these summaries doesn't give you an increased sense of urgency about being proactive, I don't know what will. Focusing on all of the small details will help prevent big events. As you read about these events, think about the importance of leadership, people, systems, and culture. Don't ever let "the big event" happen to you or your company.

The Great Texas Freeze of 2021

In February 2021, the state of Texas experienced a deep freeze that doesn't occur very often. Officials of manufacturing and utility plants had a false sense of security that the plants were protected against the freezing weather. Many power plants, water supplies, gas processing industries, refineries, and chemical plants shut down operations due to the freeze. Millions of people suffered for days without power and water, and there were many deaths associated with the loss of electricity.

There was significant finger pointing for who was to blame and what the causes were. But one cause, for certain, was that many of the facilities were not as protected for the freeze as management had thought they were or expected them to be. For example, the requirements and procedures for installing heat tracing and insulation for instrumentation for hard, extended freezes are much different than for a light freeze.

Although not a common occurrence in Texas, there had been similar hard freezing conditions in 1983 and 1989. Companies failed to institutionalize the learnings from these past freeze events.

The companies must investigate this current freeze, implement corrective actions, document the learnings in their management system, properly train people, and maintain assets in the right condition to be properly prepared in the future. The economic loss, human misery, and loss of life for this 2021 Texas freeze were significant. These failures reminded me once more why the concepts in this book are so important for documenting and building on past knowledge to prevent severe consequences from occurring during unexpected, repeat events.

Blue Bell Ice Cream

Blue Bell Creameries, founded in 1907 and headquartered in Brenham, Texas, is one of the most popular ice cream brands (my favorite) across Texas and beyond. In 2015, a crisis for the company occurred when listeria was discovered in some of its products, resulting in illnesses and three deaths. The result was product recalls and the eventual shutdown of the company's facilities. Blue Bell suffered incredible reputation damage. Federal investigators stated that Blue Bell had found evidence of listeria as early as 2013 but had failed to implement corrective actions sufficient to prevent a recurrence from happening.

The company pleaded guilty to two misdemeanor charges and paid nearly $20 million in settlements. The company was involved in voluminous litigation and various settlements. The CEO was charged with seven felonies. The board of directors was criticized for not having a board-level food safety committee and not providing appropriate risk management oversight. Corrective actions included equipment redesign and improvements in employee and hygiene practices.

Boeing

In March 2019, the Boeing 737 MAX passenger airliner was grounded worldwide after 346 people died in two crashes: Lion Air Flight 601 on October 29, 2018, and Ethiopian Airlines Flight 302 on March 10, 2019. The plane's stabilizing software, known as the Maneuvering Characteristics Augmentation System (MCAS), is widely considered to be a principal cause of both crashes. Investigations revealed technical design flaws, insufficient pilot training, leadership failures, and a lack of transparency with regulators and customers.

How could this system failure happen to such a great company? The crisis was a serious blow to Boeing's reputation. The confidence of customers and the flying public was shaken, which will take years to recover. The result was the grounding of the entire 737 MAX global fleet. Boeing issued statements regarding the various corrective actions it took including strengthening the safety culture in the company, improving aircraft software and pilot training, and creating a Safety Committee for the board of directors.

BP Texas City

On March 23, 2005, a hydrocarbon vapor cloud ignited and violently exploded at the BP Texas City Refinery. The explosion killed 15 workers, injured 180 others, and severely damaged the refinery. The hydrocarbon release resulted from liquid overflow from a blowdown stack. This chemical release followed overfilling and overheating of a process tower during startup operations. The majority of the fatalities occurred from people working in a portable building in an area adjacent to the operating unit.

Numerous investigations by a variety of entities—the BP internal investigation, the Chemical Safety Board investigation, and the BP independent investigation by the Baker Panel— concluded the causes of the incident, injuries, and fatalities were numerous and represented a breakdown in BP's management system. Deficiencies included lack of addressing previously identified risks, insufficient training, lack of competent people on plant startup, lack of infrastructure investments, use of ineffective procedures that were often not followed, inoperative alarms, and siting of portable buildings too close to the unit. These are all management system, people, and cultural items that are thoroughly covered throughout this book. Suffice it to say, this incident was devastating for the families, BP, and the industry.

BP Deepwater Horizon Oil Spill

BP experienced a second disaster five years later on April 20, 2010, at the Deepwater Horizon drilling rig in the Gulf of Mexico. Methane gas expanded in the marine riser and rose into the drilling rig where the gas ignited and exploded, engulfing the platform in flames. Eleven workers died in the explosion and 94 others were rescued by lifeboat or helicopter. The resulting oil spill continued until the release was finally capped on September 19, 2010. The environmental damage was widespread, and the event dominated the U.S. and world news for many months. The incident is widely considered the largest marine oil spill in the history of the petroleum industry.

The investigations that followed determined deficiencies such as schedule and cost pressures, operating practices, insufficient integrity assurance, leadership and employee actions, and fear of reporting safety issues by personnel. BP was accused of lacking an adequate company safety culture.

Pacific Gas & Electric (PG&E) Fires of 2017 and 2018

Fires sparked by equipment owned by the California utility company, PG&E, killed more than 100 people and destroyed more than 15,000 homes in northern California in 2017 and 2018. One of the fires, the 2018 Camp Fire, devastated the city of Paradise (population 26,000). The fire was supposedly started when a worn piece of metal known as a C-hook broke free from a transmission tower, dropping a high-voltage power line that sent molten embers onto the dry brush below.

In addition to filing bankruptcy and incurring huge liability claims, PG&E pleaded guilty to 84 counts of manslaughter for the 2018 Camp Fire, making PG&E one of the few U.S. corporations to be convicted of homicide-related charges. Investigations revealed the company had known for years that some of its transmission lines posed serious risks but didn't properly address the risks. PG&E was accused of insufficient inspections, poor maintenance, and employing inspectors with improper training.

Buncefield Fire

The Buncefield Fire was a major fire and vapor cloud explosion that occurred at an oil storage terminal near Hertfordshire, England on December 11, 2005. The terminal was owned by Total UK Limited (60%) and Texaco (40%). Massive explosions occurred and the event was described as "the largest incident of its kind in peacetime Europe." The oil terminal supplied 30% of Heathrow Airport's fuel, creating severe implications for air traffic.

A series of events led to the fire and explosions. A tank with unleaded petrol overflowed, releasing an estimated 300 tons of product. Eventually, an ignition source ignited the flammable product. There were two immediate causes for the overflow: first, the failure of a manual level measuring device, and second, a failure of a high-level switch that should have activated and shut off fuel from entering the tank.

As is typical in investigations of these types of incidents, numerous other leadership and system issues were identified. The incident served as another reminder of the necessity of attention to detail at all times.

2008 New York Crane Collapse

Numerous construction accidents and fatalities have occurred involving the operation of cranes. One such accident occurred on March 15, 2008, in Manhattan, New York City. A tower crane, model M440E, was being utilized in the construction of the 32-floor 303 East 51st Street skyscraper. The crane collapsed during construction, killing seven people.

The building was under construction when the luffing-jib tower crane snapped off and fell. The OSHA investigation following the incident stated that the manufacturer's instructions for lifting the stabilizing collar were not followed and there were problems with rigging. The overloaded slings failed, causing the collar to drop and dislodge two lower level collars from the building. This left the crane unsecured, allowing the crane to collapse.

Preventing the Big Event

The sense of urgency for action in these companies immediately after their big event was incredibly high, as you can imagine. In addition to caring for the families of injured and deceased individuals, a company expends an enormous amount of effort in correcting the damage, dealing with lawsuits, and implementing corrective actions to prevent such an event from ever occurring again. But why do companies wait until *after* such an event to develop a sense of urgency for Operational Excellence?

Big events such as quality problems, food contamination in the food industry, and fires are life-threatening and devastating to any business. You must make every effort possible and never lose focus on preventing tragedies from ever occurring in your company.

The refining and chemical industry has made continually good progress in reducing personal injury rates. These companies are continuing to improve in the area of human factors and individual behavior. However, the number of process safety incidents in the industry has plateaued. If you dissect the industry further, some companies have made excellent progress in reducing process safety incidents, while others still need significant improvement.

I contend that the differentiating factor among these companies is a disciplined, comprehensive approach to Operational Excellence and the model I have previously described of leadership, people, systems, and culture.

As described above, major incidents are typically the result of a seemingly minor defect or a series of defects. This multiple failure analogy is commonly referred to as the Swiss cheese model in which the holes (defects) line up in a manner that leads to a significant event. We often referred to this as an incredible chain of events. Therefore, the best way to prevent a big event is a constant focus on elimination of all defects, a Goal ZERO approach to Operational Excellence.

Obviously, a relentless focus on Operational Excellence will drive improved performance and it also provides the defensive mechanism to help prevent incidents. By continually eliminating variation and improving consistency, quality improves and the risk of a major event occurring is greatly reduced.

Maintaining a vibrant risk management program is critical. The practice of risk management is widely known; however, when the risk management process gets too complicated, it becomes ineffective. The preferred approach is to strictly prioritize and clearly identify the highest potential risks, assign responsible owners for each risk, and then make sure that special precautions are in place, well understood, and executed to perfection at all times.

Companies should regularly train and remind employees (and especially leaders) of these top risks and the potential consequences if the big event were to occur. This training should include a summary of the proactive measures that must be maintained to perfection at all times.

Over the years, there have been too many major incidents from lost knowledge and experience due to people moving on to other jobs or retiring. Terrible incidents continue to occur because people forget or become lax in maintaining any and all preventative measures. As time goes by, people tend to focus on other areas and forget the learnings of the past.

This loss of institutional knowledge should never occur. For the most critical risks, you can't afford to rely on people's memories, which is exactly the reason why a robust management system is so important at loss prevention, protecting people, assuring product and service quality, and protecting the wealth of a firm. A management system provides a constant, systemic focus on proactive measures to assure operations are conducted the right way, every time.

EXCELLENCE NUGGET:
Create a sense of urgency
in your organization.

Environmental, Social, and Governance (ESG)

As your company grows, it will get increased scrutiny from outside stakeholders. When I became Vice President at Dow in 2000, I was asked to spend one-third of my time externally and to lead the development of the company's corporate strategy for Sustainable Development. I worked closely with the US EPA, OSHA, the President's Council on Environmental Quality, and various governmental regulatory agencies in the Europe and Asia. It was important to know the leaders of each organization and to build mutual trust.

I spent considerable time in dialogue with individuals at non-governmental organizations (NGOs) such as the World

Resources Institute, Environmental Defense, Sierra Club, Resources for the Future, Friends of the Earth, and Greenpeace. Although we rarely agreed on philosophy, I always enjoyed the interaction and gained a better understanding of their viewpoints on various issues.

As the leader for Sustainable Development and ESG in our companies, I became involved externally to become an active part of the discussions. As time progressed, I was appointed to the board of directors of the World Environment Center and the International Leadership Council for the Nature Conservancy. Leading the Dow delegation to the World Summit on Sustainable Development in Johannesburg, South Africa was an interesting experience.

I enjoyed my interactions with many fascinating global opinion leaders such as John Elkington, founder of SustainAbility, Bjorn Stigson, President of the World Business Council on Sustainable Development, Tom Burke, author of *Ethics, Environment and the Company*, Julia Marton-Lefevre, Director General of the International Union for Conservation of Nature (IUCN), Maurice Strong, Executive Director of the United Nations Environment Programme, and Jonathan Lash, President of the World Resources Institute..... just to name a few.

On one occasion, I invited the Washington, D.C. government relations director of Greenpeace, to speak to our Dow Public Policy leadership team. He thought I was crazy inviting him to talk at a Dow meeting, but he eventually agreed. As I was introducing him at the meeting, he pulled a quick surprise by handcuffing himself to me. Then he said, "We are often handcuffed to fences or in the back of police cars. Now I feel comfortable." Everyone got a good laugh out of the handcuffing and the surprise helped put everyone at ease. I always enjoyed interactions with these folks and getting different perspectives on issues. Interaction with people with different backgrounds and perspectives is always educational.

There has been much discussion and evolution through the years regarding the purpose of corporations. Milton Friedman, the 1976 Nobel Prize winner for Economic Sciences, presented the idea that the sole role of a firm is to make money for its shareholders. Concepts were changing in the late 1980s, when Responsible Care® became the chemical industry initiative to continually improve environment, health, safety, and security performance. A term commonly used in industry was Corporate Social Responsibility, which was a form of corporate self-regulation.

As time progressed, in 1998, John Elkington published *Cannibals with Forks: The Triple Bottom Line of 21st Century Business.* In the book, he emphasized environmental, social, and economic issues and coined the phrase "triple bottom line." I was beginning to get involved in this space at the time and thought that the triple bottom line was a brilliant approach since he brought the three major special interest groups (environmental, social, and business) together for discussions and to work on the world's leading issues.

Sustainable Development was the terminology most often used at the time. In 2005, Environmental, Social, and Governance (ESG) became the term commonly used for investing purposes. I believe changing Elkington's "Economic" component to a much broader "Governance" focus was another improvement. Governance is much more of an encompassing term, thereby attracting increased attention of investors. ESG has led to more consistent reporting of performance and is used by the capital markets as a tool for responsible investing.

After all of these years, many people still ask the same question, "How do you define sustainable development and ESG? What do these terms mean for us as a company?" Confusion is understandable since it seems like almost anything can fit under the broad umbrella of ESG:

- **Environmental** can include topics such as climate change, emissions, depletion of resources, waste reduction, energy intensity, and water management.
- **Social** can cover human rights, child labor, safety, diversity, equality, inclusion, public and community support, animal welfare, and how a company manages relationships with employees, suppliers, customers, and the communities where the company operates.
- **Governance** deals with items such as a company's leadership, management systems, audits, compliance, internal controls, operational excellence, executive pay, and shareholder rights.

Tens of thousands of non-governmental organizations (NGOs) exist around the world. These groups focus on and drive their specific topic of interest. Social media has made it much easier for global communication and focus. You'll never have to worry about lack of attention from the public on any particular issue that you choose.

Stakeholders monitor the ESG ratings of companies through various rating agencies such as Morgan Stanley Capital International (MSCI) ESG, Dow Jones Sustainability Index (DJSI), Sustainalytics, and many others. Environmental and social performance are easiest to measure, but governance is softer and not as measurable. This is why leadership, Operational Excellence, and the principles in this book are so important for ESG risk management. Without good governance, it's difficult to get anything else right. A high sustainability rating may look good to stakeholders, but that doesn't necessarily translate to performance. Pacific Gas and Electric, for example, had been rated by ESG rating agencies as best among its peers prior to its serious fires in 2017-2018 and filing bankruptcy in 2019.

During my years of involvement and leadership in the area of sustainability and ESG, I learned invaluable lessons. One of the most important factors for you is to become extremely educated on the ESG issues facing society and your organization. Your company must determine which of the issues are real and which ones are just noise. Some ESG issues may be a threat to your organization, while others provide value creating opportunities. You must define your organization's proactive strategy for how you will approach ESG and not let others define it for you. Defining your strategy puts you on the offense, meaning that you can articulate what you are and are not doing.

A crucial point is to maintain a balanced approach with ESG. Remember, drive progress on the environmental and social challenges but don't lose focus on governance and Operational Excellence. Integrate an ESG strategy into your business strategy and everyday work, not just an add-on. Too many companies have lost focus on the basics of their company's operations and, in the process, no longer exist.

Remember to monitor ESG progress in your procurement and supply chain management. Protecting human rights in the supply chain, minimizing the impact on the environment, and strong governance are all critical traits of reliable suppliers.

To help in developing your ESG strategy, it's helpful to consider "Quality of Life" models. Your organization can address these for the communities in which you operate and the broader public in general. Quality of Life factors help during discussions with community leaders by keeping the discussion focused on the big picture. The major Quality of Life factors in a community are:

- Economic: income, jobs, taxes, etc.
- Housing
- Health
- Environment
- Education
- Security
- Civic engagement

The bottom line is that there doesn't have to be confusion or mystery when addressing sustainability or ESG. Be proactive, remain balanced, define your strategy, set reasonable goals, deliver measurable results, and communicate often. Now more than ever, employees (and other stakeholders) want to feel deep engagement with their work, their fellow employees, and the impact their company is making locally and globally.

EXCELLENCE NUGGET:
Integrate an ESG strategy into your business strategy and everyday work.

"The Public" Has Diverse Opinions

Responsible Care® is the global chemical industry initiative to continually improve environmental, health, safety, and security performance. The initiative began in Canada in 1984 and was adopted by the U.S. chemical industry in 1988. Participation in Responsible Care® is a condition of membership in the American Chemistry Council and all companies have made CEO level commitments to uphold the program elements.

One of the principles is to openly engage with stakeholders regarding their perspectives on various issues. Chemical industry manufacturing sites across the country, and around the world, have formed Community Advisory Panels; a terrific forum for engaging the public and encouraging interaction.

At the corporate level, Dow Chemical was an industry leader by creating a Corporate Environmental Advisory Council (CEAC) in 1992. The name was later changed to the Sustainability External Advisory Council (SEAC) and is still in existence today. The purpose is to bring a diverse outside-in perspective on issues. Council members come from around the world and include influential experts and leaders from NGOs, academia, the business community, and governments.

When I became Vice President of EH&S at Dow and began working with the CEAC members, I was incredibly impressed with these individuals and the depth of experience that each of them brought to the table. These global individuals were highly respected and enjoyed dialoguing with each other as much as they did with the company. Every meeting was filled with deep discussions on the important issues of the day.

The purpose of the meetings was to hear and exchange views on various topics. The CEAC members did not vote or try to bring consensus on how Dow should proceed on any issue going forward. These guidelines allowed each member to freely express his or her opinion since there were no decisions or commitments to be made.

We discussed all types of issues such as climate change, dioxin, human rights, and testing of products. I remember my first meeting in which we presented a touchy issue we were dealing with and our planned approach. When we completed the presentation, the first CEAC member to speak gave a passionate talk on how wrong we were and why she thought so. She had my full attention.

However, the next speaker took the opposite view and said we were taking exactly the right approach. He gave an equally energetic talk on the issue. Each of these CEAC members were extremely eloquent and presented his/her case passionately. My most valuable learning was that for practically every topic, there were diverse opinions on both sides of the issue. The value of these discussions was to dialogue, listen, and learn, and then make our own decisions on which way to proceed.

These CEAC discussions were extremely helpful to me personally and to all of us in the company. One of the clear learnings was to be careful when someone says "the public" feels one way or another about a topic, or "the public" demands or won't accept something. The fact is there is a diversity of views among people that make up "the public" and you must educate yourself on the issues to make good sound decisions. Don't allow people to generalize how "the public" feels or what "the public" is thinking.

This principle also applies to communities where you operate and the employees in your company. There aren't many community issues in which all residents have the same opinion. Take time to dialogue and learn, make decisions based on good information, and be prepared to communicate, discuss, and support your decisions. Be cautious of falling into the political correctness trap on every issue that comes along. You will never be able to please everyone. The key is to understand the issues and then decide on your approach. Incorporate all of these items into your management system and drive your culture of excellence with a sense of urgency.

An Expectation of Excellence
A SUMMARY

- Focus on all four aspects of the Operational Excellence Model: leadership, people, systems, and culture. These are the factors that lead to excellence in reliability, safety, quality, and productivity.
- Decide if you want your organization to be bad, good, or great. Determine what it takes to be great and get everyone aligned to make it happen.
- The small things count. You can't be great at the big things if there are high numbers of relatively minor defects.
- You can never allow the "big event" to occur in your organization. These events hurt people, impact the environment, damage company reputation, and destroy value. The only way to prevent these is a constant focus on excellence in everything that you do.
- Environmental, Social, and Governance (ESG) should be incorporated into the company strategy and everyday work. Don't treat ESG as an add on or separate initiative.
- Don't generalize when it comes to what the public or your employees think. There is incredible diversity in large populations, and it's often not accurate to say "the public" feels this way or that. Listen and learn the various viewpoints, and then act based on knowledge.

CHAPTER 3

A Passion for Leadership and People

*"Leaders don't force people to follow
—they invite them on a journey."*
– Charles S. Lauer

We've spent a lot of time up to this point on you becoming more effective in your life, at your job, and in driving excellence in performance. We now turn to the people you work with and ways you can help them to perform at their best and achieve desired outcomes. Whether you are a supervisor or a peer, you can have an incredible impact on others. When discussing leaders in this chapter, I'm talking about *you*.

My grandpa used to tell stories to me about the changes that occurred during his lifetime. He'd talk about his first exposure to the television, the telephone, the airplane, electricity, and running water in his home. I used to think he was old since those conveniences seemed normal to me. And, of course, he always reminded me, "I had to walk to and from school barefoot in the snow, and it was uphill in both directions."

I guess that I'm getting to the old category myself. Taylor and Henry, our grandchildren, remind me of my age frequently. In my freshman Chemical Engineering class at The University of Texas, our widely popular professor, Dr. John J. McKetta, told us to buy a good quality $30 slide rule because we would use the tool for the rest of our career. Little did he know that the handheld calculator would be introduced only a few years later.

In our early days at work, we carried beepers so that we could be reached. When the beeper went off, we had to find the nearest telephone and call in. Beepers lasted until mobile phones became commonplace.

Global communication took weeks or even months to occur. Telephone lines across the ocean were available but service was poor, and a transoceanic conversation was very expensive. Today, we watch live broadcasts from anywhere in the world and talk to each other as if we were in the next room. Other inventions such as the internet, email, and social media have changed the way we all work and live. It's amazing that so many aspects of our lives have changed in a relatively short time. Technology is improving daily, and future changes will be mind-boggling.

People, however, are still basically the same. Sure, we have the different demographic groups: Baby Boomers, Generation X, Millennials, Generation Z (Zoomers), and Generation Alpha (those born after 2010). Each generation grows up with the technology of its era. My grandchildren are Generation Z, and they were comfortable with their electronics before they could even read or write. However, people still have the same basic needs that they've always had.

Organizations can have the best management system and processes available, but without competent and motivated people implementing the system, nothing will get accomplished, and you won't win. Successful leaders understand these needs and have mastered the art of motivation and bringing out the best in their people. It all begins with leadership.

Chapter 1 was about you as an individual. This chapter focuses on your ability to influence others. The success of any organization begins with leadership and, of course, tone at the top.

For years, I have enjoyed a quote by Pat Riley, a five-time National Basketball Association championship coach. He described his job as a leader perfectly: "I am a management person. My job is to create an environment where my players can flourish. My players are the ones that truly get the job done. I do what I can, through organization and guidance, to put them in a position to be successful. I am at my best when I am of service to them. Not subservient, but of service. As much as I can, I remove my ego. In the long run, I know that I will benefit from their success as much as they do. It is the same for all managers."

How many times have you seen an organization that is not performing right, and a new leader comes in and quickly turns things around? Quick turnarounds by a new leader happen all the time at all levels in an organization: CEO, corporate staff, business units, site, and functional leaders.

People want to follow leaders who are honest, competent, future focused, visible, and inspiring. A good leader doesn't do it all him or herself, but, rather, leads and creates an environment where the team achieves more than they ever dreamed possible.

Companies spend a lot of time and energy designing, installing, and maintaining their assets. Technical people love this aspect of the business and employ countless metrics to monitor equipment operations and efficiency. The people component, however, is much more abstract, challenging, and rewarding.

You can be a leader and influence others no matter what your position is in your company. Leadership at all levels in the organization is a prerequisite to establishing a culture of excellence. All leaders, employees, and contractors must be committed to achieving excellence in every aspect of performance. Results focused leaders set high expectations, hold others accountable, and provide feedback on performance. Competent and motivated people operate the assets and execute the system. Any company can have good equipment and strategic plans, but the winning companies develop a culture in which their people thrive.

My style as a leader was to be a "player coach." I always felt I was one member of the team even though I might have been the boss over thousands of people. My job was to be a catalyst for innovation and creative thoughts to drive improvement. I believed every member was important and critical for our success and I always wanted his or her honest input. By empowering the members of our team, my job was much easier in the long run, which in turn always led to more successful outcomes.

My most important advice is to be yourself and develop a leadership style that feels natural for you. Some people try to act differently as a leader than their natural state off of the job. You can generally see their personal stress from this dichotomy, and it doesn't typically turn out well. Be yourself, be authentic, and be consistent.

People have good intentions but need guidance and leadership. Provide them with the skills, competencies, and tools to do their job with confidence and satisfaction. Continue to push responsibility to the front line by setting high expectations and empowering people. Don't micromanage. People will respond enthusiastically and will deliver.

Successful leaders create alignment. Good leaders communicate clearly and often. People want to know "why" something is important and, "What's in it for me?" Take time to engage with employees and listen to concerns. Discussion and debate are healthy for people to understand philosophy and direction. Help people to understand the big picture and how their work impacts overall results. Leadership is most essential when things don't go right and when problems need to be overcome. The good leaders help their people remain calm and confident when dealing with adversity.

Building trust in the organization takes time. You must gain the trust of your people and your people need to have trust in you as their leader. Trust begins with a clear understanding of expectations and regular communications. Allow the people on your team to solve their own problems and then praise them for it. Empower them to make decisions within an agreed upon framework or limits. Realize that no one is perfect and make sure your people know that you will have their back if things go wrong.

Help, encourage, and expect people around you to be their best and improve every day. Each person should take ownership and remember that he or she is the face of the company to others. Motivated people are terrific ambassadors for the organization. Employees should do whatever it takes to exceed customers' expectations. Create a workplace environment that is exciting and optimistic. Pride in the company is contagious. By doing so, you will have an organization in which people are proud to work and others want to join the team.

Results focused leaders may deliver results in different ways, but everything these leaders do falls under the concepts of motivating people and of passionate execution of a management system, whether they call it that or not. Strong leaders establish clear expectations, develop strategies and plans, choose the right team members, hold people accountable, instill consistent work practices, and measure results.

The culture that develops in a company is critical in driving consistency and long-term sustainability. In a large company, local cultures in different countries and at different locations are strong and will dominate. Your approach to developing a consistent company-wide culture should be to enhance the local culture with a few critical expectations that people can understand. Simplicity and clarity should be paramount. Having and enforcing a strong Code of Conduct is essential. A succinct management system that is practical and not overbearing provides the framework. A culture of excellence and a drive for perfection translate well globally.

Performance improvement comes from effective change management. Change management requires strong leadership, an inspiring vision, a sense of urgency, and constancy of purpose. Change management leadership is not a popularity contest. When you are driving change, some people will love what you are doing, and others will hate it. Many people naturally don't like change; however, keeping people future focused on the vision works wonders in motivating teams.

Bringing your organization along together during times of change and giving people an opportunity for input will help to gain understanding and support. Frequent communication of all types is extremely critical for good leadership and to establish alignment through the organization. People tend to accept change much better if they understand *why* the change is being done. Don't expect your people to understand with the first communication that goes out. Repeat the key messages over and over in various formats.

As I approached my global jobs, I spent considerable time evaluating our site managers around the world. I clearly knew that we needed to have the right leader at each manufacturing location if we were going to meet our expectations. Needless to say, we made a number of changes resulting with a final group of world-class plant managers. My evaluations also applied to the other leaders at each site. The right person in the right job has a major impact on performance and morale. If you know that a leader is not getting the job done, move quickly to improve or replace the person. After making a change, most leaders will say they wish they had made the change sooner. Don't delay.

One of the most important aspects of leadership is the ability to influence the behavior of others. Through the years, I spent a considerable amount of time exploring the concepts of behavior management. It's a challenge to motivate individuals across diverse organizations to align on common themes and perform to their highest potential.

This is the longest chapter, which includes many proven methods for bringing out the best in people. Leadership techniques will be shared for motivating people, improving performance, driving improvement, and building a winning organization.

Organizational Alignment

Each of our three multinational companies was unique in its own way and had different starting points regarding Operational Excellence. In all cases, we made great progress with significant improvement in results. The consistent approach was in creating a compelling vision and driving rapid change to achieve the vision. I always wanted to go faster with a higher sense of urgency. We continually fine-tuned our approach to increasing efficiency and driving rapid transformation.

Successful change management requires considerable discussion, communication, and flexibility to bring the entire organization along. In the end, you want people to truly believe in the path forward and feel they have been an active part of the change. It's terrific when your team is aligned on a common mission, and everyone works enthusiastically towards the same goal.

One of the most important factors in making major change in an organization is to assure there is *understanding, alignment, and support of the organization's leaders.* To be most effective, Operational Excellence needs to be company-wide and cut across traditional functional boundaries. Breaking down functional barriers is an important concept and difficult to achieve in many companies that have strong functions. It's critical that leaders at the top understand and insist on a company-wide approach with each function working closely together and in alignment. Minimize turf battles that create friction, inefficiency, and value destruction. The competition is external to the organization.

A common challenge in large companies is an independent focus on improvement within each individual function rather than company-wide. Functions such as Manufacturing, Quality, Personal Safety, Process Safety, Environment, Reliability, and Human Resources often have independent strategies and plans for improvement. The people in each function are working hard but not necessarily in a smart and coordinated manner. This independent approach often includes different terminology and concepts which add complexity and confuses the organization.

A better approach is to keep the focus at a higher level under the umbrella of Operational Excellence. Operational Excellence provides an overarching expectation from the top of the organization which improves consistency and clarity for your people. This approach allows each function and location to work within an overall framework to provide proper attention for their specific areas of responsibility. Operational Excellence eliminates the debate and confusion about which is most important: safety, reliability, quality, cost, functional responsibilities, etc. The achievement of Operational Excellence will deliver desired results in each of these important areas.

EXCELLENCE NUGGET:
Effective change management requires strong leadership alignment.

The Case for Change and a Clear Vision for the Future

Most people are naturally reluctant to embrace change. Resistance can come from any area of the organization: front line operators, supervisors, department managers, and C-suite leaders. People are busy and focused on other initiatives. People don't trust that the change will work, so they don't want to put in the extra effort. A common question is, "What's in it for me?"

Creating a good case for change and addressing the concerns of all parties is critical. People are more willing to accept change if they understand "why" the change is important and the benefits the change will bring. Change takes energy. You must either have a major discomfort with your current state or have a clear vision for taking your organization to the next level of performance

Therefore, the beginning of any major change management initiative involves creating a compelling case for change. The context for change is important. Are you fighting complacency from consistent yet mediocre performance, or are you responding to a recent serious incident? Why are you implementing the change? What is your vision for the future? What problems are you trying to solve? Different people get motivated in different ways.

As a leader, you will encounter all kinds of excuses. "We don't have the people to do this work, we don't have the budget, we have other priorities, and we don't have the time." I've heard them all. These excuses remind me of the person that was chopping wood with a dull axe and someone suggested that he sharpen the axe. He responded, "I don't have time."

The choice is clear; do you want to continue inefficiently, or do you want to take a step to become better organized so you can accelerate progress? I would much rather spend the time developing a good system to prevent defects rather than endlessly investigating problems over and over. You will figure out how to prioritize and get the job done if you have the right tone at the top and Operational Excellence is important to your organization,

It's relatively easy to develop a case for change for Operational Excellence. Poll your people for their input on the problems they face and ideas that could make the organization better. People don't have much difficulty coming up with what is wrong. I'll bet you can recognize and relate to some of the following statements that make a compelling case for change:

- Too many people are getting hurt.
- Reliability is not what we expect.
- We have too many customer quality incidents.
- Operational problems occur in one area while the solution is very well known elsewhere.
- Repeat incidents occur from the same root causes.
- We don't have a good system to capture best practices.
- We are not fully utilizing best practices in all areas.
- Rules and requirements are too long and complicated.

- We keep reinventing the wheel and working on the same issue in different places.
- We are too people dependent, and we lose knowledge when key people retire or leave.

Make your own list that summarizes your case for change. All of these issues can be resolved with good leadership, a good management system, and the right culture.

Once you have clarified the case for change, it's time to develop your vision for Operational Excellence. People respond to future focus when they understand clearly what you are trying to accomplish and more importantly, what success will look like.

A few bullet points that will help turn your current problems into vision elements for improving Operational Excellence are:

- Fewer people will get hurt.
- Operations will become more consistent and predictable.
- Employee engagement and commitment will increase.
- Costs will decrease.
- All facilities will operate with best practices.
- We will become the best in class supplier to our customers.
- Redundancy and duplication of work will be reduced.
- We will spend less time investigating incidents and more time on incident prevention.
- We will have a consistent framework for documenting the management system.
- Information and knowledge will be easy to access.
- We will have a light touch from corporate with more detail at the sites.
- We will eliminate confusion.
- We will win

I can't overstate the importance of frequent, clear communication throughout the entire change management process. Establish some graphics and a consistent set of communication materials. Experts state that you have to say something 10 times, in different ways, for people to fully understand a new concept. I wholeheartedly agree. By gaining alignment with top leaders, and everyone utilizing common terminology in a confident, consistent manner, the organization will progress to the new normal. Just remember to communicate, communicate, and communicate.

In summary, leaders must create a strong vision for Operational Excellence, which means operating safely, reliably, consistently, and cost effectively. Desire and expect to become the best in your industry. Approach Operational Excellence in all that you do through an integrated management system. The reward will be ZERO defect performance, world-class reliability, and significantly increased financial value. All departments, employees, and contractors have clear roles and responsibilities in executing the management system. Differentiate your company from all other companies through flawless execution.

EXCELLENCE NUGGET:
A dynamic case for change creates
excitement in any organization.

Tone at the Top

Tone at the top and walking the talk are incredibly important aspects for any leader of an organization. A good CEO establishes the expectations, works relentlessly to assure expectations are met, and removes obstacles and barriers to success.

I joined LyondellBasell in 2009 when the company had been in bankruptcy for a few months. LyondellBasell is one of the world's largest plastics and chemical manufacturing companies. When Jim Gallogly, the new CEO, asked me to join the company, I responded, "Why would I want to join a bankrupt company? The only way that I have ever approached my job is to do things the right way. I don't want anything to do with a company that has to cut corners due to lack of money and take unreasonable risks that would put people in harm's way."

Jim smiled and said he fully agreed. His leadership philosophy was that safety was his highest priority and that we would spend whatever it took (in a cost-conscious manner, of course) to increase the reliability and safety of our plants. He said growth and expansion would initially take a back seat to establishing Operational Excellence (a bold statement for a CEO). Growth would come later.

I accepted the job as Global Vice President for EH&S and Operational Excellence reporting to the CEO. Jim endorsed my Goal ZERO concept and established Operational Excellence as one of the six pillars of our company strategy. He established a strong tone at the top. We created a culture of dedication, hard work, safety, focus, teamwork, and winning.

Jim Gallogly's strong support for Operational Excellence and our outstanding LyondellBasell global personnel helped our company to develop a culture of excellence and become one of the most reliable, safest, and profitable companies in the industry. We emerged from bankruptcy in April 2010 and went public in October 2010 on the New York Stock Exchange at an initial stock price of around $17/share. By 2015, the stock had reached a peak price of $115/share. The private equity firm Apollo Global Management was one of the creditors that stepped forward during bankruptcy. When Apollo divested, the company made approximately $9 billion in profit on a $2 billion investment. In August 2014, a *Forbes* magazine article stated LyondellBasell had been the best private equity deal in Wall Street history.

Gallogly received external recognition for his leadership. Dr. David Michaels was the U.S. Assistant Secretary of Labor for the Occupational Safety and Health Administration (OSHA) from 2009-2017, roughly the same time I worked for LyondellBasell. Dr. Michaels oversaw the safety for literally thousands of companies across the country, and we interacted with him on many occasions. In the March 21, 2018 edition of the *Harvard Business Review,* he wrote an article entitled, *"7 Ways to Improve Operations Without Sacrificing Workplace Safety."*

In the article, Dr. Michaels complimented Jim Gallogly as being a CEO that "did it the right way," saying, "When Gallogly arrived at LyondellBasell, the firm was in bankruptcy; his job was to return the company to profitably, which he did. At his first meeting with his employees, however, he announced that he wasn't going to begin by talking about the firm's financial challenges. Instead, the new CEO wanted to focus on something far more important: his absolute commitment to safety."

Bob Patel succeeded Jim Gallogly as CEO of LyondellBasell in early 2015 and hit the ground running. Bob continued to drive Goal ZERO and Operational Excellence in the organization. As an example, LyondellBasell acquired A. Schulman, Inc., a leading supplier of high-performance plastic compounds, composites, and powders in 2018. At the time of the acquisition, the OSHA injury/illness rate for the A. Schulman workforce was 1.54 (about 1 injury in a year for every 65 workers), over seven times higher than the injury/illness rate at LyondellBasell. Patel demonstrated his passion for people and communicated his Goal ZERO expectations from the beginning to the A. Schulman employees joining LyondellBasell.

To fast forward, the acquisition of A. Schulman was successful. The new employees and businesses fully integrated into LyondellBasell's management system for conducting work and the Goal ZERO culture. And most importantly, the previous A. Schulman sites made rapid improvement in safety performance, nearly matching the performance of the legacy LyondellBasell sites within two years of the acquisition. LyondellBasell (including the A. Schulman acquired assets) had a combined total workforce injury/illness rate (employees and contractors) of 0.20 in 2020. That's one injury in a year for every 500 workers, world-class safety performance.

Bob Patel's leadership was well recognized by the public and his peers. Patel was recognized in 2018 by receiving the prestigious global chemical industry ICIS Kavaler Award. (Jim Gallogly received the award in 2014). The award is selected by industry peers for the senior executive making the greatest positive impact on his/her company and the chemical industry. Patel won the award again the next year, 2019, the only two-time winner in the history of the award.

Bob Patel and Jim Gallogly provided excellent examples for proper tone at the top, putting safety first, and driving business success through strong Operational Excellence.

EXCELLENCE NUGGET:
Growth and expansion should come after achieving Operational Excellence.

Future Focus

One of the Seven Fs that I described in Chapter 1 is to be future focused. Future focus is important for individuals and for teams. By being future focused, it helps to put today's problems and challenges into perspective, maintaining hope and optimism for the future.

When we moved to The Netherlands for my European expatriate assignment, our son Brandon was 13 years old. We were leaving the town where he was raised and had lived all of his life. He had many friends, enjoyed hunting and fishing, and played lots of sports. Life was good! The first few months in Europe were challenging. Although he was excited about the European experience, he was a bit depressed regarding the big change that had taken place in his life.

My job was director of process engineering and process control for Dow Europe, which required considerable travel. Brandon was able to come along at times and visit new places. The Antwerp International School that he attended was terrific and the school had many activities for the students. However, there were also slow days during which there weren't many activities.

To help Brandon become future focused, I bought two items to pin on the wall. One was a European map that we could write on and wipe off. The second was a year-at-a-glance calendar. We got together and began discussing our plans for the future. First, we put his school activities on the calendar, which included his sporting event trips to neighboring cities such as London, Hamburg, and Paris—all cool places. We added home trips we would be taking back to the United States. Then we spent time marking the map for these trips and discussing other places to visit. We'd agree on a plan and add these to the calendar.

Eventually, Brandon became so interested in the future that he would look months ahead and ask, "Dad, what are we going to do on this weekend?" He was excited and wanted to fill the entire calendar with activities. Getting Brandon future focused changed everything and he thoroughly enjoyed our 2 1/2 years in Europe.

Sports teams are the master of future focus. Their game schedule is well-defined and excellent coaches motivate their teams to give their best to win. By being laser focused on the future, players work extremely hard in the present to get in good shape and perfect their skills. The team may lose a particular game and it's easy for the team to get depressed. However, the sun always comes up the next day, and by the coach keeping the players future focused, the players bounce back and focus forward rather than on the past.

Low morale in organizations has often been the result of poor leadership and lack of hope for the future. Create and share a vision of winning and communicate what success will feel like. Paint a bright future, create optimism, and approach work with enthusiasm. Enthusiasm reflects confidence, spreads good cheer, raises morale, and helps to inspire others. Generating enthusiasm within yourself is an important first step towards success. Everyone is attracted to the magnetism of enthusiasm. Keep your people future focused and you will enjoy the results.

EXCELLENCE NUGGET:
Motivate people through future focus.

Human Factors

Throughout the years, we analyzed many cases of injuries, quality incidents, and near misses. A very small percentage are caused by asset failure, but most fall into the people and system categories—human factors. By digging deeper into the incidents, understanding the causes, and taking corrective actions, you are more able to proactively prevent incidents from re-occurring in the future.

Our evaluation of the data has shown that most incident causes fall into five areas of human factors and not in any particular order:

1. **Competence.** Lack of the basic skills and knowledge to do the job or task. Lack of understanding of requirements, procedures, and expectations.

2. **Compliance.** Failure to follow rules and lack of a compliance culture. Ineffective self-assessments, auditing, timely corrective actions, and gap closure.
3. **Behavior.** Carelessness, lack of attention to detail, mistakes, and lack of focus on the task. Failure to take time to recognize hazards. Lack of intervention for unsafe acts.
4. **Leadership.** Unclear expectations, inadequate skilled resources, ineffective monitoring, and lack of individual accountability and consequence management.
5. **Risk Management.** Inadequate identification of risks, improperly mitigating risks, and poor equipment maintenance.

As you can see, each of these areas deals with human behavior. A focus on human factors is key to reducing risk and eliminating defects in your company. Human errors are inevitable, but proactive measures can help reduce errors. Work processes, procedures, and standards should be written with human factors in mind to help minimize the risk of human error.

The teachings in this chapter and throughout the book provide suggestions for managing each of the areas of human factors. As I've repeatedly mentioned, you must have a good management system as a foundation and a strong culture of excellence. This then sets the stage for competent people to execute the system, drive performance, and achieve results.

Rather than experiencing a terrible incident with one of these five causes, it's better to *be proactive in each of these areas to prevent incidents and drive excellence.* Focus on the primary elements of human factors: competence, compliance, behavior, leadership, and risk management. Turn these root causes into action. Use these five causes as a checklist for education and focused attention across your organization.

Mentorship

"Most knowledge is gained at the foot of the elderly."
–Anonymous

I was privileged to meet the famous W. Edwards Deming, who I discussed earlier. I attended his conference in 1988 when he was 88 years old. Deming was an American engineer, statistician, professor, author, lecturer, and management consultant. We spent a week with Deming and the learnings were immense. Deming called it "divine wisdom."

Throughout my career, I took every opportunity to learn from more experienced people. There are numerous ways to learn from others. You can attend training courses, participate in conferences, read books, such as Deming's book or the one you are reading now, or simply spend some quality time with a mentor.

Mentorship is an excellent way to learn from others. Mentorship is the concept of someone who teaches, coaches, or gives advice to a younger, less experienced individual. I took the time to share my learnings in this book, but many people around you have many of the same experiences and are willing to share them with you.

If your company has a formal mentor program, you should take advantage of it. However, informal relationships are just as good. Seek out additional opportunities to learn from the elderly, whether these individuals work in your company or not. I've had many young people throughout the years invite me for lunch or to have a cup of coffee and just talk about various issues they are dealing with. I always found these engagements enjoyable and willingly shared my advice. Look for people that you respect and give it a try. The worst that can happen is they say no, but I bet they won't.

For those of you that have been around a while, pick younger people that you have an interest in and initiate a conversation over lunch or coffee. Ask them about their interests, their career goals, or any issues they are dealing with, and the conversation will flow. You will feel good about sharing any advice that you may have.

Individual Ownership, Accountability, and Responsibility

One of the most important elements in a culture of excellence is to establish a high level of individual ownership, accountability, and responsibility in every person across the organization. Every person should focus on what he or she individually can control and his or her individual behaviors. You want an organization in which every person conducts him or herself in the right manner, even when no one is around.

The first few hours, days, and weeks for a new employee or contractor are the most influential time for establishing an understanding of expectations and the organization's culture. *Leaders, employees, and contractors are responsible for following company rules and expectations, working safely, avoiding mistakes, and meeting the customers' needs.* This statement may seem obvious. Tragically, significant incidents and defects often occur simply because someone hasn't followed a rule, adhered to a procedure, or paid attention to detail while performing a task. Each and every individual must comply with the expectations of the organization and not repeat the same mistakes of the past.

Develop a culture in which individuals ask themselves, "What can I do to make things better?" and "What can I do to make this job successful?" Following something going wrong, the pertinent question is, "What could I have done to prevent the incident?" The emphasis is on "I" as opposed to making excuses and blaming someone else. Taking ownership is essential. Develop this expectation from the beginning with new people.

One of the simplest examples is if I am walking down the hall and slip on a banana peel. Sure, someone should not have left the banana peel on the floor—an issue that should be addressed, but don't blame others. I should be on the lookout for banana peels on the floor and other hazards. Hazards exist all around us, and we must be proactive and responsible in addressing them in the right manner. One of our manufacturing plants had a mirror on the wall with an excellent inscription:
"This person is responsible for my safety."

By creating a healthy culture of individual accountability in every person, and by not criticizing people for mistakes, people begin to take on more responsibility for their actions rather than looking for others to blame. Set clear expectations, offer public praise when people do well, and address the issue quickly when they don't perform as expected. If you treat people like adults, they will respond.

Each person in the organization must perform up to his or her full potential. It's very effective when every person in your organization can answer the question: "What are you personally responsible and accountable for in your job?" Answers such as, "I help with," or "I'm part of," or "I assist with" are not sufficient. Your organization becomes much more effective when each person has individual accountability and works with a sense of *ownership*.

Creating personal accountability begins with each position having a clear job description stating responsibilities. In the job description, be sure to avoid watered down verbs such as "help, assist, participate, advise, consult, etc." Instead, use action verbs such as "lead, manage, coordinate, etc." Make the responsibilities action oriented with well-defined deliverables. Be crisp and don't make the job description too long. Ensure that every person has an *active* role with responsibility in daily work, on projects, and on teams. Train people to look for what needs to be done instead of waiting to be told. This approach builds commitment, a positive attitude, and pride.

I'll share a simple example to illustrate my point. In the early years of my career, we held an annual picnic for employees and their families. A handful of individuals would serve on the picnic committee and work themselves to death, of course always doing a wonderful job. We noticed that the rest of the people in our department would just show up and enjoy themselves, but the energy level wasn't very high.

One year, we agreed that each person in the department would have at least one item at the picnic for which he or she was individually responsible. We wanted 100% of the employees to feel some amount of accountability for making the picnic successful, instead of just showing up. We had to be creative in dividing the tasks to create enough items for everyone to have something to do. One person was responsible for soft drinks, one for balloons, one for bingo, one for registration; you get the picture.

Well, this picnic turned out to be the best one that we ever had. Every person had a job to do and didn't want to let down the rest of the team. Every person was able to demonstrate his or her responsibility to his or her family. You could see the pride and enthusiasm that the individual responsibility created.

The neatest part of the story relates to Herman, one of our quieter individuals. Herman took on responsibility for mosquito control since the picnic was held outside. He did a great job of having the grounds clear when the picnic started. Later during the picnic, when everyone was playing bingo, Herman started up a loud gas-powered mosquito blower out near the bushes surrounding the park area and began to spray for mosquitos.

Everyone chuckled to see quiet Herman proudly doing his job. The funniest part of the story happened when he went upwind of the bingo tables and the fog drifted across where we were playing bingo. We got a laugh out of the fog, and you could see the pride and sense of ownership in Herman's eyes that came from having individual accountability and meeting expectations.

Never fall into the trap of the story about four people: Everybody, Somebody, Anybody and Nobody.

There was an important job to be done
and Everybody was asked to do it.
Everybody was sure that Somebody would.
Anybody could have done it, but Nobody did.
Somebody got angry that Nobody had done it.
After all, it was Everybody's job.
Everybody knew that Anybody could do it,
and Everybody realized that Nobody would.
In the end, Nobody took responsibility.
Everybody blamed Somebody
because Nobody actually asked Anybody to do it.
–Author Unknown

The primary message of this section is that each person should have clear accountability in his or her job. Don't allow anyone to just attend and be present. He or she needs to have individual accountability and be able to explain what the accountability means to others. Most people are always capable of doing more, but they aren't asked or expected to do so. This expectation is very powerful in building an organization where everyone is contributing to their fullest. You will see them feel better about themselves and their contribution to the team. Their pride and self-esteem will shine.

If you supervise others, accept complete ownership and accountability for your team. Be strong and enforce compliance with rules and standards at all times. Be pleased with your team's progress but never satisfied with your current status. Give your team credit when things are going well. When things aren't going so well, don't blame others; take ownership, accept responsibility, and take action to improve.

EXCELLENCE NUGGET:
Instill a sense of ownership in every person on the team

Sense of Urgency

I always worked to establish a sense of urgency among our people. I was commonly known for saying, "Go faster!" Results focused leaders constantly create a future vision and determine what needs to be done to improve, and then they get after it. When we decided in a meeting on actions to take, I often said, "This afternoon would be a good time to start."

It's important to continually prioritize and determine the actions that will make the most difference in driving desired results. Once prioritization is complete, develop a sense of urgency in your people to focus on and execute the actions for these highest priorities.

A sense of urgency also applies to closing gaps in performance. You never want the same type of incident or defect to occur when the incident has already occurred at your workplace, in another area of your company, or in another company. If a problem occurs, take immediate action to address the issue and develop a sense of urgency to act on improvement. Acting and communicating quickly sends a clear message throughout the organization of the ZERO incident expectations. Learning from incidents and then rapidly implementing corrective actions are critical for preventing recurrence.

To add emphasis, we replaced the commonly used "safety moment" at the beginning of meetings with a "sense of urgency" moment. We didn't require a sense of urgency moment for all meetings, but only when there was a current topic to highlight. Safety moments can quickly become old, stale, and ineffective. I've seen safety "moments" turn into a 15-minute discussion in an hour-long meeting. The safety topic had nothing to do with the purpose of the meeting. In the end, the safety moment took up a considerable amount of time that could have been used to address other, more important issues.

A sense of urgency moment addresses a wide variety of topics that need emphasis. A sense of urgency moment can pertain to an issue in your workplace, or a current incident that occurred elsewhere and how the incident relates to your operation. A sense of urgency moment builds a sense of awareness in areas where the event didn't occur and helps spread the word. It stresses why it is so important to resolve problems as quickly as possible.

Keeping Safety Awareness High

Protecting people in any organization is vitally important. The best leaders know to always lead with a strong emphasis on safety; leading with safety is the right thing to do, and it helps impact performance of everything else.

Nothing is worse than someone getting seriously injured. It has a devastating impact on everyone involved. Safety of yourself and those around you begins with you. You can set the right example and influence others more than you realize.

As you progress towards becoming a Goal ZERO company, injuries and incidents will be much less frequent. In fact, smaller departments and locations should statistically never have an injury. A location without injuries is terrific, but the side effect is that people can become complacent and drop their guard.

Through the years, I saw how a particular location reacted following a serious injury. People in the organization developed an intense focus, conducted all types of safety discussions, and started emphasizing the basics. The sense of urgency was high. Everyone was extremely careful not to have another incident and get hurt. If you've ever been in an automobile accident, you know the feeling. For a long time thereafter, your level of attention is at an all-time high when driving, and it's quite a while before you become relaxed in a car again.

On the other hand, complacency can set in at locations that haven't had an injury for a long time. Extra focus is necessary to maintain a high level of safety awareness in injury-free locations and companies. Bad things can still happen in the best of organizations.

One technique for keeping the safety focus high is the use of a "Safety Flash." This one-page email blast is sent to everyone in the company immediately following an injury, incident, or near miss elsewhere in the company. It's critical that the communication goes out quickly to have the maximum effect.

A Safety Flash typically has a flashy, attention-grabbing header. The Safety Flash contains a photo of the incident or something similar. The Safety Flash only states the facts that are known at the time. Since investigations have not yet been performed, don't speculate on the causes or corrective actions. The intention is to show a sense of urgency and the importance to the organization. For significant incidents, the results of the investigation can be sent out later as a follow-up.

At each location, supervision prints copies of the Safety Flash to post on bulletin boards and display at various places such as lunch tables. If appropriate, the incident should be discussed during various meetings. These flashes generate considerable discussion and help to keep safety and attention to detail on the minds of the people. The main theme should be: "Let's act like this incident just happened here. What actions would we be taking if the incident had occurred in our workplace?"

There are much improved communication platforms today that integrate emails, social media, and intranet materials—and these tools even translate the messages for you. This is particularly important for non-English speakers.

Another useful tool is a "Safety Alert." A safety alert is typically sent for incidents that occur in another company. Every incident should be used as a learning and improvement opportunity. Send Safety Alerts to the organization to remind people of the items in your management system that would have prevented the same type of incidents. These Safety Alerts serve as a periodic reminder of why your requirements and processes are so important.

Proactive vs. Reactive Behavior

Leaders and employees have many competing priorities for their time. We've all heard the concepts of important and urgent. People may be well aware of items that are important to the organization, but the urgent items commonly get the most focus. I'm going to generalize, but most people operate in either the **proactive** or **reactive** behavior mode pertaining to Operational Excellence.

I'll begin with the **reactive behavior** mode. Leaders and individuals tend to spend the majority of their time on the urgent issues of the day. These activities may consist of major projects, change initiatives, or responding to crisis situations that may arise. Reliability, quality, and safety don't receive much attention when operations are going well. Low consequence incidents or near misses don't receive much response. Leaders say the right things, but the organization picks up on their lack of intensity and acts accordingly.

Reactive behavior mode people don't increase their level of attention to detail until something significant happens such as a fire, explosion, serious injury, impact to the environment, major noncompliance fine, or a significant quality event with a customer. If such an incident occurs, reactive behavior individuals get upset and turn all their attention to managing the incident. By then, it's too late.

I've seen manufacturing plants operate with a frequent number of minor leaks and spills. This poor level of performance becomes the norm. Reactive behavior leaders don't take these defects seriously *until* one of the spills becomes large, ignites, and a major process safety incident develops. It's not unusual for major process safety incidents to result in several hundred million dollars of damage and business interruption.

Some companies operate with frequent minor service or customer quality complaints. Two unfavorable results can occur from this type of performance. First, the company can develop a bad reputation with its customers. More importantly, one of the quality incidents can develop into a major problem for a customer, resulting in a significant economic impact and the loss of a large customer.

I see this kind of reactive behavior on the highways every day. People drive too fast or tailgate too close. Drivers don't give themselves time to react if something goes wrong in front of them. These people don't think about the severe consequences of a major auto accident. These drivers don't get serious about safe driving *until* an accident occurs. As a result, approximately 40,000 people lose their lives in U.S. traffic accidents each year.

The behavior mode practiced by organizations with a culture of excellence is the **proactive behavior** mode. Proactive leaders maintain a good balance between the urgent and important activities. Proactive behavior leaders make a big deal out of seemingly small incidents and defects and set extremely high expectations for Operational Excellence at all times. These leaders know and understand that attention to the smallest details is important for achieving safety, quality, and ultimate customer satisfaction. I personally always drove progress the hardest when times were good— my philosophy was to challenge during good times and support during bad times.

The people in your organization must focus on the urgent items at hand; that's understood. However, you must also create the environment where the people in your organization have passion and maintain a sense of urgency to proactively eliminate relatively minor problems, defects, and noncompliance with requirements in order to prevent any one of them from becoming major.

Drive a culture of excellence. Strive for perfection. It's your choice as an employee or leader in the organization—you can be **proactive** with a Goal ZERO culture for the smallest of details for achieving Operational Excellence. Or you can be **reactive** and spend your time and money responding, investigating, and managing the impacts of major incidents and defects and losing customers in the process.

EXCELLENCE NUGGET:
Be proactive to prevent complacency.

Openness, Honesty, and Transparency

Openness and honesty are vital in any organization. You want to know the problems so you can take action to improve. You must know about emerging issues and trends before the issues become more significant.

Transparency implies openness, honesty, communication, and accountability. Transparency is essential in a Goal ZERO culture, but transparency is not achieved overnight. Rather, transparency develops over time until it becomes a habit. Transparency takes a considerable amount of trust. The manner in which leaders respond to bad news or opposing views significantly impacts transparency. Transparency is a challenge in cultures where people don't like bad news exposed, i.e., people don't want to air their dirty laundry. This reticence is especially true in certain countries of global organizations.

Transparency begins with clear expectations. In our company, we set the expectation that every incident must be reported and investigated as appropriate so that we could take corrective actions for improvement. When in doubt, report the incident. This practice prevents bad surprises later on. Take the attitude of learning as opposed to being defensive about any problems that occurred. Reporting of high potential incidents is as important for learning as when something really bad happens. Reporting incidents is the only way you can investigate the problems and take actions for continuous improvement. Leaders should be fully aware of all significant issues and trends.

Leaders at all levels play a critical role in establishing transparency. The objective is to learn from mistakes and problems, not to place blame. If someone reports a problem and then gets scolded, human nature dictates he or she will be less likely to report the next time. Leaders need to remain calm when receiving bad news, respond in a professional manner, and focus on improvement. Your response as a leader will impact the willingness of people to communicate bad news in the future. You are in deep trouble when your people stop telling you the bad news.

The following story illustrates the importance of early reporting. Joe is a friend of mine who left our company to take a significant position at a major automobile manufacturing company. One day he called and said, "Sam, I'm going to change your name to Water. You don't miss water until you don't have it." I asked why and he told me about a tragic incident that had occurred at one of their facilities in South America. An employee had punctured a drum of flammable materials with a forklift. The spill resulted in a fire that burned 75% of the person's body. Sadly, the person died after ten painful days in the hospital. Joe said that corporate leadership didn't hear about the incident until *after* the forklift operator's death.

During my discussion with Joe, he stressed the impact I had made on our company's culture. We talked about the difference in transparency between our two companies. In our company, we discussed all global incidents, even minor ones, at every Monday morning Corporate Leadership Team meeting. At his company, the culture and behavior seemed to be quite different. Many incidents didn't get reported until the consequences became "very serious." I wondered to myself if this culture was one of the reasons his company was the subject of so many class action lawsuits. Were problems kept at lower levels too long until the problems became widespread and out of control?

Another story on lack of transparency involved one of our company's manufacturing plants in China. We received a report through our employee hot line that there had been a cover-up of an injury at the plant. We launched an investigation and unfortunately determined that an employee had cut his hand requiring sutures. The employee's supervisor and the EH&S manager decided to hide the injury and took the employee to a private doctor for treatment. Fortunately, an honest and concerned fellow employee reported the incident to leadership.

The female manager of the plant was extremely good and one of my favorite managers in China. We worked with her on the situation and decided to terminate the supervisor and the EH&S manager. We had high expectations for honesty and transparency and would not tolerate such a deliberate act of hiding an injury.

To complicate matters, we received another employee hot line communication a few weeks later indicating that the plant manager had actually been in on the incident cover-up. After the supervisor had been terminated, he had met with the plant manager to discuss the incident and had secretly recorded the conversation. This recording provided all of the evidence we needed to confirm that, sadly, the plant manager had agreed to the incident cover-up.

Of course, we let her go and lost a previously very good plant manager with high potential for this deliberate dishonest deed. Letting her go was difficult since the terminations left us without three key leaders in a relatively small plant, but we had no other choice. It was the right thing to do.

We communicated these dismissals across our entire company. This incident was a teachable moment for all. We talked about our Goal ZERO aspirations for eliminating injuries and that we wanted to accomplish our vision the right way, not by hiding injuries. We never took any action for someone experiencing an injury unless he or she deliberately violated safety rules. We made it very clear that we expected openness and honesty in reporting of all incidents so that we could learn. I can assure you that everyone got the message, and this action was another step forward in establishing the culture that we wanted.

Companies must also be transparent with the public, especially in local communities where you operate. The longer that you hold onto bad news, the worse it gets. People get over bad news after the initial shock and, in the long term, respect the transparency. Be open and honest, and report incidents and problems when they occur. Take ownership and be responsible. Communicate the actions you are taking to correct the situation and prevent the incident from happening again. Honesty, integrity, and transparency will serve you well.

EXCELLENCE NUGGET:
Always communicate the bad news.

Communication

Effective communication is essential for establishing and nurturing the culture you desire. You must spend a considerable amount of time teaching, communicating, and, most importantly, listening to others in your workforce. There's an appropriate old Cherokee proverb, "Listen to the whispers and you won't have to hear the screams." Two-way communication is vital. Communicate regularly and clearly both upward and downward in the organization. Take enough time to help people understand *why* something is important and the vision for the future.

Effective and efficient communication is imperative because people are busy and have an enormous number of items competing for their attention. Strike a balance between communicating enough and not overloading the organization. Don't overcommunicate like so many organizations do on social media by sending unsolicited messages every day. I delete those immediately when I see them.

Make sure the messages that you communicate are well understood by the audience. Just because you say something doesn't mean the message is clearly received. Check for understanding. For those of you communicating to people with other native languages, be especially careful.

I always included a representative from our communications department as a member of our leadership team. We wanted people in the communications department to understand our actions to drive Operational Excellence performance and why this work was so important for the success of the company. Through their active participation, we provided an unlimited amount of material for company-wide communications which helped in developing the culture and behaviors we desired.

Communication upward to your supervision is as important as communicating with the people in your organization. I always took the approach of wanting to make my boss successful. It was important for me to understand what was important to him or her and for them to know what was important to me.

Ensuring good alignment builds trust and clarity on priorities and objectives. Communication clarifies how everything fits into the big picture and helps create a productive relationship with each other. There should never be any uncertainty between someone and his or her boss or direct report. Keep your boss informed to build trust and ensure an aligned approach toward the important objectives of the organization.

Here are a few recommendations that will help improve the effectiveness of your communications:

- **Be sincere, honest, and direct.** It's hard to regain credibility once you lose it. Always provide information like it is and don't sugar-coat. When a problem arises, acknowledge it, and then quickly talk about the actions you and your team are taking. People are smart and know when a person is not being honest. And one selfish motive is: if you are always honest and consistent, you don't have to spend any time trying to remember what you said the last time.
- **Develop a communications plan.** Create a schedule to prevent too much time elapsing between messages and utilize various methods of communication: face to face, email, videos, webcasts, and social media.
- **Constancy of purpose.** In his book, *Out of the Crisis*, W. Edwards Deming discusses the need for constancy of purpose. Take your time to establish simple and easily understood principles and stick with them. Repeat them over and over. Nothing is more useless than flavor of the month programs.
- **Utilize different sources for communication.** The CEO, leadership team members, department leaders, and others should all share in communicating key messages. Mix it up.
- **Keep the audience in mind.** Remember, it's not about the message you send; rather, it's about how your audience perceives the message.
- **Simplicity in writing.** Keep your written communications clear and easy to read. The Flesch Reading Ease Score is extremely helpful. (See Chapter 5.)
- **Say it 10 times.** I'm a strong believer in communicating a consistent message and repeating it often and in different ways. Many people send out a single communication for a change initiative and believe everyone "gets it." That's

hardly the truth. Many times, in my career, I witnessed someone hearing a message for the 3rd, 4th, or 5th time before the light bulb finally went off. Perhaps the person had other things on his or her mind and wasn't truly listening earlier. You must catch the receiver of your messages in the right frame of mind at the right time.

- **Eliminate confusion.** Casey Stengel, a baseball right fielder and manager, best known as the manager of the championship New York Yankees team of the 1950s, once said to his team, "All right, everyone, line up alphabetically according to your height." Leaders unknowingly create confusion at times by the way they communicate. Be sure your messages are clear and don't get misinterpreted.

- **Technical writing is different than writing a novel.** In my college English literature classes, the professor constantly instructed us to elaborate more, stretch out the verbiage, and extend the use of vocabulary. My technical communications class, on the other hand, emphasized shorter sentences, elimination of unnecessary words, consistency in choice of words, and bullet points. Both styles have their place, so be sure to understand your audience and choose the appropriate style.

- **Make it persuasive.** I learned long ago to make every communication persuasive. If you write an article or send a message, don't just make it interesting. Take the opportunity to always include action statements for whatever you want to happen. Never pass up an opportunity to persuade others.

- **Watch the harsh words.** We all get frustrated at times. It's best to sleep on it before lashing out at someone or sending a harsh email. My friend, Rhea, told me that saying something you regret later is "like squeezing toothpaste out of a tube. Once it's out, you can't get it back in!"

EXCELLENCE NUGGET:
Communicating change—say it 10 times.

Make It Fun

The workplace doesn't have to be serious all of the time. Think of creative ways to loosen up the organization to help accelerate your agenda. Here's a story to illustrate the point. When I returned from Europe to Texas and became the EH&S leader for Dow's Texas Operations, the relations with the local unions had become somewhat contentious over the previous years. We began conducting numerous meetings with union leaders to discuss various issues of concern and to rebuild relations.

One of the priorities for me was improving safety performance across the site of 5,000 employees and a considerable number of contractors. At the end of one of our meetings, I issued a challenge to the union leaders that all of the union employees could not work the entire summer injury-free.

Of course, everyone likes to take on a challenge, so the discussion became interesting. The union leaders proposed that if their people worked the entire summer injury-free, company leaders would wash their personal vehicles at the company fire station. I countered and said, "This sounds good, but let's do the contest monthly, June to August, and we will wash your vehicles each month if you work injury-free. However, if there is an injury in a month, you will wash the leadership team's vehicles." The union leaders shook their heads a bit, but finally accepted the challenge.

It was amazing how their focus and attitudes over the next three months shifted to making sure their people worked safely, which was exactly what we wanted them to do. The month of June ended as an injury-free month. We went to the fire station and the union leaders were sitting on lawn chairs ready to watch us wash their vehicles, which were primarily trucks. The union leaders really enjoyed watching us, took a lot of pictures, and we all had fun that day.

In July, a pipe fitter unfortunately experienced a finger cut requiring stitches. Now it was time for the union leaders to wash our vehicles. Again, we all proceeded to the fire station and just as the union leaders were about to wash our vehicles, they pulled out paper bags with the eyes cut out and put the bags over their heads. The union leader said, "There is no way we are going to be seen washing management's trucks." We all got a good laugh out of that.

August turned out to be another injury-free month and we gladly washed their trucks again. This entire three-month challenge turned out successful in many ways. Safety performance improved and was sustained going forward. We all had a lot of fun, and the entire site was interested in the monthly outcome. Finally, our relationship with the union leaders improved immensely. This turned out to be a win-win situation. Have fun in your workplace.

Work hard to create an esprit de corps amongst the people, a shared spirit of camaraderie, enthusiasm, and dedication to the organization. With the right culture, everyone gets better. "A rising tide lifts all boats." Treat people with respect and keep them future focused. Create an organization in which people are lined up to enter instead of wanting to leave. Most importantly, keep it simple and make your organization a place where people are proud to work.

Build Loyalty

During my university years, I worked 15-20 hours a week in the Chemical Engineering Department stockroom to help pay for my education. Our work consisted of printing materials for the professor's classes, handing out equipment for research projects, and just about anything else that the faculty and staff in the department needed. My job was great, and I felt very fortunate to be able to earn the money that I badly needed.

One of my toughest courses was Organic Chemistry in the Chemistry Department. We performed laboratory experiments that were associated with our course material. We were each issued a set of glassware (beakers, flasks, cylinders, etc.) for the course that we used in the experiments. One day when I arrived at the lab, I opened my locker and the box of glassware fell to the ground and quite a few pieces broke. I was devastated. The value of the glassware was about $300. This was an incredible amount of money for me since I was earning about $2.00 an hour in my part-time job.

After the class, I went back to work and told my boss, Bill Tatum, the story and how much I had to repay the Chemistry Department. I didn't know it at the time, but he called his counterpart in Chemistry and worked a deal for the Chemical Engineering Department to replace the glassware. When he told me, I couldn't believe he had done this and was so relieved. That small gesture meant an incredible amount to me. I've never forgotten Mr. Tatum's actions to this day.

Another example of building loyalty was in my early years at Dow. I was managing a project to design and install some new process equipment into an operating unit. I was all in and loved the assignment. During the middle of the project, my father-in-law, at the age of 59, suffered a heart attack and was life-flighted to Houston. We raced to the hospital, and he was in critical condition for several weeks before passing away. To complicate matters, my wife, Stephanie, was pregnant with our first child and delivered our new baby ten days after her father died.

It was a traumatic time for us all. I spent 2 weeks at the hospital with Stephanie and her family. I kept my boss, Dexter White, up to date with what was going on. Stephanie's two brothers said they would have to use their vacation for the workdays that were missed, and I expected the same. It really didn't matter.

However, to my surprise, when I returned to work, Dexter said I didn't need to use vacation for the time off. I couldn't believe it and was extremely appreciative. I was already loyal to the company, but this action by my supervisor took my loyalty to a new level.

I remember how I was treated still to this day, and I paid Dow back countless times for all the nights, weekends, and long hours I gladly worked to help make the company great. Do everything you can to develop loyalty in your employees; it's incredibly powerful! Small things matter.

EXCELLENCE NUGGET:
*Take care of your people
and build loyalty.*

Motivation

A favorite story of mine is about a plant control board operator named Harry. Harry was a smart guy, but he typically did the minimum and was never proactive. A supervisor would tell him to make a change in the flow rate, so he'd make the change and then sit back down. Harry was just doing what he was told. Harry was seen by others as a mediocre performer with little enthusiasm.

His supervisor, Robert, went bowling one night with some friends. As he entered the bowling alley, he heard someone yelling on the far left lane. It was Harry! He stood there and watched Harry as he bowled. Harry couldn't wait until his turn to bowl. He'd get up excitedly, grab his bowling ball, and give it his total concentration. Then he'd roll the ball down the lane, watching intently. As the ball struck the pins, he'd jump for joy and shout out. Robert had never seen this side of Harry. How could Harry act so differently at work from the way he did at bowling?

With bowling, you hear the sounds and see the pins as they get knocked down. It's immediate feedback on your performance. You record your score, which creates an element of self-satisfaction and competition. You constantly try to get better and improve.

In contrast, imagine the game of bowling if there was a soundproof curtain in front of the pins. You roll the ball down the lane, and the ball travels under the curtain. You don't see or hear anything. You don't keep score. You just sit back down and await your next turn. That would take all of the excitement out of the game and that's how Harry felt at work.

The difference is feedback. Harry was not getting feedback at work regarding the company or unit performance and the results of his actions. If you want your people to be excited and enthusiastic about their work, give them constant feedback about their individual performance and the performance of the unit, department, or company. Show them the score. Feedback is the breakfast of champions.

EXCELLENCE NUGGET:
Provide constant feedback on individual and organization performance.

Create Flow

The book, *Flow—The Psychology of Optimal Experience,* by Mihaly Csikszentmihalyi, is one of my favorites. The theme in the book is about the essence of life. The author describes a state of mind called "Flow" in which time flies by. We've all been involved in activities where it seemed like time flew by. How many times have you been doing something that you love, and you look at your watch and realize how late it is? People will spend all night enthusiastically working on their favorite hobby or reading a good book. On the other hand, we've all been in a boring meeting where the minutes and seconds drag by, thinking that the meeting will never end.

The author outlines his theory that people are happiest when they are in a state of Flow—a state of concentration or complete absorption with the activity at hand and the situation. Flow is a state in which people are so involved in an activity that nothing else seems to matter. The Flow state is an optimal state of intrinsic motivation, where the person is fully immersed in what he or she is doing.

Csikszentmihalyi performed research with thousands of people trying to determine what creates the state of Flow. Of course, Flow is different for different individuals. Results showed that activities such as hobbies, sports, sex, and a challenging job can all create Flow.

The secret is to find the activities you love the most and create Flow in your life. You can even adapt your activities, such as your work, to create Flow for yourself and for your team. As a leader, make work fun, make work a game, keep people future focused, create challenge, and recognize accomplishments. These actions can help create Flow. All of the people I worked with understood the concept of Flow and we worked hard at it and loved it.

Hire, Develop, and Inspire

Some human resources organizations define the employee life cycle as hire, develop, retain, and offboard. I've always had a problem with the word "retain" when it comes to people; the definition of retain is "to keep in one's possession." I don't like the idea that I am being retained. Instead, I like to replace retain with the word *inspire*.

Younger people have the belief that they will work for several companies throughout their career. Changing companies may be the case, but it doesn't have to be that way. Some people work for the same company their entire career and others change for various reasons. I always told new employees to work every day as if they would work for the same company their entire career. I approached my work with the same attitude.

People should work every day to make their company better. If the work situation doesn't meet expectations or if someone gets an outstanding offer elsewhere, the person has the right to leave. But if you treat people the right way, challenge them to be excellent at all times, recognize and reward good performance, and inspire them, you stand a better chance of them remaining with your organization.

Unintended employee turnover is extremely costly for your organization in many ways. Losing talented and experienced individuals is a threat to operations and to productivity. Disgruntled employees post unfavorable comments on social media, making qualified replacements difficult to find and time consuming. You must continually nurture a challenging and exciting environment, and never allow the morale to deteriorate. Low morale in a company is contagious and spreads rapidly. If you have this situation in your organization, you must take rapid actions to understand the issues and turn the tide.

Do everything possible in your company to excite your employees about their jobs and the future. Create the environment in which people enjoy coming to work every day and are passionate about helping to make the company better. Listen to employee concerns and act on what you learn.

Developing an excellent employee value proposition is one way to inspire people in the organization. The old question is always true: "What's in it for me?" Create an employee value proposition so strong that there is no other place your people would rather be. You want a company where people are lined up to get in. Inspired people brag to others about your workplace. Take care of your people and they will take care of the company.

The war for talent is real. Every organization needs talent, and every competitive organization is searching for the same types of individuals. You need outstanding people in order to achieve Operational Excellence and win. Hiring skilled talent is especially important when working with hazardous materials such as the industry we worked in.

Mack Brown, the longtime football coach of The University of Texas, wrote a good book named *One Heartbeat, A Philosophy of Teamwork, Life, and Leadership.* The book is an interesting read and the part that struck me was how much his organization placed a deliberate focus on recruiting in *everything* the organization did. A consistent focus on recruiting makes perfect sense because every team is trying to attract the same star athletes.

Mack illustrates that *every* part of their program had a recruiting element to it. Their facilities, their annual media pamphlet, and their media interviews all had a recruiting lens to them. An intensity on recruiting makes sense in sports and why shouldn't a strong focus on recruiting also apply to business?

Hiring the right individuals is the most important function a leader performs. I personally put a tremendous amount of effort into recruiting. I made sure we were doing a good job of identifying talent, personally interviewed thousands of individuals, selected the best candidates, and assured the new employees got off to a good start for a long, successful career. I always wanted to make sure individuals had the right technical skills, the right social skills, and would be the type of person we would enjoy working with.

Why would someone want to work at your company? What do your facilities look like? What are people's first impressions when they set foot on your property? Why would someone want to stay? What would make someone want to leave? These are all important questions to address on a continuous basis. If you make these a priority, you will be far ahead in making your company attractive not only for recruits, but also for your existing employees.

EXCELLENCE NUGGET:
Inspire the people in your organization.

Know Your People

An old saying is popular about what it takes to become a professional golfer. All it takes is good technique, determination, lots of practice, and God-given talent! There isn't much we can do about the God-given talent we were born with, so most of us will never become a professional golfer. However, almost everyone has some type of skills that need to be recognized and utilized.

I've seen many new leaders in an organization quickly replace almost every person on their team. The new leader is looking for people that fit their mold and their expectations. The team loses years of experience in the process. The new leader often lets his or her search for perfect get in the way of good. I've seen many of those same leaders fail or take longer to make progress.

I assumed leadership of many teams throughout the years. One of my first priorities was learning as much as possible about our people rather than making rapid changes. I wanted to understand the skills each individual thought he or she was good at and how the person brought value to the organization. I often found many of the people had years of valuable experience in the department or company and some unique talents had been overlooked. I appreciated the past contributions these people had made and the potential of their unique value. I clearly understood that none of us was as smart as all of us.

Some individuals were superb leaders. Others were individual contributors—competent, reliable, and consistent performers that constantly delivered on their commitments. Some were outspoken and critical, and I appreciated their input, as long as they were positive in speaking up and not constantly complaining. A few were exceptionally creative, typically a little different from the mainstream conservative types. I called these "stallions" and tried my best to harness their talents into making the organization great. I loved people that were proactive and self-starters; I enjoyed saying "whoa" a lot better than "giddy-up." Some team members didn't live up to expectations or were detrimental to the organization, and I didn't hesitate to quickly make a change.

Each of my teams ended up different than the one before. I believe that with this approach and playing to each person's talents, we always came up with a diverse, high performing team that drove rapid transformation. All these people needed in most cases was good leadership. The bottom line is not to overlook the hidden talents people may have and do your best to capture and utilize these talents for the benefit of your organization.

As a leader, the people on your team want to know that you care about them and have their best interests at heart. The greatest respect that you can show for someone is to have time for them. I developed a simple introductory questionnaire to help speed the process of getting acquainted. This questionnaire was given to the people of teams I inherited and to new people that joined our team. A sampling of the questions include:

- Birthday?
- Family information?
- Personal background: where are you from, what are your hobbies, what are your outside activities, and what are other interesting things about you?
- What are your special work talents and interests that you have or enjoy doing?
- Which areas of our department and company do you feel are working very well or you are particularly proud of?
- Which areas of our department and company do you feel need focus for improvement?
- What would be your initial focus if you were in my job?
- How can I best help you to be successful in your work?
- Are there any additional comments, insights, or suggestions for me?

People enjoy the fact that you care enough to ask these questions. If the individuals didn't want to answer certain questions, that was perfectly fine. The answers provide valuable information for discussion that helps build strong relationships quickly. This information helps you to understand where the employee feels his or her talents are and how best to utilize them in the organization. And people always appreciate when you remember their birthdays.

Recognition and Appreciation

People want to be listened to, trusted, given responsibility, and thanked for a good job. Everyone enjoys a pat on the back or an occasional thank you. I've often told our leaders that we don't have a budget for giving out praise and personal recognition. Recognition is so easy to do and yet so underutilized.

Personal handwritten notes of appreciation were very effective when I saw someone doing something special. On one occasion, we had an operator named Gary who had been a problem performer just a year earlier. He was beginning to show excellent initiative, so I wrote a letter complimenting him on some of his specific contributions and his value to the team.

During a visit to my parents' home a month later, my mother showed a copy of the letter to me. I asked how she had obtained the letter. She said Gary had been so proud of the letter that he sent a copy to his mother. She, in turn, being a proud mother, sent copies to her two sisters, one of whom lived in the same town as my mother. Her sister knew our family and gave a copy to my mother. This letter was just one example of how much impact a simple note of sincere appreciation can have.

On another occasion, I had assumed leadership of our Polycarbonate Production Plant at Dow. Polycarbonate is a high-quality thermoplastic used in a wide variety of applications such as DVDs, bullet proof glass, automobile applications, electronics, appliances, and even the clear front cover on soft drink machines. This production plant had considerable operational problems and work was a daily grind in the early days just to keep the plant operating. There was a lot of pressure from the commercial organization, and morale was extremely low when I arrived.

As we began to make progress, we decided to serve ice cream one day when we established a new daily production record. We wanted our people to know how much we appreciated their hard work and contributions. My boss happened to arrive while we were eating ice cream and told me sternly, "We don't celebrate daily records around here." I said, "Well, I do. We have to start somewhere." Our people appreciated the ice cream very much and the recognition helped to recognize the hard work they were doing.

At LyondellBasell, we presented annual recognition plaques to plants for outstanding performance. This recognition became a highly anticipated annual event because we would heavily promote and communicate the awards across the entire company. In addition to the site name on the plaque, we included the site manager's name to personalize the recognition even more. Those managers not receiving the recognition knew exactly what they needed to do to receive it the following year. This recognition technique was just one of many motivational items we had in our toolkit.

Individual recognition programs are particularly effective. If conducted in a sincere, credible manner, individual recognition for a job well done or for a significant accomplishment can work wonders. I've seen many, many times the personal impact that recognition has on people and how being thanked makes them feel. Recognition is extremely powerful.

Companies may have many established reward and recognition programs in place, but don't let that stop you from going further. Proper recognition serves so many purposes: it's meaningful to the team or person receiving the recognition, it serves as motivation to others in the organization, and it doesn't cost much. Make sure recognition is sincere and given as immediately as possible.

Be specific regarding the reason for the recognition and communicate why the accomplishments are valuable and important. As the American poet Maya Angelou once wrote, "I've learned that people will forget what you said, people will forget what you did, but people will never forget how you made them feel."

EXCELLENCE NUGGET:
Everyone enjoys a pat on the back.

Spouses, Partners, and Families

Spouses, partners, and family members are extremely important in how well an employee functions. We always considered the family a part of our extended team. When there is trouble at home, the trouble is constantly on an employee's mind. If there are lots of problems at work and employees are working long hours, these problems can take a toll on the family.

During times of plant troubles, I often sent flowers to the spouses to let them know how much I appreciated their support. Also, some of the best recognition was something that included the spouse or family rather than just the individual, such as a nice dinner or paid weekend trip. Attention to the family paid huge dividends many times over.

We always enjoyed conducting a family day at the plant. Before we began these, family members had no idea about the work of their loved one. We always received tremendous feedback when we held these events. You could see the pride in our employees' eyes when they showed their families where they worked and talked about their responsibilities.

On one occasion, one of our control board operators, Johnny, was telling his wife about his work. He told her that he had to know everything about the plant and be able to respond to any of the hundreds of alarms that might activate. At first, she said, "No, I don't believe it." I replied, "Yes, it's true. Johnny oversees this entire control board." She was definitely impressed but was a little puzzled. She turned to Johnny and asked, "Then why do you act so dumb at home?" We all got a good laugh out of that one.

Finally, keep the children in mind. For any event, make a special effort to make it fun for the children. If you take care of the kids, mom and dad are happy, and everything else falls into place.

Try to Say Yes

I was fortunate through my career to receive a considerable amount of excellent leadership training. At Dow, some of our locations were salaried operations and some had unions representing the hourly workforce. I enjoyed working in both types of organizations. In my opinion, people are basically the same and respond well to good leadership and attention. Of course, we preferred salaried operations to avoid the hassles if you have unreasonable union leadership. We had frequent training workshops on how to maintain a salaried operation. One of the principles was to take good care of your employees or else the union will.

In one of the early training sessions, there was an ex-union negotiator named Ralph teaching a section of the course. Ralph was a tough guy and had a long history of giving companies a rough time. He worked for our company now, conducting training sessions. During the session, he asked, "Which of you believes you are a good supervisor?" Of course, everyone's hand went up. Then he asked, "If a plant operator came to you and said his child had been run over by a car and he needed to go home, would you let him go?" We all raised our hands and said of course we'd let him go take care of his child.

Then Ralph posed a third question, "What if an operator came to you and said that his cat was feeling bad this morning, and he needed to go home to check on the cat?" Only a few of us raised our hands. That's when he became heated and challenged our supervisory and decision-making skills. The discussion became lively. Ralph said that we were passing our personal judgment on what was important to our operator. He said we should let him go home and check on his cat. Ralph's comments were very surprising to all of us.

As we continued the discussion, it became clearer that Ralph was right. This cat may have been the highest priority in the operator's life. Any pet owner understands that feeling. If it's important to your employee, *try to say yes* if you can. Your employee will be much appreciative and more loyal in the future. If you say no, he'll be bitter and remember forever that you turned him down. More damage will be caused in the long term than letting him go home in the first place.

On the other hand, maintain a watchful eye for bad behavior. If a person starts to abuse a privilege such as this, you'll know he's playing games and you should approach him differently. You can never allow your willingness to say yes get out of hand. Just don't punish the entire group for one or two bad actors.

The point of this section is that the natural tendency of many leaders is to immediately say no to requests. Be careful and give a request or suggestion some thought. If something is very important to someone and the request is reasonable, try to say yes even though it's not important to you. You will be delighted at how positively the person reacts.

Challenge During Good Times, Support During Bad

Everyone that works in a manufacturing environment knows that you can be on cloud nine as you drive home one day and as low as a snake the next. Nothing is better than when your operation is running smoothly and you are setting production records. On the other hand, when something breaks and the unit shuts down, the disappointment hits you quickly. Sometimes in extreme cases, the problem is serious or the cause unknown, and these are the worst of times as you and your team work to resolve the issues and get the plant back online.

Your job as a leader is to provide a sense of calm, confidence, and assurance to your team during such times. Shelter the heat from upper management pressure and provide a calming influence for your people. Your people already have enough pressure dealing with the urgent issues at hand. The people want to know that you have their back and will support them. Avoid panic and help your employees to keep their heads straight, so they can think clearly and do their best.

At the same time, people up the line who are responsible for sales, customers, and profitability naturally get concerned and want to know what is being done. It's critical to communicate proactively and regularly to keep everyone up to date. The last thing you need is unnecessary pressure from above during times of trouble.

As I advanced to higher leadership roles, my philosophy was always to drive progress and improvement extremely hard when times were good and to be as supportive as possible when times were rough. I always remembered what it was like to be on the receiving end when things weren't going right. I've had plenty of site managers tell me how much they noticed and appreciated the support during difficult times.

Many leaders sadly take the opposite approach. Poor leaders become complacent and take good operations for granted, and, alternatively, become overly upset when there are problems. These leaders are reactive, not proactive, as I discussed earlier.

My message is to be proactive. Drive Operational Excellence very hard and set high expectations during good times. Be as supportive as possible during the difficult times. Any manufacturing person knows what I'm talking about; we've all been there.

EXCELLENCE NUGGET:
Challenge during good times,
support during bad.

Plan and Execute

We often used two simple terms for driving progress, PLAN and EXECUTE. Results focused leaders know that the art of getting things done is to focus on both. Spend an appropriate amount of time to develop a strategy and action plans, and then focus the majority of your time on relentless EXECUTION of the plan. However, over time, I coined an additional term for some of the inefficient teams I observed: "TALK ABOUT IT." After developing a plan, some teams and individuals continued to go back and "talk about it" rather than focusing on executing the plan. These people would revisit the plan over and over again instead of executing what needed to be done.

We typically approached our work on an annual cycle and liked to have the new year's plan completed before the end of the previous year, so we could hit the ground running on the first of January. We would review performance data, evaluate areas for improvement, and then all agree and align on the path forward.

As the new year progressed and some type of incident occurred, inevitably someone would want to spend too much time talking about what had happened and tell their stories from the past. They would go through the history of incidents all over again and spend endless time telling war stories and talking about what we needed to do to improve. The result was often a waste of time and duplication of the planning work we had already completed.

Once your plan is in place, focus on building the right culture to execute the plan. Over time, teams become disciplined to use the annual planning exercise as the time for open discussion, looking back, and planning actions going forward. Setting an end date for the planning process is essential. Once the planning exercise is complete, stick with the plan with relentless focus on execution, and don't keep looking back. Modification of the plan is acceptable if conditions change considerably, but make the changes in an efficient manner and move on. Efficiency and productivity improve as the team learns to eliminate the "talk about it" part of PLAN and EXECUTE.

Divide and Conquer

How often have you seen that most of the work and responsibility falls to just a few people? A few individuals step forward, while some sit back and allow others to do the work. I've seen it in departments, work groups, and in teams. This imbalance of workload doesn't utilize every participant's talent and is not efficient. People normally have much more capability than leaders realize. This outlook is especially true for operators on the front line. I have seen many operators who are leaders in their communities or run side businesses but then are micromanaged when they are at work. This is an incredible misuse of talent which is demotivating for the individual. I've always kept a watchful eye for this type of situation and did my best to spread the load. I call this "Divide and Conquer."

During my Boy Scout days, I was the patrol leader for our patrol. We attended various camporees where we competed with other patrols and troops. One of the events was communicating messages by Morse code. Of course, this era was way before cell phones. Using Morse code, you could communicate to others by using a flashlight or a flag. Each letter of the alphabet had a specific code, a combination of dots and dashes.

The competition consisted of dividing our patrol into two groups. One group was given several paragraphs of a message which they were to communicate over to the other group by flag signals. This communication was a huge challenge as it was extremely difficult memorizing the entire Morse code.

To address the challenge, I created my first "Divide and Conquer" approach. Instead of each person trying to memorize the entire code, I divided responsibilities by having each person memorize only ten letters and numbers. That way, we collectively had the entire alphabet and all numbers covered. Each scout did his part and accepted his individual responsibility. The sending and receiving groups each operated as a TEAM. We were proud to win the event on a regular basis and every scout knew he had contributed to the team's success. *None of us was as good as all of us.*

Another story comes from early in my plant management days, which included management of about 70 employees in a union operation. I was disappointed if an external audit team found deficiencies and noncompliance items. And my reaction was even worse if we ever had an incident or an injury with a root cause of not following a requirement. I expected perfection. Yet knowing and complying with the hundreds of pages of the many legal, regulatory, and internal requirements seemed impossible. So, I decided to apply the Divide and Conquer approach.

We assembled the documents and divided responsibilities among our entire staff including operators and maintenance personnel. Each person's assignment was to read and understand his or her assigned document, continually self-assess our plant for compliance, correct any noncompliance, or write work orders for any deficiencies. If the person found any noncompliance items that couldn't be managed, he or she simply had to bring the problem to my attention, and I'd take care of it.

The results were amazing. It was probably the first time that *all* of the documents had been closely read by anyone. Our team submitted hundreds of work orders during the first few months for items to get corrected. Everyone on the team had individual accountability and thrived on it. Incident rates went down, reliability went up, audit results were good, employee engagement went to an all-time high, and we were on our way to a culture of excellence and achieving Operational Excellence. You could see increased engagement and pride of ownership with each employee. Divide and Conquer works!

In my global leadership roles, I always reminded myself that there were thousands of employees around the world and only one of me. Divide and Conquer works at any level and in any team, local and global. Make sure that everyone has an individual role to play. Make expectations very clear and hold people accountable. Push decision-making down to the lowest level. Empower people within a defined framework and limits. The people will rise to the challenge and will be much more motivated.

Focus as much as possible on individual accountability and be careful with "shared accountability." Shared accountability becomes fuzzy and too many important items fall through the cracks. Create a high expectations environment and most people will succeed. For those few that don't, perhaps these individuals are in the wrong job and a change is needed. Everyone must do his or her part to deliver on individual accountability.

Create Friendly Competition

By now in the book, you know that I place a lot of value on competition. I believe a good competitive spirit and a desire to perform well and win is extremely motivating. Of course, you can overdo competition and unintended consequences can result, so manage and monitor competition carefully.

People figured out long ago that competition helps sports to be more interesting. Enormous benefits are derived from playing sports. You get plenty of exercise, you learn about the importance of teamwork, and you learn to execute your individual responsibilities. You learn about "the thrill of victory and the agony of defeat." When every member of the team does his or her part, it's a terrific feeling.

Keeping score and competing is much more exciting than just participating. Some college football stadiums attract 100,000 people for games on weekends. I wonder how many people would attend if the two teams just played a game without scores—like a scrimmage. There would most likely be a lot of empty seats. Every team begins the year with enthusiasm, wanting to win the championship. Results are posted each week providing the top teams with pride and the lower teams with incentive to do better.

Why shouldn't the same concept be true with any organization? In the business environment of our free enterprise system, the external competitors are easy to identify and there are numerous ways to measure and compare performance. The competitors are always working hard to produce a better product or service, increase sales and market share, lower their costs, and improve profitability. Competition and keeping score motivate us all to do better. Everyone on the team should know the score and how the team is doing.

Nonprofits, education, and government organizations should use the same concepts. I haven't worked in these organizations but have spent a lot of time with them. These organizations have a different challenge because their "competitors" may not seem so obvious. Many people in these organizations don't seem to have the same competitive spirit and it's easy to develop a culture of complacency. Don't allow this to occur in your organization.

Look for specific things you do, stakeholders you care about, and identify organizations that are performing similar activities. You may not be competing with them directly, but you can benchmark, compare specific activities, look for best practices, and measure everything that you can. Benchmarking and taking action to improve is always helpful. A competitive spirit is good for the people in any organization in creating a culture of excellence.

Friendly competition is also helpful *within* an organization. We used to compare performance results of our operating locations on all types of parameters. We felt that if each of the locations was working to be best in class, we would be in good shape as a company. We used friendly competition frequently between countries where we operated. I enjoyed going into a plant in Texas and highlighting how the Germans were doing something better than the Texans were. I was probing into their competitive spirit and pride. Then I'd go to a similar German plant and find something the Americans were doing better and challenge them. I had fun creating these challenges and I could see behaviors change.

As with any good intentions, there can be unintended consequences. Intense competition can incentivize people to do things that aren't best for the company and drive reporting of problems underground. Keep the competitive spirit positive and with the purpose of motivating everyone to do better. Leadership and culture are the keys to openness and transparent reporting.

Competition yields many benefits. Competition teaches us to put forth our best effort and helps us to learn to win and lose gracefully. Nobody likes a boastful person, and nobody likes a whiner or pouter. Competition gives us the opportunities to cope with feelings of pride and disappointment and to learn to process them in healthy ways. People learn to recover quickly when things don't go their way. Competition helps people to try harder and helps to build self-esteem. Learn to utilize competition effectively.

Behavior Management

The only way anything gets accomplished in an organization is through the behavior of people (human factors). Whether you want to improve reliability, increase production, reduce quality defects, eliminate injuries, or take advantage of value creating opportunities, people need to change their behavior. Employees need to do more of certain behaviors, less of other behaviors, or change their current behaviors. Therefore, one of the most important subjects for leaders to understand is human behavior.

Human behavior is one of the most studied concepts of all time. Why do we do the things we do? What drives us? When do our behaviors become habit? How much influence can we have on the behavior of others?

As a leader, create an environment where people conduct themselves ethically. You want them to work the right way even when no one is watching. People must comply with the Code of Conduct and follow the rules and procedures. To eliminate injuries, unsafe behaviors must be eliminated. In short, you want predictable performance and confidence that people will do the right thing and make the right decisions at all times.

Many books have been written on the subject of human behavior. One outstanding book written by Aubrey Daniels is *Bringing Out the Best in People*. One of the behavioral models he describes is the Antecedent-Behavior-Consequence (ABC) model. His book has much more detail, and I'll provide my simple summary. You may need to read this section several times to fully understand this powerful concept.

The three primary terms used in the model are:

A = Antecedent
B = Behavior
C = Consequence

- **Antecedent** includes conditions before we act, how we think, the rules, the expectations, the situation we are in, and our past personal experiences.
- **Behavior** is the action we take: do we perform as expected, follow the rules, and work with care or do we perform unsafe acts, take shortcuts, break rules, and take unnecessary risks?
- **Consequences** occur from every behavior; consequences can be positive or negative and intended or unintended.

The ABC concept is quite simple and powerful. An antecedent comes before a behavior and a consequence is a result of the behavior. Our behavior is shaped by pre-existing conditions (antecedents) and by the potential consequences of our behavior (both past consequences and future potential consequences). Consequences of previous behaviors become antecedents for future behaviors.

An example of ABC is one of driving an automobile. Our daughter, Sharon, loved her dance classes and I loved watching her. Let's assume a situation in which Sharon has a dance recital tonight; however, I am leaving work late and might not get to the recital on time. I have a choice regarding how I will drive (my behavior). The antecedents are that I am running late, I want to get there on time, I love watching her, I know the speed limit, and I know roughly how much a ticket will cost if I get caught speeding. If I speed, I might make it to the recital on time (positive consequence for a bad behavior).

However, I also might receive a speeding ticket and even worse, I might get involved in a traffic accident (two negative consequences to a bad behavior).

On the other hand, if I drive the speed limit, I know I will be late for the recital (negative consequence to a good behavior), but I won't get a speeding ticket and will reduce the risk of a traffic accident (two positive consequences to a good behavior). These antecedents and consequences will impact my decision-making.

These are the types of situations and decisions we face every day. In the above example, the decision of my behavior to obey the speed limit or not will result in possible negative or positive consequences. Of course, a much-preferred earlier behavior would have been for me to have left sooner and not put myself in this situation to begin with. All behaviors have consequences, and consequences turn into antecedents for future behaviors. The cycle of ABC—ABC—ABC—ABC goes on and on and our behaviors get shaped by the antecedents and consequences we experience.

In your organization, it's critical to have antecedents in place such as clear expectations, a Code of Conduct, practical rules, easy to understand procedures, and Goal ZERO expectations. Most companies are good at creating antecedents and letting people know what they want them to do; that's the easy part.

In addition to good antecedents, there also needs to be a culture of consequences. Most consequences in your organization should be positive for good behaviors and good performance (praise, reward, recognition, and thank you). What gets rewarded, gets repeated. Positive reinforcements are powerful. A frequent occurrence is when someone *does something good and nothing happens.* You'll often hear, "No one knows or appreciates anything I do around here. Why should I follow the rules? Why should I go the extra mile?" Don't pass up opportunities to issue sincere thanks and appreciation when you notice someone doing something right (positive consequence for a positive behavior).

Effective leaders create designed positive consequences that then become effective antecedents. We always had effective recognition programs for production plants that achieved production or safety records. We made a big deal out of the recognition and communicated it widely, showing sincere recognition to those that deserved it. This communication was a positive consequence for those that received the recognition, and the recognition also served as a powerful antecedent for others to work harder to achieve the recognition the next time.

On the other hand, negative consequences are extremely important, but hopefully not used as often. In a culture of excellence, you must *never* ignore or neglect to act when observing bad behaviors. Bad behaviors (unsafe acts, rule breaking, noncompliance, etc.) must always have consequences and people need to understand them. The consequence may be as simple as a quick intervention or a short discussion. Negative consequences don't need to imply punishment. Remember, if you ignore bad behavior, that's a positive consequence to the person for a negative behavior and the person is more likely to repeat the same undesired behavior again in the future. Put most of your energy into positive consequences, but don't hesitate to apply a negative consequence when needed.

The most effective consequences are those that are *positive, immediate, and certain.* People love "positive" reinforcement (a pat on the back) and recognition. Perform the recognition as "immediately" after the behavior as possible and be specific. Providing feedback to someone for something he or she did a year ago has much less impact than for something done earlier in the day. And finally, "certain" means people expect consequences for particular behaviors. "Certain" consequences are a prerequisite for establishing a culture of excellence. People know they will be positively recognized for good behaviors and know there will be negative consequences for negative behaviors.

Culture and leadership are the keys. The culture of any organization definitely impacts the way people behave. The Goal ZERO concept helps create the right culture and serves as an incredible antecedent. A Goal ZERO expectation leads to Goal ZERO performance.

The ABC methodology is powerful. There are consequences to every behavior, whether the consequences are intentional or not. It's a sign of a poor leader when his or her people consistently don't follow rules or make poor decisions without consequences. By consistently applying the techniques of

ABC and communicating clearly and frequently, people will understand the expectations within your organization and adapt accordingly.

EXCELLENCE NUGGET:
Antecedents and consequences drive human behavior.

Behavior—Task Specific

An essential factor in good performance is an individual's personal behavior on each and every task. Many routine tasks that individuals typically perform are considered to be low risk. However, mistakes in these types of tasks can often lead to personal injury, operational impact, quality incidents, or negative customer consequences.

Have you ever noticed that a person may be acting differently today than he or she did yesterday or last week? Many factors can affect the human brain. A person may have had a bad night's sleep, he might be getting sick, or she might have a major family issue taking place. And, of course, people may be influenced by drugs or alcohol. It's important to know the people on your team and be aware of subtle changes in their behavior.

The expectation of a Goal ZERO culture is for individuals to perform every task with zero defects. Working with zero defects is much easier said than done. No one is perfect and people make mistakes, but you can implement programs and practices that significantly reduce the risk of error.

Football is an excellent example. The top coaches understand the team has the best chance of winning if each play is executed to perfection, one play at a time. For each play, every player needs to concentrate on the signal count so that he doesn't jump offsides. Then he needs to perform his individual assignment to perfection. If each player on the team executes well, the play has a good chance of being successful. If every play is successful, the team has an excellent chance of winning the game

Business is the same. You want each of your employees to perform each task to perfection, one task at a time. Carpenters understand this concept very well, and you'll hear them say, "Measure twice, cut once." Work hard to develop a culture of excellence in performance.

Daydreaming is something we all do. How many times have you gone into another room to get something and when you got there, you forgot what you went to get? Have you ever been getting dressed in the morning and forgot whether you brushed your teeth or not? Doing one thing while thinking about something else can lead to mistakes that can have significant consequences, especially in the workplace.

Throughout the years, I've come across many themes and programs designed to keep people focused on the task at hand. Many of these are safety related but can be applied to an emphasis on quality and reliability. Here are a few examples:

- **Take Two.** Take two minutes to think through a job before you start it. Slow down to avoid errors.
- **Pre-task Analysis.** Many companies utilize this analysis, which requires the employee or work group to think through the job and make sure individuals understand the risks, are taking the right precautions, have the right tools, and can do the job safely. A pre-prepared checklist is often utilized. A downside is that a checklist can become so routine that employees begin to "check the box" without giving the risks the thought that is needed. Therefore, keep the approach fresh and rotate processes from time to time.
- **Check Signals.** This mental process requires every employee to answer three questions before each task:
  1) What can go wrong?
  2) What precautions do I need to take?
  3) Can I do the job correctly?
- **Eyes on Path.** People should use this simple technique when moving from one location to another to avoid tripping hazards, especially when going up and down stairs.
- **Look up, look down, look all around.** This practice helps employees identify potential hazards by becoming more aware of the surroundings in their workplace.

- **Do what you are doing.** This technique simply reminds people to concentrate on the job they are doing at the time. If you find yourself thinking about something else, stop! Take some time to process your other thoughts and then get back to the task at hand.
- **Focus—Start to Finish.** This mantra helps to reinforce the need for individuals to focus on what they are doing, from start to finish, when conducting a task. Avoid distractions that can lead to mistakes and defects. Check your work for errors.
- **Intervention.** This technique allows individuals to feel free to give or receive an intervention if someone is performing an unsafe act or is not concentrating on the task at hand. We all need to help each other.

All of these approaches help drive incident-free performance. Keep your approach fresh since everyone can become complacent over time. Use frequent examples of bad incidents and results as reminders of consequences that can occur by inattention to detail. These techniques are various ways to help people prepare for jobs properly and keep their minds on the task at hand at all times. Individual behavior and inattention to detail are some of the leading causes of incidents.

Skills Development

*"Train people well enough so they can leave.
Treat them well enough so they don't want to."*
–Richard Branson

"What if I train them and they leave?"
"What if you don't and they stay?"
–W. Edwards Deming

Companies spend an enormous amount of time and money training personnel. Employees must have the skills and knowledge to perform their jobs effectively. Far too many incidents occur in which one of the root causes is lack of adequate skills.

Effective training is a challenge. I prefer to place the emphasis on learning as opposed to training, thereby focusing on the pupil learning rather than the teacher teaching. A couple of techniques we have found to be extremely effective are chalk talks and competition.

You've all participated in your share of ineffective classroom training. The instructor is speaking, and the audience looks like they are barely awake, about to die from boredom. The minutes on the clock seem to be at a standstill. It seems like the people are being spoon-fed, but don't want to eat. A similar situation is computer-based training, as people speed through the course to finish as quickly as possible. People check the box for the training, but do these individuals really learn?

An effective technique for improved training is utilizing "chalk talks." For production plant operators, we put the emphasis on the operator to learn rather than for us to teach. The operator had a training schedule that included a weekly chalk talk to demonstrate his new knowledge. The operator knew he needed to learn the material because he would have to present his learnings at the end of the week. The process consisted of the operator drawing a portion of the production plant on the chalkboard and then describing the manufacturing process and answering questions. Not only did this technique provide the student an opportunity to demonstrate what he had learned, chalk talks also provided coachable moments for areas in which he needed help.

It's amazing how this simple approach changed the behavior of students and the effectiveness and speed at which people learned. You could see the pride and confidence build as the person demonstrated his or her newly acquired knowledge.

We utilized another successful technique for more experienced personnel who attended trainings or workshops lasting several days. At the beginning of the program, we divided the students into teams. At the end of the course, the teams were expected to present an overview of a case study associated with the training material. The presentations were judged by senior leaders and the results were highly publicized. The teams worked on their presentations each day and night of the training course.

The energy level for learning was much higher since the participants knew they had to learn and present. More importantly, participants enjoyed the competition, which created a level of pride in their work. Try these techniques in your development programs and you'll see the difference.

Getting Leaders and Others Up to Speed Quickly

I'll describe a new manager onboarding program that we found to be extremely effective. Manufacturing plant managers have a tremendous number and variety of responsibilities. Plant managers deal with technology, projects, reliability, budgets, communications, people, the public, and the safe operation of their facility. When a person is assigned a plant manager role (or any new job), he or she drinks from the fire hose for the first six months or so, with so much to learn; and, typically, the urgent issues of the day get the most attention. The danger in this is possibly overlooking some very important items, which may not be urgent at the time.

My most important expectation for any new plant manager was to manage risks and to operate the plant safely. To help with this objective, we developed a New Plant Manager Review, a process for new manufacturing plant managers which you can use for any new leader. The primary theme of the review was process safety since the consequences of a major event can be so severe.

We wanted each new plant manager to clearly understand the major risks at his or her new plant and to ensure proper precautions were in place to prevent incidents. However, the review was much broader and focused on understanding and execution of the plant's management system and the status of their culture of excellence.

We developed a list of items as a guide for the new manager's review. The assignment was for the plant manager to give an interactive presentation within 90 days on the items listed. The audience would be his or her team, a plant manager from another location, additional key leaders, and a few subject matter experts. At first, our process safety experts got excited and wanted to develop training for these topics. But I said, no, "The intent is for the new plant manager to work with his or her team to develop the answers and presentation." The experts would be available as a resource if needed.

The items the manager had to address with his or her team and include in the presentation were:

1. Overview of the plant management system
2. Basic knowledge of the plant process
3. Top risks and hazards of the process
4. Approach to managing process safety hazards and risks
5. Outstanding action items and mitigation risks
6. Competency and experience levels of the staff
7. The culture of the organization
8. History of incidents at the site
9. Latest audit reports and action items
10. Process Hazard Analysis (PHA) management
11. Asset integrity of the unit
12. Unique site or community issues
13. Top 10 technology lessons learned that should prevent future incidents

This New Plant Manager Review was one of the most successful activities we conducted for helping new plant managers quickly assimilate into their new job. By working closely with their team on an assignment with a deadline, the new manager developed a close working relationship. In addition to the new manager learning how work was conducted at the site, he or she was also able to identify and correct any deficiencies in the management system before presentation time. The power was in the team working together to develop the answers rather than sitting back and having someone teach them.

All managers that went through the process said it was tough, but well worth the time early in their new assignment. Most of the plant managers implemented the same process for new people coming into their department.

I highly recommend this type of approach for getting new leaders in your organization up to speed quickly. Create an outline of items and expectations that any new manager in your organization should consider. Give the new manager a designated amount of time to work with his or her team and then prepare an overview presentation on how each topic will be managed. The new managers will make faster progress and will most likely identify several key areas for improvement during the process.

Teams—Confidence in Self / Confidence in Others

Teams are an essential aspect of any organization. A model I learned years ago was a grid with "Confidence in Self" on the X-axis and "Confidence in Others" on the Y-axis. The ideal state for a high-performance team is to have high confidence in both categories. If you have a strong team in which individuals each have self-confidence and confidence in others on the team, there is no limit to what the team can achieve.

For teams at higher levels in the organization, there typically isn't a problem with self-confidence. Individuals have been successful in their careers and have made it to this level. Confidence in others, however, is often a challenge. If you have a team of self-confident individuals who don't have confidence in others, there will be a severe lack of trust.

In your various approaches to team building, keep this concept in mind. Confidence in others is built in many ways. Confidence in others comes when team members are competent, honest, take responsibility for their mistakes, meet their commitments, and are willing to step up and do whatever is necessary.

Bruce Piasecki, in his book, *Doing More with Teams,* makes some excellent observations. Piasecki states, "One way in which teams are magical is that they allow all types of individuals to succeed. People who would not normally be able to succeed on an individual basis can reap the benefits of success and reach peaks they would not be able to climb alone."

Some team members may be planners, other may be doers, and still others may be natural born leaders. "The planners and doers are often people whose creativity and contributions may go unnoticed because they do not have the internal spark to market themselves or stand out like the natural born leader. Nonetheless, the mix of differences meld, and as the group comes together, the team becomes one as it triumphs." Piasecki got it right. Understanding each other and respecting each other's talents go a long way towards building confidence in self and confidence in others.

Increasing Effectiveness of Subject Matter Experts

As people progress through their careers, they advance as a single contributor or rise up the leadership ladder. The successful single contributors develop strong expertise in a subject and progress into roles with titles, such as expert, scientist, specialist, technologist, or chief. These individuals are very important to the organization and are recognized for their individual knowledge and/or their previous contributions.

Supervisors get the most attention and direction from top management. Subject matter experts can fade out of sight, out of mind. Many of these experts are self-starters and will look for opportunities to improve the organization. Other subject matter experts who have developed significant expertise, but are a bit shy, tend to wait to be called when needed. These individuals may become complacent and live on their reputation. These people need focused attention as well since they have such a high level of expertise and are necessary for improvement in performance.

Keeping these individuals challenged and motivated to drive hard for improvement is vital for success. I've seen many subject matter experts become too comfortable in their jobs and develop a responsive mode, going wherever they are asked to present at meetings or whenever someone calls on them. I've seen many rest on their laurels from past contributions.

One of our research scientists from Dow in my early years was a crystalline morphology expert. I saw him give the same presentation a hundred times over the years, and I always wondered what contribution he had made lately. A professional baseball player may have been the league's Most Valuable Player a few years earlier, but his contributions this year are what's most important. Why shouldn't it be that way in business?

Many techniques exist to keep these types of individuals challenged and on their toes. Keep them motivated and you will get much more value out of their contributions. Utilize techniques previously discussed such as ownership, individual accountability, responsibility, proactiveness, goal setting, and expectation of deliverables. Ensure a job description exists so everyone is aligned on expectations. The responsibilities should be action oriented and steer the specialist to drive towards intended results.

Job titles are important. I have never been a fan of passive job titles such as advisor and consultant. I always preferred titles with more teeth and ownership in them. A consultant provides help and advice but doesn't have ownership or accountability for results. Subject matter experts should be held accountable for broad performance trends in their area of expertise.

Subject matter experts should demonstrate ownership and overall accountability for their area of responsibility. This accountability gives them a healthy perspective for how to approach their job. The subject matter experts are not accountable for performance at each individual workplace or location, but the expert should be held accountable for their particular expertise and how the company is performing. This helps provide them with "skin in the game" and a motivation to be proactive. These individuals should be working to eliminate problems, not just come in for investigations to talk about what should have been done.

Some individuals feel that the knowledge they possess represents power. Some subject matter experts are reluctant to document their knowledge or to share their knowledge widely with others. This behavior is not healthy and shouldn't be tolerated. In a company with a good management system, everyone must contribute to the success of the management system to continually improve. Subject matter experts should have pride and personal satisfaction when they have created a management system that is helping to deliver superior results in the organization.

In addition to the organization's performance improvement, subject matter experts should be recognized and rewarded for keeping the management system (standards, processes, procedures, training materials, etc.) up to date and effective.

Challenge them and then provide sincere recognition as appropriate. Technical professionals can be a major success factor in performance improvement of the organization.

If you are a subject matter expert, be proactive with the items I have just mentioned. Take ownership for how the organization performs within your area of responsibility. Take pride in your work and the company's performance. Develop a sense of urgency for continuous improvement and the elimination of defects. You are extremely valuable and important for the success of the organization.

Fear of Losing a Job

Many companies have been on an endless path of reorganizing, restructuring, and downsizing ever since the early 1990s as described in my history lesson in Chapter 2. Some companies never learn their lesson. During good times, these companies lose discipline and hire too many people. Then when times get tough, the companies are forced to downsize the organization and implement layoffs.

I learned early on to maintain the headcount of our teams on the lean side. People would come to me and say we needed more resources and I'd tell them, "No, you don't. It's always better to stay slightly understaffed." Our people learned to appreciate a lean organization when the bad times came around and we didn't need to do much cutting of budgets.

On one occasion, Dow announced there would be a reduction in headcount. After a few weeks, our best Instrument & Electrical technician came to talk with me. He was shaking and said he was extremely worried about losing his job and couldn't sleep at night. I told him, "Danny, you are our best technician, and you would be the last person to lose your job." He said he understood but still couldn't get over the fear of the possibility. Some of the best people worry the most.

On many other occasions, I saw organizations take months to begin executing downsizing plans after announcements had been made. The pending employee reductions kept hanging over everyone's heads and impacted morale in significant ways. For the first time, some of the very best and loyal people updated resumes and started proactively looking elsewhere for a job. The damage was incredible.

Downsizing has an incredible impact on the people leaving. However, don't underestimate how much downsizing impacts the people that remain. Avoid the need to downsize in the first place. However, if downsizing must be done, move quickly and communicate as clearly and as often as you can. Downsizing can be "slow and painful" or "fast and painful," so go fast.

EXCELLENCE NUGGET:
*Major change can be
"slow and painful" or "fast and painful."*

The Poor Performer

Many leaders lack the skills for dealing with poor performers. These leaders let poor performance continue which results in morale loss with better performing employees.

I've had my fair share of poor performers through the years. I'm proud that in most cases, we were successful in turning their performance around. We always approached poor performance as quickly and as directly as we could, time being of the essence. A poor performing employee needs to improve or move on. Most leaders will look back and wish they had moved faster when dealing with a poor performer.

The biggest detriment of a poor performer is how much he or she negatively affects others in the workplace. When someone is not performing well, he or she knows about the poor performance and everyone else knows it as well. Our work was too important to not have every individual doing his or her fair share and contributing.

I had a simple technique in dealing with a problem performer. I always explained our expectations and where the person was falling short. Instead of focusing on the negative, I would say that I wanted him or her to succeed and clearly explained what had to be done to improve. I offered to help in any way I could.

It was always important to get agreement and alignment with the individual, and that improvement needed to be made quickly. If the performance didn't improve, we'd conduct another session and tighten up expectations and timelines. Every step of the way, documentation of our discussions was important and applied to both union and non-union personnel.

In many cases, no one had ever been so clear and direct, which is a common problem made by many supervisors. By making expectations very clear, most problem performers closed the gaps and significantly improved. However, in some cases, the person was a mismatch for the job and a change was necessary. Telling an individual about losing his or her job was never a pleasant experience, but employees often thanked me for everything I did for them. At least I knew I had done my best to help them succeed.

Zero Tolerance; Be Careful

In a Goal ZERO company, full compliance with all internal and external requirements is an expectation. The phrase is positive, and the expectations are very clear. Ensure the rules are fair and reasonable, and hold people accountable.

Some leaders like to use the words "zero tolerance." These leaders use zero tolerance as a simple way to deal with noncompliance and want to send a clear message to the organization. These are good intentions, but I personally don't like the zero tolerance terminology and never used the term; zero tolerance sounds like a threat and comes across negatively. The phrase typically means automatic termination for noncompliance. Zero tolerance limits your flexibility when dealing with an issue. Many types of consequences are available, short of termination, that are just as effective and are actually more powerful.

Many unintended consequences exist with a zero tolerance policy. One of the biggest is the potential loss of a person with considerable experience. If you use proper consequences the right way, short of termination, you can be assured the person will never repeat the same behavior again and will, in fact, become an ambassador to the organization for the importance of doing things the right way.

I'm not saying to never terminate individuals for poor behavior. Rather, make sure that termination is the right consequence for the particular individual and don't forget about the myriad of other potential consequences you have the ability to utilize.

You are My Ambassador

In my early years, I transferred to many different operating units within Dow's Texas Operations. Compliance and following the rules were a couple of my basic principles. We didn't want a single person to ever get hurt. However, I was disappointed at times to find a loose approach to compliance in new groups I joined. I often heard the same excuse from supervisors for a particular rule such as wearing required personnel protective equipment: "We just can't get the operators to follow the rule." These were systemic and cultural issues that needed to be addressed quickly.

So, I began what I secretly called my compliance ambassador program. I would begin by conducting an employee meeting to discuss our strategic plans. In the meeting, I'd make it crystal clear that I expected full compliance with all rules. We could change or eliminate a rule if we felt the rule was unreasonable or didn't add value. Following the meeting, I'd send a note to everyone with a clear message about a particular rule in which noncompliance was common (such as required safety goggle areas). The note was important to document the communication.

I'd admit that we had not been in good compliance with safety goggle requirements in the past and why safety goggles were so important from a safety point of view. I'd emphasize that we will never risk someone getting blinded from an unexpected release of a toxic, corrosive chemical. I'd say, "From this moment on, I expect full compliance with the safety goggle requirements in specified areas." It was always important to personalize the message and help people to understand "why" a particular rule was important.

I knew a single note wouldn't change everyone's behavior, so I asked the supervisors on our team to watch closely and find the first person who breaks the rule. (Note, this is opposite from my typical approach of trying to find people doing something right.) Due to old habits, it didn't take long before we'd catch the first person breaking the rule. As an example, I'll tell you how I would handle the situation with Charlie, who was first to break the rule.

The supervisor would tell Charlie that he needed to report to Sam's office at 3:00 p.m. to discuss the rule breaking incident. This delayed meeting notice was intended to give Charlie time to think about what he had done and for him to discuss the issue with the other operators. I wanted everyone to know the meeting was going to take place. By the time Charlie arrived in my office at 3:00, he would be concerned about what we were going to talk about and have his story all prepared.

I considered these opportunities as teachable moments and actually looked forward to them. My routine was fairly typical, and I tried my best to urge the person to do most of the talking. In a very calm manner, I'd welcome him into my office. "Please sit down, Charlie." Charlie would sit and after a pause, I'd start the conversation, "You're one of our very good operators, but I understand you were in a safety goggle area today without goggles, breaking the rule. What do you have to say about this violation of the safety rule?" Charlie would squirm around and say something like, "Everyone breaks that rule all of the time." He'd make all kinds of excuses.

I'd say, "That's true, Charlie. Our people didn't follow the rule consistently in the past. That's why I held the employee meeting and then sent the note saying that, from now on, we are changing, and everyone must follow the rule. I am never going to allow anyone to get hurt by breaking a safety rule." I'd urge Charlie to say more about the incident. Then I'd say, "Charlie, have you ever given serious thought about getting blinded by a toxic chemical spraying into your eyes? What would it be like to never see your children again?" He'd think about the scenario for a while and say, "I can't imagine anything worse."

Then I'd get more serious and say, "I can't take a chance with this kind of behavior anymore and risk that you might get blinded in our workplace. You know that I'm going to have to take some disciplinary action. This violation is so serious that I'm thinking about firing you for breaking the safety rule."

Of course, this statement would be a shock to Charlie, and he'd say, "Please don't. I'll never break rules again." Again, I'd remain silent by giving him time to think about it and speak. Then after further discussion I'd say, "Well, how about some time off without pay? We have to send a strong message about compliance around here and that expectations are changing." Charlie didn't like that suggestion either and I'd give him more time to talk. Of course, by now Charlie was becoming very uncomfortable.

After enough deliberation, I'd suggest, "Charlie, what if we don't take any disciplinary action, but you agree to go back to work and be my ambassador for full compliance in our plant? I am not going to tolerate noncompliance and we have to change our team's approach." Charlie, looking relieved, would say, "That's a great idea, Sam, and I'll be your ambassador. I'll tell everyone. Thank you!" We'd shake hands and with a smile I'd say, "Thanks, Charlie. I'm counting on you." After Charlie left, I would document the discussion and file it in his records. Charlie didn't receive a lecture or punishment, but he surely didn't want to go through an uncomfortable discussion like that again.

The interesting, predictable part was that Charlie would then go out into the control room where his colleagues would be anxiously waiting for him. They'd ask, "What happened, Charlie? Did you get chewed out? What kind of disciplinary action did you get?" Charlie, still a bit shaken and confused, would answer, "No, I didn't get chewed out or get any punishment, but I'm never going to break any rules again and you better not either. Sam is serious about safety and compliance."

I repeated this process many times in my career, stepping from one noncompliance item to another until we had the right culture of full compliance. This method works and is a positive way to address problems. The employee appreciates not being punished and the intended results are achieved. There's something powerful about the reverse psychology of a person being held accountable and not being punished, rather than being resentful from receiving punishment. This technique gives terrific results and helps build a culture of excellence. Punishment should be a last resort when all else fails.

Logbook Warfare

Our manufacturing plants operated 24 hours a day. In the "old days" before email, texting, and electronic devices, we kept logbooks in the control rooms of our operating plants for communication. Operators and supervisors would enter notes about events that occurred during their shift and anything special the next shift needed to know or do. The logbook was a simple and easy way to communicate from shift to shift.

Periodically, someone would get upset about an issue and write a negative note in the logbook. Often, the negative note concerned someone leaving their workplace with poor housekeeping or suggesting that the other shifts are not doing their fair share of the work. Such a note would start a back-and-forth war of words in the logbook that continued to escalate.

It didn't take me long to put a stop to that kind of behavior, which we called "logbook warfare." Everyone knows the power of the written word and how words can be easily misinterpreted. That's normally the way it begins—someone writing a note he or she thought was innocent and someone else interpreting the message as a personal attack.

As email, text messages, and social media have become more prevalent, it's much easier for miscommunication to occur. I've seen many email debates on a particular subject where there was disagreement and the discussion got out of hand. Bantering back and forth in writing causes many problems, ends up with hurt feelings, and certainly doesn't help teamwork.

Don't let this negative interaction occur in your organization. My advice is to always STOP and pick up the telephone and talk about the issue. For topics that involve several people, call a quick meeting to discuss the situation. It's important to monitor this kind of behavior closely and end the discussion quickly. Documents written in haste and without proper review can create unintended liability for the organization.

Retirement and Exiting Employees

High employee turnover in an organization drives up expenses, drives down productivity, and erodes culture and corporate memory. Practically everything in this book will help to create a culture of excellence and reduce employee turnover in your organization. However, we all know that there will always be some individuals leaving the company for various reasons. People are willing to open up a lot more when they are leaving the company. This is a time that you can learn an incredible amount of information.

I personally enjoyed visiting with individuals who were leaving. Not only was the visit an opportunity to thank them for their service, but I could also solicit their thoughts for ways we could improve. Visiting with these individuals was time-consuming, but I learned considerable information, which was especially true when the exiting person was several layers down in the organization.

One example involved an operator named Steve in the Polycarbonate Unit that I managed. Our unit was located in a very large union site with over 90 operating units. Operators could bid for a job in a different unit based on their site seniority, work a minimum of two years, and then bid on another unit. When I began working at Polycarbonate, the problems were considerable, the morale was terrible, and there was fruit basket turnover of plant operators. We realized quickly that we had to turn this frequent turnover of personnel around and stop the loss of experience. We worked very hard on addressing operator issues. After a couple of years of improvement, we were proud of our accomplishments and the way the plant was operating.

One day, Steve gave notice that he was going to bid on another unit, so I scheduled some time with him to ask why he was leaving. He said when he had arrived, the work environment was so bad that he had marked his calendar to leave after two years; his mind was made up from the very beginning. I asked for specifics, and he began to describe his complaints. Steve talked about one of the front-line supervisors and how disrespectful he was. I said I agreed, and we had moved the supervisor out 13 months ago. He named item after item, and it turned out we had corrected each one.

After a while, Steve had a puzzled look on his face and said, "I guess everything is better than I thought. I didn't realize how much things have improved, and I think I'll stay. I need to go talk to my co-workers about this. We all thought things were still bad."

I was shocked. This conversation opened my eyes to the fact that people may not notice gradual change and you must communicate often to make improvement obvious to the organization. Steve and the other operators had focused on complaining and talking about the same old problems but failed to notice how much things had improved.

HR departments typically conduct exit interviews, but the data is often lumped together and not as useful as the data could be. Nothing is better than getting information directly from a person when he or she is most willing to talk.

Bringing Out the Best in Functions

In small companies and organizations, individuals wear many hats and perform a wide variety of activities. In larger companies, functions are created so that individuals in the function can become true subject matter experts (SME) and provide services to others in the company. Functions such as procurement, human resources, EH&S, legal, and finance exist in all large organizations.

When I became the Vice President of EH&S at Dow, I found that many people in the EH&S function referred to themselves as subject matter experts and their job was to "help" the plants by providing tools, processes, advice, and tracking results. All were very good people, but I was surprised the function was not held accountable for the resulting EH&S performance results and didn't believe it had the accountability. I commonly heard that manufacturing plant supervision was accountable for their results and the EH&S personnel were just advisors. I definitely agree that direct supervisors are primarily accountable for their organization's results. However, my question to the team was, "What if our tools, processes, and advice are not good and don't contribute to improvement? How will we measure the end result and our associated accountability?"

A common understanding in the industry is that an operating plant should not depend on the safety organization for its safety performance. The plant management has accountability for safety, not the function. However, many people in the function take this concept too far and begin to act in an advisory and consulting role. These functional people say that if the line management is accountable, then the function is not accountable. You can see this understanding in behaviors too; many will perform their work in their allotted time, instead of a manufacturing behavior of doing whatever it takes, regardless of time, to achieve desired results. A huge difference exists between these two behaviors.

Based on my past manufacturing experience, I realized a change was necessary. We wanted each of our functional employees to have "skin in the game," so we added a strong accountability element for the function and each individual. To be clear, each individual manufacturing plant was clearly accountable for its operation and EH&S results, but we said the function's scorecard would include overall EH&S improvement for the company. If the function was providing the proper tools, processes, and support for improvement, then the measurable results needed to show it.

We eliminated titles such as advisor and consultant and changed to more action-oriented titles. These changes were a major shift in philosophy for the function in that the individuals were being held accountable for bottom line EH&S results for the first time in their careers. Most people rose to the challenge. The increased enthusiasm in their behavior was evident. For the first time, these people had a measurable scorecard that would show the results of their efforts.

All functions (EH&S, human resources, etc.) need to understand what success looks like and have clear accountability for expected results. In addition to providing the basic services of a function, these groups need an accountability element for overall results. Accountability provides a focus for driving improvement and creates a stronger function. Accountability also significantly improves morale. People enjoy being held accountable, working hard, and seeing the results of their work. Good people will respond well if they have the right work environment, incentives, and clear expectations.

Support functions need to maintain a good balance in their work; I call it "support and challenge." Individuals in functions need to provide support through their expertise, work processes, tools, and advice. Most people are very good at support and enjoy helping others. However, functional individuals must also have the courage to challenge people in the organization when necessary. Their added accountability for results provides them with a mandate and lays the foundation for providing challenge. It's not enough to give advice like a consultant and then allow people to do whatever they wish.

Functions need to do more, be strong, and not give up until the right actions are taking place. Persistence is key; functional people must create a level of discomfort at times to drive initiatives and the right behaviors. The actions add to effectiveness and credibility of the function and the results the people will achieve.

Choosing the right leader for functions is critically important. Do you want a staff person to just manage the back office of a function or do you want a strong leader to drive and achieve measurable improvement across the entire organization? There is a huge difference between the two. If the wrong person is assigned to lead a function with no history of driving bottom line results, then don't expect a paradigm shift in company performance. A good functional leader requires strong interpersonal skills.

A person with no proven history of influencing others and driving improvement will find it difficult to lead a function that has to work through influence of others to achieve results. The leader will do a good job of the basics; however, he or she might fall short in the skills it takes to improve company performance. A subject matter expert doesn't necessarily become a strong leader.

I observed contrasting behaviors in functional leaders at other companies as I participated in numerous industry forums, task forces, teams, and conferences. You could easily tell the leaders who had a strong sense of ownership for achieving results and the ones who acted more as an advisor. My observation was that only about half of EH&S leaders had the passion, drive, and accountability for actual improvement in their companies.

The same principles apply to other functions, too. Human Resources is a perfect example. Most Human Resources leaders are excellent at their functional administrative processes, such as compensation, benefits, hiring, and termination. However, the truly exceptional HR leaders accept ownership and accountability for driving improved measurable employee and leadership performance across the organization. These HR professionals do whatever it takes to assure talent in the organization is improving, leadership skills are developed, robust succession plans are in place, the company is identifying and developing young talent early, and the workforce is engaged and motivated. These leaders understand what is trying to be achieved, they measure progress, and they are accountable for driving improvement.

Just to be clear, departmental supervision should always have primary accountability for their people and the performance of their organization. However, a terrific functional leader accepts accountability that his or her function's systems and tools are working well and that the broader organization is delivering desired, measurable results. The right person in the job must influence others to achieve these results.

To all of you currently working in functions, you can control your own destiny for advancement. It's great if you want to be a subject matter expert in a particular field. However, if you want to become a leader, you must begin early to develop leadership skills and demonstrate a track record of ownership, passion, and results. Work closely with others to drive measurable results. You can gain these skills in a variety of manners such as through leadership development programs or leading teams and task forces. The key is to be seen by others as having the skills to lead and influence, then you will be an outstanding candidate for advancement.

You Have More Resources Than You Think

My career took a major shift when I moved into a global functional leadership role. In prior roles, I always had clear accountability with an appropriate number of direct reports and staff to do the job. In my new functional role, with only a small group of direct reports, I quickly realized we had to operate through influence of others to be successful.

An important success element was creating my "virtual" organization chart. In my mind, the CEO and his team "worked for me" for the purpose of promoting Operational Excellence and driving performance improvement. I knew that if we created an exciting and reasonable vision, strategy, and plan that was well understood, our people would get on board and execute. We needed leaders throughout the company to consistently deliver our message. We utilized every person in the organization who could help us spread the word and implement the programs.

I included each of these people as "working for me" in my "virtual" organization chart:

- CEO
- Corporate leadership team members
- Board of directors
- Site managers
- Site leadership team members
- Manufacturing
- Engineering
- Communications
- Human Resources
- Procurement
- Supply Chain

If we could influence these people to align and work in the same direction, how could we fail? For example, we kept the CEO well informed and up to date, providing him with talking points for driving the programs we were implementing and making sure he kept our messages front and center in everything he did. The phrase I used when working with him was, "Whatever interests my boss, fascinates me!" I always kept my boss and the rest of the corporate leadership team interested so they could keep their people fascinated!

The point of this section is that no one can accomplish results in a company alone. I hear individuals in functional roles often say, "I don't have enough resources." I find that to be a poor excuse. You have people all around wanting to do the right things. If you have a functional role, create the right vision and practical supporting programs, communicate well, and ask others (or tell them) what you want them to do, and the people will deliver. At any level in the organization, you can create your own virtual organization of support to accomplish your objectives. Be a catalyst for change and drive improvement.

EXCELLENCE NUGGET:
You have more available resources than you might realize.

Salaried Operations, Unions, and Works Councils

I've had the benefit and pleasure of working in locations of salaried operations, locations represented by a union, and locations with works councils, primarily in Europe. I enjoyed them all. People are people and the same principles apply everywhere pertaining to honesty, respect, fairness, and communication.

Most people are good, but you'll always find a few individuals who are difficult to work with in both union and non-union operations. It's not the system, but, rather, how your people are treated that makes the difference.

The origin of unions dates back to the 18th century in Europe. The purpose was to represent workers, protect their common interests, and give them a stronger voice. Unions provided a check and balance with company management. Unions have helped all of us in many ways through the years, such as negotiating wage increases, establishing reasonable work hours, gaining employee benefits, and improving workplace safety. Union membership peaked in the early 1970s and has since been in steady decline. Some individuals in union leadership positions are very reasonable, fair, and enjoyable to work with. These leaders do their best to protect the rights of their workers and negotiate for increased pay and benefits. Others, unfortunately, don't look at the big picture and constantly create friction by making totally unreasonable demands.

Most companies understand that "If you don't take care of your people, the unions will." Another common saying is that "You will get the union that you deserve." We preferred non-union operations over union representation because we had more flexibility. We kept our salaried operations pay and benefits better than the union sites, yielding no good reason a site would vote for union representation unless the site had poor leadership. I'm proud to say that I've never had a site vote to be represented by a union.

The people you work with make the difference. I've worked with some union leaders that do everything they can to protect workers, even those that blatantly break the rules and are very poor performers. On the other hand, some union leaders are primarily concerned with fairness for their workers and don't hesitate to address problem performers directly.

One union operations example was when I became plant superintendent for the epichlorohydrin production unit at Dow. Epichlorohydrin is a versatile chemical intermediate used in downstream applications such as food products, beta-blockers, epoxy resins, and plastics.

Every union has a contract with the company that details specific agreements and rules agreed to by the union and the company. One of those agreements was that overtime and overtime pay should be distributed fairly, and the individual units could determine how to accomplish the distribution. The epichlorohydrin plant had a fair system for distributing overtime. If you were offered and turned down an overtime shift, the turn down would count the same as if you had accepted the overtime. In addition, a clause provided that if you had vacation scheduled the day before or after one of your long weekends, you would not be charged for overtime you turned down during that long weekend.

One of the operators, Dan, was gaming the system and upsetting his co-workers. Dan's behavior had become a huge issue in the unit. At the beginning of each year, Dan scheduled a day of vacation adjacent to each of his long weekends. As the year progressed, he would cancel his vacation the day before it was scheduled, after overtime for the weekend had been offered. He had "gamed the system" so that he had his long weekend off and wasn't charged for any overtime offered. Naturally, Dan's actions made the other operators furious. When I arrived and heard about the problem, I read the union contract carefully and saw that another agreement stated supervision had the option to approve or not approve vacation that was scheduled or canceled. Turning down vacation cancellation requests rarely happened. To address the situation, I told Dan I would not approve any more of his vacation cancellations.

Of course, Dan was upset and called the union boss who went by the name of "the Duke." The Duke was a tough guy and had a huge reputation across the site. The other operators and I listened as Dan talked to the Duke on the telephone and told him how unfair I was being. Dan then handed the telephone to me and said, "The Duke wants to talk to you." The Duke told me, "Sam, this doesn't sound like you. You aren't being very fair. Sometimes people change their plans, and you should allow them to cancel their vacation if they want to."

I then explained to the Duke that Dan had not told him the entire story and explained what Dan was actually doing. After hearing my story, the Duke agreed with me and said I was doing the right thing. I hung up the telephone and Dan asked with a smirk on his face, "What did the Duke say?" I answered, "The Duke said I can do whatever I want," and walked away. We never had another problem with Dan and the overtime system again. I also gained a lot of respect from the other operators.

The point is to be as fair as you can with your people, but also to address problem performers head on. The Duke was a tough guy, but also very reasonable which I appreciated. Another lesson, if you work in a union represented facility, read every line of the contract. The contracts are written to protect both parties.

Dealing with problem performers can be almost the same in a union or non-union environment if you deal with people the right way. The main principles are to treat people fairly and to address problems openly with the individual. If you take measurable actions to improve performance, most of the time the employee will improve. It's critical to document every step of the way. By following this process, we never had a problem terminating an individual that didn't respond and improve, both in union and non-union operations.

Works councils in Europe are required by law in many countries. The works council consists of employees voted into the council by their peers. The primary cause of major problems with works councils is when company management decides major change is needed, such as organization change or downsizing the organization, and creates all plans before consulting the works council. The company surprises the works council, which immediately sets up conflict and a bad confrontation.

The preferred method is to engage works councils early in the process. Explain to the works council the objectives and why the measures are important. "Tell" the council members what you need to accomplish and engage them on "how" best to accomplish it. This early collaboration provides a preferred starting point for the discussions and always leads to better results.

EXCELLENCE NUGGET:
Address individual issues rather than punishing the entire team.

Contractors

Most companies utilize a fair number of contractors in their operations. It's just as important for contract employees to have the proper skills and competencies for their jobs as your employees. A contractor with the wrong skill set or work practice can cause significant problems.

OSHA requires companies to report injuries and illnesses for their own employees. Contractor companies are responsible for reporting their own injuries and illnesses. When OSHA rules first came out, it was not uncommon to hear: "There was an injury in the plant, but it was *just* a contractor." The injury didn't count on the company's statistics. Most of us hated hearing this statement, and contractors were often treated as second-class citizens.

Fortunately, the better companies began to record contractor injuries and illnesses the same as their own employees, providing a total worksite injury/illness rate. If your company isn't already reporting a total worksite injury/illness rate, I strongly encourage you to do so.

We made special efforts to treat all of our contractors with respect and eliminate any second-class citizen mentality. We worked hard to reduce the number of contractor companies we utilized and built strong partnerships with the companies we selected. We did everything possible to indoctrinate contractor employees into our Goal ZERO culture from their first day on the job.

Legal considerations should be followed when working with contractors such as co-employer situations. Follow the legal guidelines and make the contractors feel like part of the team. Hire the right contractor companies; make sure their top management clearly understands your expectations; be firm, but fair, and always treat their employees with respect. Contractors are an important component for your success.

The Board of Directors

A board of directors is a group of talented people with excellent and diverse experience. If you are working at an executive level in your company and interacting with the board of directors, this section is for you. Utilize the talents of the board members.

Leaders in some companies primarily tell the board good news and hold back on some of the problem areas. At LyondellBasell, we took an entirely opposite approach and were totally open and transparent at all times. We went lightly on the highlights (and we had many to tell) and instead focused on our problems, challenges, and what we were doing to improve. This approach worked great, and the board members became much more engaged in the discussion. And, of course, good board members are always willing to make suggestions and discuss their experiences. I found this approach to be extremely effective and helped build mutual trust.

The principle of total transparency has been reinforced by the Boards I'm on today. Board members bring a wealth of experience and are more than willing to help. Board members have the added benefit of working with other companies, which is extremely helpful in providing outside perspectives. Management takes courage, confidence, and integrity to discuss crucial issues with the board. Leaders should not be defensive when receiving input or feedback. The discussions must be kept professional and not become personal. We appreciate openness and honesty, which helps us to build trust in leadership. The board and company management should work together for the improvement and success of the organization.

An important governance topic for boards is risk management. The Audit Committee focuses on the financial risks of the company. Companies with high operational risk activities, such as energy and chemical manufacturing companies, typically have an EH&S Committee. This committee provides an appropriate amount of time to be spent on operational matters to help prevent major incidents.

It's always interesting to me how many companies create an EH&S committee *after* a major incident occurs. Boeing is such an example, forming a Board level Safety Committee for the first time following the two fatal crashes of the 737 Max.

People Metrics

As I have said so many times, you won't be able to accomplish anything without a highly skilled and motivated workforce. Many factors change over time, both inside and outside of your company, that can impact your employees. For example, as I write this book, global issues include the COVID-19 pandemic, the Russia-Ukraine conflict, high inflation, and extreme supply chain issues; each of these has drastically impacted the workplace environment.

People are one of the four leadership keys to achieving superior performance, so maintain a laser focus on them. To continually monitor the workforce and navigate trends as they occur, you should identify the people metrics that are important to your organization. Two of the best areas of focus are employee morale indicators and adherence to your Operational Excellence Expectations document. State your intentions as clearly as possible and then measure results regularly.

People metrics I've found to be helpful are:

- **Operational Excellence Expectations (Chapter 4).** Pick some of the critical expectations you have listed for people and track your progress.

- **Employee satisfaction.** Employee surveys are an important way to gain a broad understanding of your workforce opinions. Address concerns in the workplace expeditiously. Comments are especially useful. Integrate your Operational Excellence Expectations into the survey questions. Break down the data by location or department. Averaging the data over a large company dilutes the real messages you are receiving.

- **Employee turnover.** A considerable amount of time and energy is spent hiring and developing the right employees. The loss is significant every time a good employee leaves the company for another opportunity. Tracking the number of employees that leave, especially top performers, is essential. Track the exits by location and you'll be able to pinpoint issues early.

- **Absenteeism.** Motivated people show up for work unless they are sick or have another significant reason. Absentee rates for individuals or departments can be an early warning signal of larger problems.

- **Exiting employee survey data.** It's a shame when you lose a good employee, but an essential action is to interview the person and find out why he or she left. Some people leave for reasons outside of your control, such as moving closer to family or getting an opportunity that you could not match. However, many leave due to their dissatisfaction, often attributable to their supervisor and management. It's important to find out whatever you can, track the data, and act.

- **Diversity.** A diverse workforce is powerful whether it is diversity of race, gender, or thought. Challenge your team to actively identify, hire, and develop high quality diverse candidates.

- **Promotion rates.** Track the rate of promotion as a function of employee rating or performance evaluation. Make sure the top performers are advancing appropriately.

- **Compensation.** Pay for performance has long been my mantra. Track the compensation level of your employees as a function of their performance level as well as their job size.

- **Experience level.** A sufficient level of experienced personnel is essential in every organization. A healthy company has a blend of experienced and new people, but never allows the experience level to fall too low.
- **Succession planning.** A mature organization has people who have the experience and skills ready to take on the next level job and promotes from within. Succession planning is important in any organization, and you should track the health of your succession candidate list on a regular basis. Leaders should be held accountable for developing people and maintaining a healthy candidate pool within their organization.

The Talent Management Section in a Management System

The company's Operational Excellence Management System should include a Talent Management section. You can't accomplish anything without the right people with the right skills. Most organizations have many types of strategies: business strategies, growth strategies, etc. How many organizations actually have a well-defined talent management strategy? I'm talking about a comprehensive, detailed, fine-tuned approach to achieving your people objectives.

A good talent management strategy covers the entire life cycle: talent identification, recruiting, hiring, employee and leadership skills development, inspiring the people in the organization, getting the most out of each person, performance evaluation, and succession planning.

Your talent management strategy should begin with a clear vision, desired outcomes, and a set of objectives and plans. To assure the strategy and plans are comprehensive, ask important questions such as:

- How do we manage our recruiting process?
- How do we achieve diversity and equality?
- How do we train people and is our training efficient?
- How do we evaluate performance of individuals and leaders?

- How do we recognize and reward good performance?
- How do we compensate people and does this compensation plan drive desired behaviors and achieve intended results?
- How do we identify high potential talent?
- How do we give high potential individuals unique developmental opportunities?
- How do we perform robust succession planning?
- How do we motivate people to do their best?
- How do we assure employee morale remains high?

I'm sure you can add many additional questions to the list. Once your list is complete, document the processes utilized to address each of these important topics in the management system. Keep it simple; these processes should not be complicated. Regularly review the effectiveness of these processes and whether they are achieving the desired results with the company's personnel. Identify the key people metrics that are important for the organization and monitor regularly. Catch negative trends quickly and act on the data.

The key points are to identify what is important for talent management, develop processes to achieve desired results, assure that responsibilities are clear, and measure progress on a continual basis.

Without such a system, the emphasis on certain areas of people development can rise and fall over time or even fall through the cracks. Approaches to human resources processes might change every time a new leader comes on board. Leaders won't understand how the various elements impact each other and the company will never achieve consistency.

Remember that to achieve Operational Excellence, the primary tenets are leadership, people, systems, and culture. The leadership and people areas must be managed proactively and to perfection at all times just as operations and service quality are managed. Don't fall behind in this obviously crucial area.

Supervisors have the primary accountability for the people reporting to them. The human resources department has the accountability for developing, driving, and monitoring work processes that deliver measurable results in individual performance and leadership. The desired approach is to be best in class in people leadership with a management system that the company uses, delivers desired results, and gets continually improved over time.

EXCELLENCE NUGGET:
Include a robust talent management section in your management system.

A Passion for Leadership and People

A SUMMARY

- Organizational alignment is essential for achieving excellence. Communicate often. Work hard to find common ground and understanding.
- Learn the finer points of influencing behavior. Utilize the ABC model. Motivate people to do the right things because they want to.
- People are happiest and most productive when they are future focused. People need to understand the vision, objectives, and plans for the organization. They will give their best to achieve results for objectives they believe in.
- Individuals need to have clear personal responsibility and accountability. This builds pride and gets the most out of every person.
- Use the divide and conquer technique to spread the load and increase effectiveness.
- Develop a sense of urgency, excitement, and enthusiasm in the organization. This applies to driving improvement or correcting problems.
- Communication is critically important at all times. Develop a communication strategy utilizing various techniques. Be proactive in communications to all stakeholders.
- Know your people. Recognize good performance. Build loyalty. Develop skills. Identify and develop high potential individuals. Build individual and team confidence.
- Include a talent management section in the company management system and measure results.

CHAPTER 4

Establishing a Culture of Excellence

*"If you don't execute well,
it doesn't matter what your strategy is."*
– Tom Peters

Vince Lombardi was a famous professional football coach, whose team won five National Football League (NFL) Championships in seven years in addition to winning the first two Super Bowls. One of my favorite Lombardi quotes is: "Gentlemen, we are going to relentlessly chase perfection, knowing full well we will not catch it, because nothing is perfect. But we are going to relentlessly chase it because in the process we will catch excellence. I am not remotely interested in just being good."

This combination of vision and expectation is about as clear and understandable as you will ever hear. I have the same passion for achieving excellence and I hope that you do too.

A common denominator in the most successful organizations is a strong culture of excellence. **With a strong culture, people clearly know the expectations of the organization, people believe the expectations are the right ones, people do what it takes to meet the expectations, and people know that their behaviors will lead to desirable results.**

I retired from LyondellBasell as Senior Vice President, Americas Manufacturing, in 2017. I joined the company in 2009 after it had filed for bankruptcy earlier that year. Our corporate leadership team and each of our global employees worked long hours and endless weekends to bring the company out of bankruptcy and transform it into one of the safest, most reliable, and lowest-cost producers in the industry. We set extremely high expectations for the organization.

The Goal ZERO culture we established and the Operational Excellence approach were significant factors in the success of the company. LyondellBasell won the American Chemistry Council Responsible Care® Company of the Year Award in 2014 and again in 2020. This award is presented annually to the best company in the industry for innovative practices and leadership in the areas of environment, health, safety, and security. In 2022, LyondellBasell was named to *Fortune* Magazine's list of the world's most admired companies for the *fifth year in a row*. That's an incredible improvement from the bankruptcy days in 2009. Operational Excellence and a culture of excellence provide a sustainable, competitive advantage that LyondellBasell has achieved and continues to enjoy today.

Creating a positive culture was just the right thing to do. We considered culture to be simply a matter of the working environment—how the company treated its people and how the people behaved, acted, and treated each other. We treated each other with respect and dealt head on with issues as they arose.

We wanted a culture where we celebrated successes and people looked forward to coming to work every day. We wanted people to receive appropriate training, have opportunities for advancement in their careers, and perform at their best. We knew that creating the proper culture was important for morale, reducing employee turnover, and recruiting new employees.

I observed a wide variety of work cultures throughout the years, both within the various departments in our companies and in other organizations. I saw some cultures that were tough minded, very strict, and a macho type of environment. On the other extreme, I witnessed cultures that were almost like a country club, with everything focused on softer things, the easy life, and not enough focus on achieving results. Needless to say, there are a wide range of cultures across organizations and also within various departments in the same company.

However, since I wrote the first edition of this book, I have come to realize that culture is so much more than just the working environment. I know now that everything we did actually had an impact on the culture of the organization. Culture is not fixed or mysterious. The culture of an organization is alive, and we see it every day. Culture is the way people conduct themselves and is an indicator of how work gets done. A culture of excellence is absolutely critical for success and everything you do has a subtle impact on creating the culture.

What do good and bad cultures look like? I think you know it when you see it—the signs are obvious. In poor cultures, people don't make the extra effort, attitudes are bad, people wait to be told what to do, housekeeping is poor, there seem to be an endless number of problems, employee turnover is high, and customer complaints are commonplace. This sounds like a recipe for failure to me.

On the other hand, in organizations with a strong culture, there is an expectation of excellence, every minor detail is managed well, employees are enthusiastic and willing to help each other, loyal customers keep returning, and there is an overall good feeling about the place. I know the kind of culture I like to work in.

There are an endless number of factors that influence culture. We worked hard to make sure people followed the rules, we expected good housekeeping, we expected equipment to be in good working order, and we expected people to be proactive in their work. We dealt expeditiously in addressing valid employee concerns.

We simplified rules and requirements so people could easily adhere to them, and then we enforced the rules. People have a difficult time complying with rules and procedures if they aren't written in the right manner. We didn't realize at the time that *simplifying documentation in the management system was a major factor in enabling a culture of excellence.* It's critical for people to understand and be supportive of the expectations of the company.

When employees' behaviors match the company's expectations, you are on your way to a culture of excellence. If you tolerate poor behavior and poor performance, people are more likely to repeat the poor behavior again. This is often called *normalization of deviation.* You must deal directly with poor behavior. That doesn't imply you have to be mean, just create a culture of open and honest feedback and make sure it goes both ways. Culture development begins with the little things. Let me provide a few simple examples to illustrate my point.

- **Goals**—It's a good practice to set goals and track progress to assure intended results are achieved in a timely manner. If employees and departments set goals, but then are not held accountable for results, goals start to become meaningless in the organization.
- **Housekeeping**—If housekeeping is not emphasized and there is trash on the ground, people will adapt to

this environment. Many people may live in a home or neighborhood with poor housekeeping, and they may not know what good looks like. We were always adamant about impeccable housekeeping, and our people always adapted to our expectations. Their improved behavior eventually became good habits. Good housekeeping helps to create pride in the organization.

- **Signs**—If the sign on the door says eye protection required, but people frequently ignore the sign, you're on your way to a culture of selective compliance. Make sure all signs are important and that the instructions are followed. If the sign is not that important, take the sign down.
- **Rules**—Some people say rules are made to be broken. I'm definitely not a supporter of that philosophy. I believe in minimizing the number of rules, making sure each one is sensible, and insisting on full compliance. Required protective equipment, safety rules, and procedures must all be followed as required.

Culture is an integral component of the Operational Excellence Model. Culture affects not only how people treat each other, but also how people think and behave every day. The right culture helps people to perform their jobs in the right manner, minimize errors, improve compliance with rules, exceed customers' expectations, and achieve excellence in performance.

Some leaders in organizations tend to focus on their strategy and blow past the importance of culture. Executives may underestimate how much a strategy's effectiveness depends on cultural alignment. A strategy is relatively easy to understand and create. Culture is complex and hence tends to get less attention. A strategy without the right culture will fail. Companies with a strong culture tend to produce superior results as compared to those with weaker cultures.

Create a culture of excellence that brings out the best in people. Develop a culture of competent, motivated, dedicated, and loyal people. From my experience, the best cultures have the following elements:

- People like clarity; they don't like confusion and inefficiency.
- People understand their job responsibilities and the responsibilities of others.
- People are held accountable.
- People feel they are doing worthwhile work.
- People feel valued.
- People feel they have growth opportunities.
- People feel comfortable in delivering bad news.
- People follow the core values of respect, transparency, and ethics.
- People are motivated by the future focus and objectives of the organization.
- People say they work hard but also have never had so much fun.
- People like regular communication.
- People feel they are fairly compensated.
- People like to be on a winning team.
- People have pride in their company.

EXCELLENCE NUGGET:
A strategy without the right culture will fail.

A Culture of Excellence—The Secret Sauce

I was once in the hospital for five days for some tests. I felt fine, but the doctors were concerned about a potential situation. During my stay, it was incredible how many mistakes were made. The nurse started an IV and overfilled my lungs with liquid. Nurses twice brought medicine that wasn't intended for me. Nurses came in to perform procedures that were intended for someone else.

At the same time, I observed that the staff had an incredible number of rules and processes, which were intended to promote consistency and eliminate mistakes. To say the least, the hospital staff were following all of the rules and procedures, going through all of the required steps, but not operating mistake-free. The system was one of bureaucracy and the culture of performance did not match the expectations of the organization.

Having said this, there's a secret sauce for creating a culture of excellence and that's the introduction of a ZERO defect or ZERO incident theme. Quality, reliability, and consistency are extremely important. A ZERO defect theme is invaluable in organizations that provide a service, such as the hospital I just described, your favorite restaurant, or the hotel where you stay when traveling. People pay a lot for these services and expect to receive quality performance and service.

The culture in an organization can be extremely fragile. Beliefs, philosophies, and behaviors can change quickly. Culture can be soft, fuzzy, and difficult to understand. However, the philosophy of ZERO defects helps to make culture real and actionable. People can understand the concept of ZERO and rally behind it.

During my 50-year career, I researched and observed numerous programs, slogans, themes, and approaches to individual performance and achieving excellence in operations. Nothing comes close to the effectiveness of a ZERO defect culture. It's all about striving for perfection. We all understand that no one is perfect, but as Vince Lombardi said, "chase perfection and catch excellence along the way." You want people striving for perfection at all times.

In our company, we used the term **Goal ZERO.** A considerable number of companies understand the concept and use various terms for the ZERO defect theme such as Target ZERO, Mission ZERO, ZERO Harm, and No One Gets Hurt.

Positive worded themes are Excellence Every Day, Striving for Perfection, Own It, Driving Perfect Performance, or Safety First. The University of Alabama football team has a sign over the door, "Play Like a Champion." You can't be clearer with your intentions than that. These themes are all excellent.

The point is that the theme should be **memorable, actionable, and become engrained in everyone's minds at all times.** Pick a theme that works for your company and stick with it to help create consistency of purpose and a culture of excellence. If you already have an action theme in your company, keep the theme in your mind as you read the Goal ZERO concepts described throughout the book.

Culture in an organization develops over time and is highly influenced by leadership. Leader's behaviors and actions are an incredible force in creating a Goal ZERO culture. A Goal ZERO culture shapes the way people think and act. Goal ZERO serves as a way to express your combined expectations and values in a consistent manner—Goal ZERO performance, Goal ZERO behavior, etc.

Have you ever watched a football game and wondered why some teams incur so many penalties and while others seem to play almost penalty-free? The difference in the winning teams is a ZERO defect culture. Each player knows the expectations and focuses every play on executing defect-free. You can't expect the team to win or your company to produce perfect product if people operate in a haphazard manner. A ZERO defect culture takes the churn out of the organization and lays the foundation for excellence that enables people to be more confident, to be more predictable, and to go faster.

This chapter covers the philosophy behind a ZERO defect theme and how the concept is such a powerful force in helping to create a winning culture. Simply put, Goal ZERO is a driver for achieving **excellence** in any organization, and performance **excellence** contributes to top-notch value creation and risk management.

I will blend in personal stories dealing with the Goal ZERO impact on safety, but the Goal ZERO concept impacts all areas of performance and excellence. In this chapter, I explain the power of Goal ZERO and what it means to be a Goal ZERO company. An emphasis on continuous improvement may be good, but to achieve a paradigm shift in performance, a culture of ZERO sends a clearer, absolute message. ZERO means having a positive, proactive culture of excellence in which you expect zero defects, zero rule breaking, zero noncompliance, zero incidents, zero customer complaints, and zero missed value creating opportunities.

EXCELLENCE NUGGET:
Choose a ZERO defect theme that's actionable and memorable

Goal ZERO—An Overview

We first introduced Goal ZERO at Shell worldwide in 2007, and the philosophy was a major breakthrough in our ability to create a ZERO defect culture. I give credit to my friend Paul Tebo for triggering our thoughts around this concept. Paul had a successful career at DuPont, with his last assignment as Corporate Vice President for Health, Safety, and Environment. I was skeptical at first, but as I began to understand the Goal ZERO concept, I became a believer and enthusiastic supporter.

Goal ZERO is not complicated, but it's powerful. Simple things are always better. Goal ZERO is an easy-to-understand expectation of excellence in everything that you do; continuous improvement isn't good enough anymore. It's a human factor cultural change tool that works across any company and in any industry. Goal ZERO creates a culture of discipline. It's a belief that every one of us can work defect-free, every day. Achieving Operational Excellence takes dedicated leadership and a Goal ZERO approach with respect to people, systems, and culture to achieve desired results in safety, reliability, quality, and service.

Goal ZERO has many meanings and is used commonly in an organization's vocabulary. First, Goal ZERO is a noun. Examples are: "We work hard to achieve Goal ZERO," "Goal ZERO is a foundation for excellence," "Goal ZERO impacts every person in the organization," and "Goal ZERO becomes a way of life."

Goal ZERO is also an adjective. Examples are: "We are a Goal ZERO company," "The Goal ZERO culture in our company guides behavior," "People perform their jobs with Goal ZERO behavior," and "Following rules and paying attention to detail are signs of Goal ZERO performance."

One of the most important factors in the success of establishing a Goal ZERO culture is leadership alignment. Leaders and employees become enthusiastic supporters once they truly understand the concept. Goal ZERO is the right thing to do. Goal ZERO helps protect people; it reduces defects in people's work as well as being beneficial for business. Leading with safety is an intuitive way to introduce Goal ZERO and then expand into all areas of Operational Excellence.

On my first day at LyondellBasell in 2009, I didn't waste any time and introduced Goal ZERO with a single slide (Figure 3).

FIGURE 3: Goal ZERO

The initial focus was on safety, but the overall intention from the beginning was to achieve Operational Excellence in everything we did. I firmly stated that we were going to change the culture into one that expects zero injuries, zero reliability incidents, zero quality incidents, zero noncompliance, and zero defects. Nominal yearly improvement was no longer sufficient. As you can imagine, many people thought such a goal was unachievable.

What ensued was a considerable amount of discussion at all levels in the organization which I enjoyed very much. People need time to think about the concept of Goal ZERO and internalize what the philosophy actually means. This discussion is healthy and builds long-term commitment. As leaders and our people began to endorse the concept, Goal ZERO became a foundational element of the culture of our company.

In the beginning, I heard over and over that Goal ZERO wasn't possible. "It's impossible for such a large company to have zero incidents." However, that wasn't the point at all. ZERO is possible for each of us individually on any given task. Goal ZERO is not about the company as a whole, Goal ZERO is about you and me individually, task by task.

For example, if each person works each day incident free, the entire company will work incident-free, one day at a time. It's amazing how quickly the concept catches on as people begin to internalize and personalize Goal ZERO. Goal ZERO is about protecting people.Undoubtedly, Goal ZERO changes the entire mindset of every person in the organization. People start to realize they are expected to perform to Goal ZERO expectations every day, on everything they do.

EXCELLENCE NUGGET:
*Goal ZERO is achievable
for each one of us individually.*

A Word of Caution

Goal ZERO, by itself, cannot accomplish anything. Instead, Goal ZERO is a platform on which to build a culture of excellence in safety and everything else. A very poor example sometimes seen in companies is to employ a very simplistic ZERO harm safety approach. I've witnessed this tactic in some contractor organizations that negotiate a safety incentive award as part of their contract for the work.

For each month that the employees work injury-free, each employee receives an award. If someone gets injured during the month, no one receives an award that month. To make matters worse, if an employee gets injured, he or she gets singled out for causing everyone else to lose their reward.

Of course, if this ZERO harm safety approach is the full extent of a company's safety program, it's a terrible approach. This approach will lead to all types of unintended consequences. People will hide injuries, not report near misses, and the organization will never learn and improve. If this approach is your intention with Goal ZERO, forget it......*and never tell anyone that you read my book!*

Proven Performance Results

Here's an example of safety metrics to illustrate the impact of Goal ZERO. The Occupational Safety and Health Administration (OSHA) provides oversight for safety performance in the United States. The metric for personal injury and illness rate is *incidents per 200,000 work hours*. An easier way to think about it is *injuries in a year per 100 workers*. A 1.0 OSHA rate is approximately equivalent to 1 injury for every 100 workers. Figure 4 shows the average OSHA injury/illness rates for various industries in the year 2020.

Note that the American Chemistry Council (ACC) Responsible Care Companies have an extremely low injury/illness rate of 0.65. I attribute this performance to the constant safety focus by industry leaders over many years. A company in the energy and chemical industry can't be great if it doesn't have superior safety performance, which is true for many other

OSHA RECORDABLE INJURY and ILLNESS RATES 2020

Health Care	5.5
Agriculture and Forestry	4.6
Transportation and Warehousing	4.0
Manufacturing	3.1
Arts, Entertainment, and Recreation	3.0
Construction	2.5
Utilities	1.5
ACC Responsible Care Companies	0.65

Injuries per 200,000 work hours
Approximate annual injuries per 100 workers

FIGURE 4: SOURCES: BUREAU OF LABOR STATISTICS–US DEPARTMENT OF LABOR AND AMERICAN CHEMISTRY COUNCIL (ACC)

industries as well. A major incident or serious noncompliance can have devastating consequences in loss of life, brand damage, litigation, and employee morale.

The American Chemistry Council has required member companies to *publicly* report their performance in safety and other metrics for almost 20 years. This requirement is meant to enhance transparency and accountability, driving performance improvement of member companies. Another reason for the excellent safety record in the industry is constant awareness of the severe consequences that can result from a major fire or explosion. Piloting airplanes for a commercial airline company or doctors and hospitals taking care of patients are similar— you can't allow the big event to occur.

Our expectation at LyondellBasell was to be the best at protecting people. *With a Goal ZERO approach, we achieved a recordable rate at LyondellBasell for our combined workforce (employees and contractors) of approximately 0.20 on a consistent annual basis.* That's one OSHA recordable injury annually for every 500 workers. Our performance was in the top decile of one of the best performing industries—the best of the best. Our company was recognized consistently by the American Chemistry Council and the American Fuels and Petrochemical Industries (AFPM) as one the safest companies in the industry. And an added benefit, the reliability and quality of our operating plants improved considerably. We were all extremely proud of these achievements and worked at Operational Excellence relentlessly.

Making Goal ZERO Personal

I have a very good friend from Dow, Alex Pollock, who is one of the most enthusiastic and positive individuals I have ever met. Alex refers to certain individuals as being in his mental health club. He has many sayings, and one that always stuck in my mind was, "People don't care what you know, they want to know that you care."

This quote is so true, especially when you are dealing with the topic of safety. It's so easy to become obsessed with metrics such as OSHA recordable rates and lost time incidents. However, safety is not about the numbers; it's about protecting people. More importantly, it's about preventing the terrible consequences that friends and family must suffer when a loved one gets seriously injured.

Goal ZERO performance in safety is indeed possible for each of us individually. Here is a good way for you to explain the concept to others. If my good friend Cindy has one injury in 100 years of working, her personal recordable rate will be 1.0. Of course, no one works 100 years, so if she has only one injury in a 40-year career, her personal recordable rate will be 2.50— still way above the industry norm. For Cindy's personal OSHA rate to meet LyondellBasell employees' actual performance of 0.20, she will have to work *500 years* with only one injury. Think about it.

As these numbers begin to sink in, people start to personalize Goal ZERO and realize that the vast majority of workers never get injured. You can and should never get hurt—that's the fundamental belief of Goal ZERO.

We spent considerable time talking about safety with our people. A serious injury can be life changing. We asked people to think deeply about the consequences of a serious injury and the impact it would have on their family if the employee didn't arrive home from work. We used small group sessions for discussion on why Goal ZERO behavior was so important and what Goal ZERO meant to them.

Imagine never getting to play baseball with your son again or never getting to watch your daughter's dance recital. Time and time again, people said they thought they had been working safely but now realized they had been nonchalant about it. Goal ZERO took our people to an entirely new level and made them much more proactive in their work to prevent incidents and defects. We used the powerful theme, **"Goal ZERO begins with me."**

One of our most popular programs was putting pictures of family members, friends, or pets on the back of their identification badges. Along with the picture, the badge said, "This is why I work safe." We would blow the pictures up to poster size and place them along the walls of our buildings. These posters were immensely popular during large "maintenance turnarounds" of our manufacturing facilities in which we brought in hundreds of temporary contractors. The pictures of loved ones served as a constant safety reminder to each of them.

People are smart and can accept principles if they understand "why" the principles are important and have some data to back them up. People begin to change their belief about Goal ZERO and that not getting hurt is indeed possible and expected. Individuals know and believe they can achieve Goal ZERO and expect everyone around them to do the same. People recognize that by risking incident and injury, they are putting everyone they care for in jeopardy. If a person accomplishes each task, every day, injury-free, the person will work the entire year injury-free.

Team members begin to understand that the only way to achieve Goal ZERO is to follow the rules at all times (even when no one is watching), to do a good pre-task analysis before each task to think about the hazards and precautions to take, and to focus on the task from start to finish. This applies to everything we do, such as driving a car, walking down the stairs, or climbing a ladder. By focusing on incident prevention in even the smallest of activities, the mistakes affecting quality and reliability also dramatically decrease.

Any time a significant incident occurs, it's crucial for leaders to demonstrate a sense of urgency and go to the location of the incident as soon as possible. The first purpose is to show care for the people who will be understandably shaken. Comfort and reassurance during times like these are extremely important. The other reason for going to the scene quickly is to learn and see the situation for yourself. It's amazing how much you can learn immediately following an incident while everything is fresh on people's minds.

Within a short time, as the Goal ZERO culture catches on, you can see the passion in people as they begin to personally understand the concept. Goal ZERO gets imbedded in their souls and in everything they do. Injury rates rapidly decrease and so do plant operational incidents. Reliability improves and quality incidents occur much less frequently.

A Goal ZERO culture impacts everything throughout the organization. People begin promoting and explaining Goal ZERO to others. Individuals work with a Goal ZERO attitude because they want to, not because they have to.

EXCELLENCE NUGGET:
Personalize safety and Goal ZERO.

Goal ZERO—100%

Most people are good and will deliver on expectations if you communicate clearly and the culture of the company is one of Goal ZERO. However, a few individuals will always try to buck the system. Every person needs to be held accountable for following all rules and you must deal with the person individually if he or she doesn't comply.

One note of caution, leaders' actions for dealing with noncompliance need to be seen as fair and just. Don't punish an individual if there are systemic violations of rules. If the people in your organization lose trust in leadership, they will not get on board with a Goal ZERO vision.

More importantly, a broad culture of rule breaking indicates a leadership and culture issue. It's a sign of poor leadership when an incident occurs and an individual is held accountable for breaking a rule, when the rule is often broken by others.

Here's a simple example to illustrate the point of poor compliance. I participated in hundreds of visits to operating facilities. My primary objectives were to interact with the people, communicate, learn, and see for myself how the facility was being operated. I tried my best to look for good practices and compliment people. People appreciated the recognition and sincere appreciation for the good work they were doing, and I received considerable positive feedback.

However, I never hesitated to address problems when I saw them. On one tour of a facility, our group went through a door with a sign that said, "Eye Protection Required." The group started entering the room anyway without eye protection. I stopped the group and asked about the sign. The leader knew he had made a mistake and nervously gave a weak excuse, saying, "We were just going in the room for a short time."

I actually enjoyed these types of situations which served as a coaching opportunity. I replied, "What kind of example does this behavior set for others when leaders don't follow the rules? In a Goal ZERO company, everyone must follow *all* of the requirements, *all* of the time. If the rule isn't important, take the sign down. It's that simple."

Remember, the little things matter. Enforce zero rule breaking, zero noncompliance, and zero defects until the behavior becomes habit and culture. Goal ZERO—*100% of the people, 100% of the time.*

Clear Expectations

One of the most important factors in establishing a culture of excellence is to have a list of very clear expectations. Everyone is familiar with Missions and Visions. These are often long sentences that capture everything under the sun. While these documents are good at a high level, Missions and Visions don't do much to actually change behavior and drive improvement.

The purpose of Mission and Vision documents is to state the values and intention of the organization. In other words, the documents describe the organizational vision for items such as safety, quality, environment, reliability, cost, profitability, sustainability, and ethics.

A good Code of Conduct is also essential for any organization. The Code establishes the moral compass for the company and should include topics such as ethical behavior, legal requirements, conflict of interest, protecting intellectual property, dealing fairly with others, human rights, and record keeping.

In addition to the Mission, Vision, and Code of Conduct documents, I highly recommend creating a list of specific *Operational Excellence Expectations* for your organization. This document should be simple to read, be understandable, and establish very clear *expectations* for every individual and department in the company that will lead to a Goal ZERO culture. Leaders and individuals can work together to develop the expectations for your workforce. The exercise is extremely useful in creating alignment and commitment. Each expectation should be written in a clear and positive manner.

The best way to organize the expectations is to list them under each area of importance, such as leadership, people, operations, service, quality, and risk management. The number of expectations is a matter of choice. As an example, ExxonMobil has 65 expectations and LyondellBasell has 40.

The primary objective is to clearly state what you expect from people across your organization. Just remember, once you write your expectations, you then need to walk the talk! Make sure that behavior of individuals matches the expectations completely. I've included examples on the following page of items you might include in your Operational Excellence Expectations document.

Operational Excellence Expectations—Examples

1. **Individual Accountability.** Leaders, employees, and contractors are responsible for following company rules and requirements, working safely, meeting the customers' needs, and avoiding mistakes.
2. **Competency.** Employees and contractors have the necessary skills and knowledge to perform their jobs.
3. **Ethics and Integrity.** Leaders insist on compliance with laws, regulations, and internal requirements, effectively monitor performance, and take action to correct all deficiencies.
4. **Management System.** Leaders assure that their management system is kept up-to-date and that the expectations of the company are being met.
5. **Reporting.** Employees and contractors report potential violations of legal or company policy without fear of retribution.
6. **Learning from Experience.** Management systems are updated to capture internal and external learning.
7. **Risk Management Process.** Hazards are systematically identified, owners are assigned, risk assessments are conducted, and mitigation measures are put in place.
8. **Procedures.** Operating, maintenance, and inspection procedures are in place, kept up-to-date, and are rigorously followed.
9. **Management of Change.** A management of change process is followed for people, process, and equipment changes.
10. **Incident Reporting and Investigation.** Incidents and high-potential near misses are promptly reported, investigated, and corrective actions are defined.
11. **Self-Assessment.** Regular, ongoing self-assessments with timely corrective actions take place to ensure adherence to legal and internal requirements.
12. **Audits.** Independent, comprehensive audits with timely corrective actions take place to ensure adherence to legal and internal requirements.

13. **Action Item Closure.** Action items from self-assessments, audits, investigations, and risk reviews are completed by their assigned due dates.
14. **Management System Review.** An annual self-assessment of the management system takes place to evaluate its suitability, adequacy, and effectiveness.

As you can see from the examples, the objective is to clearly write the expectations that you have for people in the organization. Create an Operational Excellence Expectations pamphlet and distribute to all of your employees and contractors. The expectations document provides an excellent platform for employee discussions. Discuss your vision for achieving Operational Excellence in all that you do.

Take a Goal ZERO approach to each of the expectations listed in the document. By constant messaging and with total alignment, you will experience a rapid shift in employee mindset, customer service, and level of compliance. Good communication helps the workforce understand the company's objectives and why they were important.

I believe the most important expectation is the first one, Individual Accountability, which states the expectation for each employee to work safely and follow all rules. This expectation may seem obvious but be sure to repeat this individual expectation over and over to embed the message in people's minds. Individual accountability at all levels is critical to achieving Goal ZERO performance.

The second expectation simply states that employees and contractors must have the skills and competencies to do the job. An employee or contractor should not perform any task unless the person feels he or she is prepared. No person can give the excuse of not being trained.

It's relatively easy to write a document and then put it on the shelf. However, make sure everyone is committed to achieving the expectations that are established. To close the loop, survey each employee as to adherence to each expectation when periodic audits or employee surveys are conducted. Separate the responses from supervisors and employees of the audited department. As you can imagine, if the answers between the two groups are different, the difference gives you something to discuss further.

Be serious about a Goal ZERO approach to the each of the Operational Excellence Expectations. You will never receive any pushback on the expectations if the document is written in a commonsense manner and your people understand the importance.

EXCELLENCE NUGGET:
Great leaders make expectations extremely clear.

Global Emphasis Day

We were always searching for new ways to get people's attention and improve safety performance. One extremely helpful concept we developed was conducting a Global Safety Day each year. We perfected this program through the years and conducted Global Safety Day annually the last 11 years of my career. You can also use this concept for other topics that you wish to emphasize such as quality, reliability, and customer service.

The purpose of Safety Day was to dedicate one day each year for the entire global company to discuss and focus on safety and what it meant to work in a Goal ZERO company. The concept was primarily focused on individual behavior since behavior is such an important factor in achieving a culture of excellence. Over time, the topics expanded to other areas under the Operational Excellence umbrella. We wanted to conduct a day so powerful and impactful that every participant would leave work at the end of the day with a renewed sense of dedication to working in a Goal ZERO manner. Safety Day provided a terrific venue for establishing a Goal ZERO culture of excellence.

We began each year by selecting a theme, which always had an element of behavior and action embedded in it. Some of the Global Safety Day themes were Goal ZERO Begins with Me, Goal ZERO—Focus Start to Finish, Goal ZERO—100%, and Performing at Our Best Every Day.

We then selected a global steering team and site steering teams. We provided some high-level concepts and guidelines, but the power was in the teams thinking about and developing their own individual programs and what the department needed to accomplish. By maximizing the number of people involved in the planning, we were well on our way to an effective program.

The locations designed their Global Safety Day around maximum active employee participation and minimized listening to presentations. The most effective activities involved small group discussion sessions in which someone introduced a particular subject and then facilitated open discussions. Discussion topics included the impact on your family and friends if you were seriously injured, how you can intervene if someone is performing an unsafe act, telling others why it's okay to intervene with you, areas where we could improve in our department, avoiding mistakes, and the importance of always following rules. Creating various types of contests within units was also very successful in achieving active participation.

No other meetings were to be conducted on Global Safety Day which allowed leaders to participate fully in the day's events. Executive Team members were assigned different locations to attend and participate. Following the first Global Safety Day we conducted at Shell, our CEO, Jeroen van der Veer, told me Safety Day was the first event he had ever seen that captured the attention and participation of the entire global organization so well.

Needless to say, Global Safety Day was a huge success each year, and the day provided the right setting for communicating Goal ZERO expectations and also listening to our employees. Our employees told us they were proud to work for a company that cared so much for their safety.

Employee Surveys

As I've mentioned many times, the culture in an organization needs to align, match, and support the expectations of the company. The strategy and systems in the company describe how work should be done; the culture describes how work is actually done. A good strategy and plan without the right culture is doomed to fail.

An important technique that companies use to evaluate the culture is to conduct employee surveys. Data is critical for understanding your culture, measuring compliance, and analyzing behaviors. Surveys take considerable effort and are typically conducted every year or two. Some companies choose to use outside resources for the survey so that the company can benchmark data to prespecified, consistent questions.

A problem with many employee culture surveys is the survey falls short and focuses only on the softer elements of the organizational culture. These surveys focus on items such as employee engagement, team dynamics, trust in leadership, growth opportunities, freedom to speak up, and if the company is a good place to work. These are all good questions but only get halfway if you really want to understand the culture in the organization.

I recommend that employee surveys have two parts—one focused on human interactions and the second part focused on the alignment and actions of individuals in meeting the expectations of the company. You must find out if people believe in the expectations of the organization and, more importantly, if the people are meeting the expectations. Get real feedback on how work is actually being done.

The human resources department typically conducts these types of surveys. A common concern is in making the list of survey questions too long, so make the survey as short as you possibly can. That's why strict prioritization in selection of the survey questions is so important. A best practice is for HR departments to work with others across the organization to develop the second part of the survey.

It's important to ask questions regarding compliance with rules: are the rules reasonable, do people report incidents, do incidents get properly investigated, and do quality issues get addressed in a reasonable manner? Ask specific questions that are important for the organization to be successful. The company has a good strategy and set of Operational Excellence Expectations, so now include questions to make sure the people are actually following and meeting the expectations.

All functions should cooperate together in developing an effective employee survey and in driving excellence across the company. If you are going to conduct a survey, get the full benefit.

And, of course, you must act quickly on the findings. When there are gaps between expectations and performance, dig in deeply to understand the causes and work together to improve. Communication back to the workforce on learnings and actions is critical in gaining alignment and establishing a culture of excellence.

Establishing a Culture of Excellence
A SUMMARY

- Chase perfection and catch excellence along the way.
- Strategies and plans will fail if the culture in the organization does not deliver expected behaviors.
- The system describes how work "should be done" in the organization. The culture describes how work is "actually done" in the organization.
- A ZERO defect theme is powerful for establishing a culture of excellence. The theme should be memorable, actionable, and become engrained in everyone's minds at all times.
- Actively communicate and build on the ZERO defect theme with the people. Make it personal. Utilize communications, workshops, and various opportunities to reinforce the intention.
- Develop a set of clearly worded Operational Excellence Expectations and communicate broadly.

CHAPTER 5

Processes and Practices for Achieving Excellence (The Contents of a Management System)

Simplicity is the ultimate sophistication."
– Leonardo da Vinci

A management system consists of processes, procedures, best practices, requirements, recommendations, technology, and tools. The system defines how work should be done. This chapter provides examples of effective practices, techniques, and activities that you may wish to include in your management system. These practices have been found to be particularly effective at delivering performance improvement. Think of these practices as tools in your toolkit. Use the appropriate one for the right application.

Procedures are an established series of actions and steps conducted in a certain order or manner. The steps in procedures need to be very clear, so that people can easily follow them.

Work processes, however, tend to be written at a higher level, providing guidance for how to perform various activities. Work processes are continually improved based on experience. Processes should capture the key steps of an activity and shouldn't be overly prescriptive. My advice is to err on the side of simplicity when documenting work processes. You don't need a lot of process when you have a culture of excellence.

A regular cadence of activities provides certainty and regularity for the organization. Proven tools and processes help to provide consistency. People know what to expect and the organization consistently improves.

Change Management Process

Developing a culture of excellence requires continuous focus and constancy of purpose. A change management process should be followed when driving change, and many such processes are available. Here are the steps I like to follow for instituting effective and lasting change:

1. Develop a compelling case for change
2. Create a sense of urgency
3. Form a strong team
4. Establish clear accountability, expectations, and plans
5. Engage the organization and get people involved
6. Communicate, communicate, communicate
7. Generate short-term wins
8. Monitor and track progress
9. Sustain the change

Leaders in organizations often spend considerable time developing and planning change initiatives. However, by the time a program gets rolled out to the organization, leadership has already moved on to the next priority area. To be successful, leaders need to remain intimately involved during steps 5-8 of the process.

Just as it took leadership a while to fully understand and get behind the new concepts, it will take the same amount of time for the people across the organization. Times of change are an excellent time for leaders to lead, dedicating time to coaching, talking, and listening to their employees.

A second word of caution is to not underestimate the time and effort it takes to truly impact culture change. Stay the course and be consistent in your messaging at all times. People need to understand and believe why the change is important to them as individuals. Don't forget to communicate frequently during every step of the change process to institute the permanent change.

Terminology

One of the crucial elements in an organization is consistent terminology. As we all know, endless synonyms exist in any language, and all serve their purpose. However, in business and in large organizations, establishing a consistent set of key terms to use for important concepts is critical.

For example, in this book I use the terminology Goal ZERO. Goal ZERO is written in a very specific manner, and it is used the same way at all times. It doesn't matter what terminology you use, be consistent.

Reading books such as this one and attending conferences are important for learning new concepts and stimulating thoughts. Authors, consultants, and conference presenters use their own specific terminology for common items. That said, you must guard against people introducing new conflicting terminology at a single location in your company after reading a book, attending a conference, or hiring a consultant. You will never drive Operational Excellence and achieve consistency across a company if different work groups define key concepts in different ways, forever changing. Encourage people to bring good concepts to your organization and blend the concepts into the existing systems and terminology if appropriate.

This consistency in terminology is especially critical in global organizations for countries in which English is not the native language. People in those countries may have some English capability but their vocabulary is probably limited, just as your vocabulary would be in speaking a second language.

Clear definitions of important words are also important. I could share countless stories about major disagreements, debates, and discussions simply because people had different interpretations for the same word or concept. This confusion happens among people with different native languages and even with people that speak the same language.

A simple example is "work process." Hearing the words, some people instinctively think of detailed process descriptions with every detail defined, while others may think of a simple one-page flow diagram. Words and clear definitions are extremely important in any organization.

The bottom line is to standardize the key high-level terminology used in your organization, define terms clearly in a glossary, and be disciplined about everyone using the same terminology in a consistent manner. This simple practice will help keep people on the same page, reduce confusion, and enable faster progress.

Technology

The technology employed for producing a product is the backbone of an operation. Some technology is purchased, while other technology is developed within the organization. Regardless of the source, it's crucial to get the knowledge and information out of people's heads and into the organization's management system.

Documentation provides a solid basis for achieving consistency and continuous improvement. Everyone has a firm foundation to work from and important knowledge doesn't get lost over time. An integral step in continuous improvement of the technology is to update the documentation following each improvement.

Have you ever eaten at a restaurant and the food is terrific? Then the next time you are disappointed because the food tastes different. This inconsistency is generally a result of which chef is on duty at the time. The most successful restaurants document their recipes (technology) and insist on consistency for every meal. Other restaurants without this type of documented approach rely on the talents of individual chefs, thus leading to inconsistency.

This principle applies to all products being produced. Document your technology and insist on consistency.

Simplify Writing Style

How many times have you tried to understand the instructions for a piece of electronic equipment you've purchased? You find yourself underlining key points or even writing notes on a separate piece of paper just to understand what the document is trying to say. The instructions are extremely confusing, but the document probably made perfect sense to the technical expert who wrote the document.

Don't let this confusion exist with the documents in your organization. The author of communications and instructional documents must write in a way that's understandable.

Subject matter experts will spend considerable time generating subject matter material. Therefore, it makes sense to create documents that are easy to read and comprehend. Simplified management systems must consist of documents that are concise, clear, and easy to understand.

People are busy and don't have time to unpack overly long sentences and complex dictation. Documents should be written in the clearest and most understandable manner possible. Multiple reviews should be conducted to assure ease of readability and avoidance of misunderstanding. Simplified writing is incredibly important but is often overlooked. To prevent complex writing, document writers should be trained and aligned on good writing practices.

Literary experts recommend that documents are most effective when written at the 8th grade reading level, which the average adult can easily read and comprehend. With a little training, document writers learn the factors that provide the best results:

- Short and concise sentences
- Frequent use of bullet points
- Average amount of syllables per word

It's not about dumbing down the content, but, rather putting the content in a format that people can understand. Ernest Hemingway was the king of short, concise sentences. He made every word count and kept his sentences simple and to the point. Simplification of writing style is a terrific enabler for all documents in a management system. Train document writers and hold them accountable.

With the advent of computers, authors have gotten into the terrible habit of installing multiple links within a document to other documents. These links lead to "standards within standards," which creates considerable confusion. It's easy for the author, but difficult for the reader.

It doesn't make sense for the author of a document to do what is easy for him or her, but cause confusion for years to come for the thousands of practitioners that must use the document. The hard, up-front work of the subject matter experts on prioritization and simplification will yield time savings and significant efficiency improvement across the organization.

EXCELLENCE NUGGET:
Create documents with appropriate readability.

Technical Writing—Flesch Reading Ease Score

Two excellent tools for document writers are the Flesch Reading Ease Score and the Flesch-Kincaid Readability Test. Readability is the ease with which a reader can understand a written text. With this technique, document writers can be trained and each document graded on readability.

Higher readability eases reading effort and speed for any reader. Making reading easier is especially important for those who do not have high reading comprehension. In readers with average or poor reading comprehension, improving the readability of a text can make the difference between success and failure of your communication goals. Readability is especially true for documents such as procedures that are used by the broader population.

The scoring formula is based on the average number of words per sentence and the average syllables per word. The scoring criteria uses a scale from 0 to 100, with 0 being the most difficult and 100 the easiest to comprehend (higher score is better).

Tests have shown that the *Reader's Digest* magazine had a readability index of about 65, *Time* magazine scored about 52, the *Wall Street Journal* about 43, the *Harvard Law Review* in the low 30s, and a standard auto insurance policy of about 10.

Microsoft Word has the Flesch-Kincaid Readability Test built into the software. The Flesch Reading Ease score and the

Flesch-Kincade grade level of the document can be found in the document stats section. We targeted our documents to be in the 60-70 Reading Ease score range. Other software programs offer similar methods for obtaining Reading Ease scores.

Set clear expectations for document writers, measure their work product, and hold the writers accountable. Create easy to understand documents to help eliminate confusion and the people on the front line will greatly appreciate it.

Required and Recommended

Some industry and company documents are problematic due to the terminology used. I've seen company standards with a list of requirements, and a few are labeled "mandatory" requirements. What does that mean? If some requirements are mandatory, does it mean that others are not mandatory?

In a Goal ZERO company, take out the word mandatory; otherwise, people in your organization might think other requirements aren't mandatory. Reduce the requirements to those that are most important and insist on full compliance. Goal ZERO means zero noncompliance with all requirements—it's the culture.

Common terms in governance documents include shall, must, should, and may statements. Industry accepted definitions for these terms are:

- "Shall" and "must" are required items.
- "Should" indicates a recommended item.
- "May" is an optional item.

In some documents, authors use these terms loosely and intermix them throughout standards. This inconsistency creates confusion and potential legal liability. Standards that include a combination of shall, should, and may statements confuse the user with items that are required and those that are recommended. Use these terms in a consistent manner and you will eliminate considerable confusion in the organization.

Work Processes and Procedures

Practical work processes are important for a variety of reasons. A work process should be clear and understandable. If it's intuitive, you don't even realize you are following a work process. The way you organize your kitchen silverware, for example, is a simple process. Processes provide order, reduce variation, and improve efficiency when everyone understands and performs work in a consistent manner.

Work processes can often become much too complicated and, as a result, people don't follow them. Keep your work processes clear and practical. Organize the steps that go into a work process, keep them at a high level, and don't try to micromanage every step.

Procedures for critical activities are different and more detail should be used for work in which every step is critical. Procedures are an integral component of any management system. Procedures should be continually improved and provide a consistent and safe manner for performing critical tasks.

Write procedures from the user's point of view. Procedures written in checklist format are most helpful to the front line. People can follow the checklist while performing tasks and also write down recommended improvements for the procedure as they proceed. People should follow the procedure or else make recommendations to change it. Keep procedures up to date, practical, and intuitive, and people will follow them.

Don't bog down procedures with instructional material. Maintain instructional material and reference information in separate documents.

Exceptional Housekeeping

Exceptional housekeeping is a cornerstone in a culture of excellence. Superb housekeeping should be a basic expectation for every person in the organization, from CEO to the front-line operator.

In one of my early assignments in Dow's Texas Operations, the unit's housekeeping was terrible, and the unit manager didn't care. Therefore, many people in the unit didn't care, but the sloppy housekeeping bothered me. Around that same time, I remember taking our children to Disneyland and marveling at the wonderful housekeeping in the park. I saw employees immediately picking up any litter that hit the ground and clipping the edges of grass immaculately. The difference between our two organizations was undeniable. I wanted our housekeeping to look more like Disneyland than what we were currently experiencing.

Shortly after our Disneyland visit, a new site manager, Larry Wright, was assigned to Texas Operations. He insisted that every unit in the site maintain excellent housekeeping. We were thrilled, and we began to immediately clean up our plant. You could see the pride and morale improve along with the cleanup. Larry demonstrated the power of strong leadership.

From that moment on, I accelerated my passion and expectation for excellence in housekeeping. We conducted a 15-minute "bucket brigade" in all of our plants once per week immediately after lunch. Everyone participated. I made it a point to personally cover as much area as I could to be visible to as many employees and contractors as possible. The bucket brigade made a big impression on everyone, and our housekeeping was always second to none.

Another example was on one of my visits to China. I went to a unit our company had acquired in a large industrial complex owned by another company. The housekeeping was very poor, nothing was painted, and weeds were growing everywhere. I talked to employees at the unit and convinced them to clean up and to send pictures to me. The team followed my guidance and the improvement over the next few months was remarkable. In later months, to my delight, the Chinese team said the units around them, owned by the other company, began to take notice and were actively working to improve their areas too. Peer pressure works.

One of our plant managers in France and a good friend of mine, Jerome Mauvigney, coined the phrase "the Smolik Sweep." He said every time I visited the plant and we walked around, I would casually reach down as we were walking and pick up any piece of trash that I saw. I always felt it was an effective way to set a good example and demonstrate our expectations. I chuckled each time on these tours as other people in our group would start picking up litter too.

Good housekeeping is an important precursor for how people work in an organization. If the work area is cluttered when people begin their work, they will probably leave the site in even worse condition. However, if people start with a clean workplace, they will leave it clean.

Begin by making sure that exceptional housekeeping is an expectation across your workplace. Never clean up "because the boss is coming." Keep the workplace clean at all times. Place trash containers in convenient locations and keep them emptied on a regular basis. A good guideline is that nothing should be on the ground or floor unless it's there for a specific reason. Keep areas painted and well lit.

Housekeeping is important in so many ways. Housekeeping builds employee pride. Housekeeping is integral to safety and quality performance. Housekeeping helps with recruiting when potential employees see an exceptional looking workplace. The public sees it. Customers love good housekeeping. And, most importantly, outstanding housekeeping is a visible sign of a culture of excellence.

EXCELLENCE NUGGET:
Good housekeeping is fundamental for excellence.

Investigations

Undoubtedly, a good investigation process is one of the most effective ways to gain information and drive improvement. Investigations should be a regular component in an organization that wants to continually improve. Investigate defects and incidents, learn from them, and take action to improve. Corrective actions apply to a department where the incident occurred and also across the company. Repeating the mistakes of others makes no sense. People should have fire in their guts for excellence, a passion to learn from experience, and the drive to implement corrective actions that will take their operation to the next level of performance.

If the word "investigation" seems threatening in your culture, give the process another name such as "after action review," "assessment," or "analysis." The objective is to address problems directly in an adult manner and make improvements to prevent recurrence. Once you develop this cadence, the people understand that it's all about improvement. Your organization can't afford to repeat the same mistakes over and over again.

Investigate the "small" problems before they become big problems. Investigate defects as soon as possible following the event. Investigations should be seen as a positive experience to keep the focus on learning, improving, and getting better. Never use an investigation in a negative way by pointing fingers, lecturing, or placing blame. Investigations provide an incredible coaching opportunity.

Do you remember my earlier story about the days I spent in the hospital? There were some serious errors committed, such as filling my lungs with liquid, but we were lucky and minimal harm was done.

However, I noticed that there wasn't a practice of investigating incidents and near misses at the hospital. The hospital personal just corrected the problem and went on about their work. The hospital had clear expectations for their employees but obviously didn't have a corresponding culture of excellence. I believe if the hospital had investigated minor incidents and taken corrective actions, the organization would have greatly reduced the risk of more serious incidents occurring.

Several methodologies are available for conducting incident investigations; however, the high-level process is quite simple (and should be conducted in this order):

- **Document the facts** that are associated with the incident.
- **Determine the cause(s)** of the incident.
- **Develop action items** to prevent recurrence.

Many incident investigations take too long. Don't drag them out longer than needed. We've conducted hundreds of investigations in an hour or less. More complicated incidents take longer.

The first step in the investigation process is to document the facts. Work on collecting this information as soon as possible following an incident. During the investigation, resist the urge of people wanting to jump straight to causes and corrective actions until the documentation of facts is completed.

Then the investigation process shifts to discussion of potential causes. The causes of an incident can always be grouped into the categories of leadership, people, systems, and culture. If you keep asking "why" in the investigation, you will eventually get to system and leadership issues. However, don't lose the value of the people and culture intermediate causes.

Data shows that roughly 90% of injuries involve some type of human factor as one of the causes. If the incident is caused by human behavior, then careful analysis is necessary to determine if a particular individual's actions caused the incident or if broader system or cultural issues are at play.

There are often debates in organizations when assigning causes of an incident. Some people will determine one of the causes of the incident to be people related: the individual wasn't following the procedure, the individual made a careless mistake, etc. Others will always go past the human behavior and pin the cause on the system: the standards and requirements were lacking, the rules and procedures weren't clear, etc. Still others will say there is a cultural problem: there is a culture of noncompliance in the organization, people pick and choose the rules that they will follow, etc. Finally, all of the above potential root causes tend to be a result of poor leadership.

The truth is, excellence and minimizing incidents are the result of all these factors—leadership, people, systems, *and* culture—not one or the other. Don't waste time debating one root cause or the other. There doesn't have to be just one root cause of an incident. Instead, focus on all four factors to drive sustainable improvement and build on your culture of excellence.

If the actions of a specific individual caused the incident, call it like it is. This is definitely not about placing blame; it's about stating the facts and learning. Conduct investigations in a positive manner. However, some leaders aren't comfortable holding individuals accountable. These leaders assign system issues (procedures, rules, equipment, etc.) as the cause instead of focusing on the human behavior itself. This assignment of cause is often misguided and tends to take away from the accountability and responsibility of the individual.

If an incident was caused by the actions of an individual, learn from it, and move on. We all make mistakes at one time or another. Failure is okay as long as you learn and improve. Dealing with undesired behavior in a fair way is important in establishing a Goal ZERO culture. At the same time, evaluate improvements in the processes and procedures of your management system to help reduce the chance of human error. But remember, don't respond to one individual's poor behavior by adding costly asset changes or additional onerous rules that impact everyone else. Conducting regular investigations is a positive way to address problems and raise the sense of awareness for a ZERO defect culture.

The final step of an investigation is to assign corrective actions to prevent recurrence. Determine the improvements required to further reduce risk. Corrective actions may consist of improved leadership actions, modifications to procedures, or potential improvements to the management system.

A useful metric to track and communicate is the number of investigations conducted. Although counterintuitive, a higher number of investigations is better. Why? Investigating incidents means that departments are evaluating their issues and making improvements. If the number of investigations starts tracking downwards, start asking why. As incidents with consequences begin to decrease, more focus can be applied to high potential incidents and near misses. Keep learning and improving. Finally, all corrective actions must be completed by the due date, which is another aspect of the Goal ZERO philosophy.

Manufacturing organizations understand the value of investigations. Investigations document the facts, determine causes, and develop corrective actions to prevent recurrence. Formally investigating defects and problems in some functions is not as common due to the negative implications associated with investigations. However, a culture of investigating problems in all functions is critical for continuous improvement.

EXCELLENCE NUGGET:
Investigations are an essential process for achieving continuous improvement.

Learning from Experience Process

Many companies have a "Learning from Incidents" work process. We took learning a step further. We understood that you not only "learn from incidents," you also learn from audits, sharing of best practices, internal improvements, individual input, external incidents, and all types of additional external information. Therefore, we changed the name to a "Learning from Experience" work process. We had a process for collecting information from various sources and assigning it to the right management system person for action.

Here's a situation familiar to all of us. You attend a conference and learn some new information that would be extremely helpful to the company. You return to work enthusiastic about your new knowledge, but your daily workload and urgent items consume your time. The new information goes unshared and unutilized within the organization and often dies on the vine. It's a shame to not capture and take advantage of this new information. With the Learning from Experience process, it's easy to submit your learnings and ideas to the appropriate management system document owners for further consideration.

Reviewing major incidents at other companies is a vital source of learning for safety improvement. The Chemical Safety Board is a good source for information for the energy and chemical industries. Test each incident against your management system with the question, "Would proper execution of our management system have prevented this incident?" If the answer is no, make necessary improvements to your system documents. If the answer is yes, use the incident as an example to people in your organization for how important it is to follow the system requirements. Act as if the incident had just occurred in your organization. Always use an unfortunate incident as an opportunity to learn and improve.

The key is to create a process where learnings and information are captured and improvements are documented into an ever-improving management system. Updating the system assures the learnings are never forgotten.

Gap Assessment and Gap Closure

Gap assessment is an exercise to determine gaps with legal or internal requirements. Gap closure is the completion of action items within a defined time frame to close the gaps that were identified.

A gap assessment and gap closure process is important for two main reasons. The first reason is for compliance when new or revised documents in a management system are rolled out to the organization. The responsibility of each facility is to perform a gap assessment and identify actions required to close the gaps. The department assigns action items and gap closures are tracked to completion. It's important at a corporate level to assure 100% closure of gaps within the agreed upon time frame.

The second use of the gap assessment and gap closure process is for newly acquired mergers and acquisitions (M&A) assets. If you have developed a well-documented management system, integration of M&A assets becomes much easier. Each newly acquired facility conducts a gap analysis for the documents in the management system and then develops and executes a gap closure plan.

The principle is that newly acquired facilities will convert to the selected management system for overall consistency. Of course, the newly acquired company or facilities may have some very good practices of their own. For these situations, items are entered into the Learning from Experience work process and incorporated into your existing system as appropriate. I'll explain more details later in the Mergers and Acquisitions section.

Self-Assessment and Auditing

Three primary levels of ownership and assessment are important for full compliance with rules and regulations. The first is the personal responsibility of every employee and contractor to follow all requirements. One hundred percent compliance by one hundred percent of the people is fundamental to a Goal ZERO culture.

The second level of oversight is a regular cadence of self-assessments within each department. Of the many mechanisms for self-assessments, my favorite is one that operates on a continuous basis, which can be accomplished through the Divide and Conquer process. Divide self-assessment accountability for standards and other requirements among the personnel in your operation. Establish clear expectations. All assigned employees should carefully read and thoroughly understand their assigned requirements. On a regular basis, the employee should perform checks to ensure the organization is complying.

If the employee finds gaps, he or she should take actions to correct the deficiency. If the gap is beyond their control, notify an appropriate person that can address the issue. This type of self-assessment process spreads the workload and keeps an eye on compliance at all times. These assignments increase individual responsibility and improve employee engagement.

A well-designed and functioning self-assessment process is easy to manage and blends into daily work. If conducted the right way, the unit will remain in full compliance at times. If the self-assessment process is functioning as expected, independent audits will simply confirm that everything is in good shape.

The third level of oversight is an independent audit program. No matter how good individuals and units may be, a continuous process for checking compliance is important and good governance. Independent audits consist of auditors that are not a member of the unit receiving the audit. Assign a few individuals skilled in auditing techniques and subject matter experts to be full-time auditors. Use external resources only if you don't have the expertise or enough personnel within your company.

Staff independent audit teams with additional personnel from other areas in your company. I call these "guest auditors." Guest auditors provide a fresh set of eyes to identify gaps and to suggest improvements. The audits also serve as good learning and development opportunities for the guest auditors. People learn more when they actively participate. Keep track of the guest auditor participation and make sure everyone eventually has an opportunity to participate in audits of other units.

Most importantly, auditing should serve as a learning experience for everyone involved. Auditors have the benefit of learning from many different facilities and should share their learnings. Significant learnings should be documented in the company's management system to capture the knowledge gained.

EXCELLENCE NUGGET:
A robust self-assessment process will identify most noncompliance situations.

The "WHY Review"

Over the years, we observed that when audits were being performed at plants, noncompliance items were found, audit reports were written, plants performed corrective actions, and then business went on as usual. Auditors often found some of the same areas of noncompliance at every location they audited. We didn't feel that the company was receiving the full benefit of the audit program.

Remember that in a Goal ZERO culture, every department should be in full compliance with every requirement at all times. The department should have an ongoing, robust self-assessment process to assure all items are always in compliance. If noncompliance items are discovered, it's important to determine "why" the noncompliance items existed.

To take compliance to the next level, we added an additional step to the audit process. After an audit of a unit was completed and if significant noncompliance items were found, we'd conduct a follow-up meeting called the "WHY Review." The purpose was to learn and improve.

We didn't dwell on "what" the findings from the audit were. Rather, we focused on "why" the noncompliance items existed. The explanations typically resulted in a system problem or people performance (including leadership) issues. The participants in the meeting included the plant manager and anyone he or she wanted to bring from their team as well as the plant manager's boss, the head of Operational Excellence, and myself.

Sometimes we determined a requirement in a corporate standard wasn't clear and needed to be updated or eliminated entirely if deemed a low priority. At times, the conclusion was that the plant didn't have a sufficient process for assuring compliance in a particular area. At other times, a noncompliance was due to an individual who simply wasn't performing his or her assigned task and needed to be dealt with individually. And finally, the noncompliance was sometimes a plant leadership issue, i.e., allowing a culture of noncompliance to exist.

Regardless of the cause, these sessions always provided a terrific learning experience and a coachable moment for leadership. These reviews were an opportunity to reinforce how serious we were about Goal ZERO compliance. The sessions were not intended to be negative towards plant leadership although I'm sure none of them looked forward to the session. Instead, the sessions served the purpose and allowed plant managers to do some self-reflection on their leadership behavior and how they could work better with their teams to deliver desired results.

High Potential Incidents (HPIs)

In a Goal ZERO operation, fewer and fewer serious consequence incidents occur, which is the good part. As the frequency of incidents declines, however, the danger lies in people relaxing and becoming complacent. We all know that learning experiences continue to occur because nothing is ever perfect.

Many companies encourage their employees to report near misses. Near miss reporting helps keep employee awareness high at all times. The problem with the near miss category is that the definition of a near miss is not typically well-defined resulting in a wide variation of reporting across the organization. If a large number of near miss incidents are reported, the sheer volume inhibits a sense of urgency, and some near misses don't receive the attention they may deserve.

I highly recommend a **High Potential Incident (HPI)** reporting requirement. Instituting an HPI program is extremely effective since it creates an important incident category between an actual reportable incident with consequences and a loosely defined near miss. The HPI category is a defined subset of near misses. The definition for an HPI is a near miss that had a **high probability or reasonable potential** of becoming a serious injury, operational, or quality incident. This classification screens out the minor near misses.

There should be a well-defined list of near misses that must be reported as an HPI. Some may be associated with noncompliance of life-critical activity requirements. Several examples are:

- Fall from height greater than 6 feet
- Working at heights without proper protection
- Confined space entry violations
- Work without proper energy isolation
- Unprotected excavation work
- Breathing air incidents
- Any electrical shock with 120V or greater
- Dropped objects from heights
- Unexpected contact and exposure
- Certain defined operational incidents

In addition to the pre-defined list of automatic HPIs, departments should report any additional incident as an HPI that is deemed appropriate and deserves increased attention.

Investigate HPIs as if the worst had happened and take appropriate measures to prevent recurrence. Funnel key learnings into the Learning from Experience Process for corporate improvement. This approach helps to continually close gaps with expected performance and effectively demonstrates Goal ZERO expectations to the workforce. A Goal ZERO culture does not depend on luck. A focus on High Potential Incidents allows the organization to take corrective actions for serious near misses before incidents occur with significant consequences.

Some HPIs may have been caused by an individual's behavior. Designating the incident as an HPI sends a powerful message to the person and to others in the organization. The right kind of discussion and actions with the person and the workforce can be powerful and result in improved employee performance going forward. A good HPI process provides the organization with a sense of urgency for doing work the right way at all times. I would much rather exert these efforts on an HPI rather than waiting for an incident to occur with serious consequences.

Life-Critical Activities

My heart breaks every time I read or hear about a repeat incident from a well-known activity and people needlessly losing their lives. This type of work falls into the category of life-critical activities. These are high risk activities which unfortunately have a long history of ending with catastrophic results if not performed correctly. These types of activities and associated incidents are well known, and incidents should never occur. These incidents get investigated thoroughly each time and always end up with the same causes falling into the leadership, people, systems, and culture categories.

It is critical to identity the life-critical activities that are performed in your operations and the precautions that must be taken every time. Learn from the unfortunate experiences of others and never allow failure in these activities to occur.

A few examples of life-critical activities in the energy and chemical manufacturing industry are:

- Crane and Rigging
- Confined Space Entry
- Working at Heights
- Hot Work
- Initial Break into Equipment

All standards and procedures must be followed in a Goal ZERO culture, but life-critical activities need an extra layer of detail, protection, and diligence. Communication and review of these requirements should occur much more frequently. Keep the awareness of these activities high. Any violation of requirements or near miss with a life-critical activity should be reported as a High Potential Incident. The incident should be investigated with the same level of intensity as if severe consequences had occurred.

This focus gets everyone's attention and helps to assign appropriate corrective actions that can prevent recurrence. Ensure that everyone is aware of life-critical activities and that work is performed to perfection every time.

Initiative and Action Item Overload

Every initiative has good intentions, but the organization has limited capacity. Initiative overload can create too much distraction from the daily pursuit of excellence. If you have more initiatives than the people in the organization can handle, none of the initiatives will get done very well. Make sure you have a robust prioritization process to help manage the load. Someone must have the power to say "no" and draw the line on initiatives.

The same principle applies for corrective action items. Action items are assigned from meetings, investigations, audits, and many other initiatives. Action items are essential to correct problems or make improvements in your work. Remember, however, that each action item creates work for someone. People have limited time, and every action item will take the place of some other work that is needed.

My advice is to use strict prioritization for action items, the same as for initiatives. It's easy to proceed through a meeting or incident investigation and create action items along the way. The intentions at the time are good. However, at the end of the meeting or following the meeting, someone needs to review the action items in context with everything else on people's plates and cull out the ones with lower priority. Strict prioritization is crucial. Make sure people are always working on the highest value items that will deliver the most positive impact.

As mentioned before, every action item that gets assigned in a Goal ZERO culture must be performed by the assigned due date and tracked. The process should allow for extending the due date based on valid reasons, but these extensions should be the exception and not the rule. Deadline extensions should be documented and monitored. With this process, you should have zero overdue corrective actions at all times. Overdue corrective actions create legal liabilities, not to mention how terrible it would be if a serious incident occurred because you hadn't completed corrective actions previously identified.

EXCELLENCE NUGGET:
Remain diligent to prevent initiative and action item overload.

Metrics and Key Performance Indicators

We all know that data is powerful. Data is used to track progress, identify trends, improve performance, and reward people based on their achievements.

We found that basic definitions of key terms were extremely important to prevent confusion. A clear understanding of the difference between "metrics" and "key performance indicators" (KPI) by everyone is essential:

- **Metrics.** These individual items are measured within each area of focus. The number of metrics in an organization may be very high.
- **Key Performance Indicators (KPI).** These indicators are the "critical few" metrics most important to a company or a department. KPIs should be the high-level indicators of success or items that need special focus for improvement. KPIs can change year to year.

At higher levels in the organization, maintain a laser focus on the KPIs and drive performance hard. As necessary, drill down into the various metrics and leading indicators that support each individual KPI. At lower levels in the organization, the individual metrics become much more important in driving KPI progress.

List all of the metrics that you expect to be tracked and clearly define each one. Determine how each metric will be measured and who is responsible and accountable for maintaining the metric. Don't allow any important metric to fall through the cracks.

Data Management and Reporting

The number of metrics tracked within each area of work can be in the hundreds. A lot of time and energy goes into collecting data. However, it's amazing how little effort is put into effectively reporting data in a meaningful way that grabs people's attention and changes behavior. I've seen many reports packed with data in complicated tables and charts. It may be the easiest way to report for the person that assembled the data, but the reader doesn't get the overarching messages.

Organize data reporting so that it intuitively "tells the story." The message should jump out at the reader. Data is powerful. Simplification is the key. To be effective, data reporting should be done in a manner that is persuasive and drives behavior.

Tailor various data reports to particular audiences. The board of directors and company management may need one style of report, department managers another, and the general employee base still another. It's important to increase employee engagement by showing them the data—show the score. Feedback is powerful. Employees should see how their particular department or company is performing relative to others. Report the data that is most important and in a manner that is clearly understood by the intended audience. Avoid data overload. Use discipline to prioritize and limit the number of metrics or KPIs reported.

We used this concept extensively when reporting Operational Excellence data. A monthly report was issued that began with a single page dashboard of Key Performance Indicators. The dashboard showed the monthly, year-to-date, and the previous two years of data for each KPI. The dashboard provided everyone with a snapshot of performance on the most important parameters.

From the dashboard, the company performance was clear but didn't provide information on individual sites. To increase visibility for the plants, we followed the dashboard with Pareto charts. We included a series of Pareto charts to emphasize key areas, *with only one KPI per chart.*

Take the subject of personal safety as an example. Instead of a table with information overload, a single Pareto chart was extremely effective. We listed the safety performance of each site, from best to worst, on a Pareto chart. The sites were color coded by quartile. This type of data reporting didn't require any discussion to deliver the intended message. The Pareto chart told the story; the chart provided instant positive recognition for the best performers, highlighted the poorer performers, and indicated where additional efforts needed to be placed.

It was clear that to get off of the wrong end of the chart, a plant needed to work harder and improve performance. Reporting data in this manner resulted in significant leader behavior change and rapid improvements.

When you report data, make the intention as obvious as possible and use as many pareto charts as necessary to highlight important components. The concept of showing performance results from top to bottom is no different than in sports. You can check the sports results every day and find your favorite team's status. These rankings are an incredible motivator. Think how boring sports would be if the games were played, but the scores and rankings were never communicated. No one would care and the players certainly wouldn't try as hard.

EXCELLENCE NUGGET:
*Data is powerful if presented
in an effective manner*

Benchmarking

I am a huge fan of benchmarking to monitor performance relative to others and to capture best practices. Benchmarking is the practice of comparing business processes and performance metrics with other organizations. Best practices and lessons learned should be incorporated into your management system.

In a large company, opportunities for internal benchmarking between operating units are plentiful. Benchmarking compares parameters and each unit should utilize the data constructively in their quest to become the best.

Sam Walton's benchmarking expectations called for every Walmart store manager to periodically walk through their competitors' stores. The managers were expected to observe their competition's work processes and any new ideas and concepts that were emerging. Walton realized that his company didn't have all the answers and they were always interested in learning from others.

Companies such as Solomon Associates and Phillip Townsend Associates perform excellent benchmarking services throughout the energy and chemical value chain. Other industries have similar services. Data from external benchmarking is often presented in quartiles of performance. I don't know about you, but my expectation was never to just be in the top quartile; my objective was to be the best.

Controlling Costs, the Right Way

Throughout my career, I've seen manufacturing units that are under the responsibility of upper managers with no operating experience. Some of these leaders determine how much the business can afford and set strict top-down budgets—no excuses. Lack of appropriate funding was one of the causes of the 2005 BP Texas City incident in which 15 people perished. The process hazards had been identified, but insufficient funds were provided to correct the deficiencies.

One such example was in one of our joint ventures shortly after I became Vice President of EH&S at Dow. This joint venture had been formed about five years previously and one of the plant managers was a good, experienced Dow person. The joint venture was operated independently of Dow and the plant manager reported directly to the business vice president, an unusual reporting relationship for Dow plants at the time.

An incident occurred in which an employee was severely burned from an equipment failure in a boiler unit. Upon investigation and follow-up discussions, we realized the joint venture had not closed the gaps in compliance with Dow standards. The plant manager told me how frustrated he had been since taking the job. He had told the business vice president many times about the problems and the extra cost needed to get the plant up to standards. He said the vice president turned down the request, saying "the expense would kill the business."

The plant manager was in an unfortunate position of reporting to a bad leader and, as a result, had operated the plant in poor condition resulting in an unfortunate injury. At the time, Dow was making billions of dollars in profits. Blaming a serious injury or fatality on lack of affordability in a business unit or subsidiary was not acceptable.

This example shows that improperly maintaining an asset is sometimes due to the individual unit cost and profitability restraints of a particular business, not the restraints of the entire company. The business leader has his or her scorecard, which can cause conflicts with the core values of the company. Through the years, I often found disconnects between the CEO of a company and the leaders of units, functions, and businesses down in the organization.

I have yet to find a good CEO who wants any of his or her units to be operated in an unsafe manner. Top management is generally willing to approve extra spending if they truly understand why the spending is important and understand the potential consequences of not doing it.

EXCELLENCE NUGGET:
Cost control must be conducted in the right manner.

Mergers and Acquisitions Process for Operations

A good component in a management system for a growth company is a robust Mergers and Acquisitions (M&A) process. Mergers and acquisitions are typically conducted to expand geographic footprint, bring new technology or service to the company, expand the company's customer base, or create significant synergies.

Unfortunately, a recent *Harvard Business Review* report indicated that the failure rate for M&A deals is an incredibly high 70-90 percent. It's important to weed out the bad deals in the due diligence process.

From an operations point of view, why acquire another company unless you can operate the company better or generate increased value? Establish a strong Operational Excellence culture in your company with a robust management system before making acquisitions. Then you will be able to move quickly with the acquisition, integrate systems and work processes, achieve synergies, and drive value creation.

Corporate and commercial leadership typically negotiate the deals, but operating units have a major role in implementation. Synergies and expected value creation are developed and then the deal is executed. I was fortunate during my career to participate in several successful acquisitions and divestitures.

Following my retirement, I worked on a project with Pilko & Associates, a leading advising and consulting organization for Operational Excellence. In advising a client on a potential major acquisition, we provided an M&A work process focused totally on operations.

The operation's M&A process has three phases:

- **Phase 1.** Developing the deal, pre-signing
- **Phase 2.** Detailed preparation, between signing and closing
- **Phase 3.** Executing the deal, post-closing

Phase 1 consists of the early stages of deal preparation when due diligence is conducted with a laser focus on valuation. Potential synergies are developed during this phase. One of the important aspects of Phase 1 is to determine potential costs post acquisition. One of the elements commonly missed when developing deals is the expense or capital required to close gaps with your management system requirements.

Another deliverable during Phase 1 is to determine risks with the new acquisition and whether your organization will accept those risks or not. It's much better to identify the risks and costs early, especially if these issues prevent the deal from going forward. It's better to know the risks and costs and kill the deal rather than learning much later and having the deal destroy value.

In addition to due diligence, Phase 1 is the time to begin preparations for Phase 2. Begin to develop plans and answer questions such as how the combined company will be structured, will the deal be a takeover or merger of equals, who will be the decision-making authorities, what are the role definitions, who are the key stakeholders, and what is the communications plan?

If the decision is made to proceed, Phase 2 begins when the deal is signed and lasts until closing. Timing for this phase is typically 6-18 months, depending on the size and complexity of the deal. Regulatory approvals will require significant resources and can add uncertainty to the actual closing date. During Phase 2, detailed preparations and decisions should be made regarding leadership, people, systems, and culture.

If Phase 2 is executed properly, you will be able to make all necessary decisions and hit the ground running on Day 1 following deal closure. Phase 2 should be executed function by function with clear expectations for deliverables. Phase 2 is the time to:

- Announce legal business rules (stock purchase, etc.).
- Meet the people.
- Create functional transition teams.
- Determine objectives to complete prior to Day 1.
- Determine preliminary asset gap closure plans.
- Determine standards and processes to be followed for the new organization.
- Review organization charts and develop headcount synergy plans.
- Determine who will fill senior leadership roles and implement soon after closing.
- Begin discussing the desired culture of the new organization.
- Determine who will comprise the Phase 3 transition team.
- Develop detailed transition plans.
- Empower functional leaders and enable fast decision-making.
- Consistently update stakeholders: employees, customers, communities, unions, and shareholders.
- Maintain a strong focus on safety since people may become distracted.

- Treat all people with dignity and respect.
- Move quickly, get it 80-90% right.
- Be ready to execute beginning on Day 1.

Phase 3 begins when the deal closes. Phase 3 consists of executing the deal and begins with a successful Day 1. People will expect changes when the deal closes, and you should be ready to take full advantage of the "honeymoon" period. Speed in executing Phase 3 initiatives will be an important element of success. A well-planned Day 1 will set the stage for the future. Perform symbolic gestures such as installing new signs at facilities and issuing new employee badges. Create excitement with a good communications strategy and send key leaders to as many locations as possible.

On Day 1, or quickly following, make planned changes in key leadership. Update members of the transition team and announce expectations and timing function by function. Conduct workshops to establish the new culture and expectations. Many mergers have failed due to conflicting cultures. Understand that culture change takes time, and a considerable amount of communication is required to bring people along with the changes. Strategy and plans are useless unless the culture of the organization is supportive and in alignment.

Perform a gap analysis with the management system requirements at all new locations. Create gap closure plans and then relentlessly close the gaps in a timely fashion. Acquisitions can put the entire company at risk if facilities are not integrated into the existing culture and management system. Your company is only as good as its weakest link.

I've listed only the high-level points of the Operational M&A process, but you get the idea that each phase is unique. Of course, many details are embedded within each phase. Communicate often with your stakeholders throughout the process. The proper execution of each phase enables the next phase to move quicker and more efficiently. Proper execution of the M&A process will significantly improve your chances for success in expected value creation.

Processes and Practices for Achieving Excellence

(The Contents of a Management System)

A SUMMARY

- Continually improve the work processes that make a positive difference for your organization.
- Follow a good change management process when conducting major change initiatives.
- Utilize consistent terminology in your organization. Write in a concise and clear manner.
- Simplicity is a differentiator. Shorter and simpler is always better.
- Investigate defects, learn from them, and make improvement to prevent reoccurrence.
- Benchmark best practices and performance within and external to the organization.
- Be careful with initiative overload. Utilize a gatekeeper for weeding out lower value initiatives and too many corrective actions. Prioritization is essential.
- Clarify the performance metrics for the organization with clear definitions and owners. Select a critical few Key Performance Indicators (KPIs) that are critical for the organization's success.

CHAPTER 6

Pulling It All Together in a Management System

"For every minute spent in organizing, an hour is earned."
– Benjamin Franklin

Many individuals in companies waste too much time trying to determine "how" to conduct work and drive performance improvement. These individuals waste valuable time recreating the same processes that were used in the past or exist elsewhere in the company.

When incidents and defects happen, an endless amount of time goes into determining "why" the problems occurred and in developing corrective actions. The same frustrating mistakes get repeated over and over again. Management gets frustrated when there are too many problems and puts the pressure on their people. The people are trying hard, but things don't seem to get better.

One cause of these "how" and "why" questions is the absence of a robust management system providing a solid foundation to build on. *Every company needs a management system.* If a good management system exists, the "why" is often simply failure to execute what is already known and documented in the system. A management system and an associated culture are the enablers for people delivering consistent, quality results.

One of the causes of incidents and poor performance is loss of historical knowledge. People retire and leave the workforce. The knowledge goes out the door. Another cause is people forgetting learnings years later after a serious incident has occurred. A robust management system that captures these experience and learnings would prevent both of the situations from occurring.

Addressing loss of institutional knowledge is one of the primary reasons I have written this book and specifically this chapter about management systems. A good management system documents all learnings from the past in an understandable manner, so the learnings are constantly integrated into daily work and are never forgotten. People can leave the organization, but the knowledge remains. You should never repeat the same type of incident twice, no matter how much time has gone by.

In today's global environment with communication tools and social media, bad news travels fast. Your company is only as good as its weakest link. Incidents occurring in a single location in the world can have devastating consequences across the entire organization. We used to say, "When part of the skunk stinks, the entire skunk stinks." Therefore, you can no longer afford to have every location operate its facility entirely its own way as companies did in the ancient past. Changing operating practices each time leadership changes has inherently higher risk, increased turmoil, and never leads to overall company consistency and Operational Excellence.

The principles in this chapter provide clear guidance for development and organization of materials that go into a management system so that people can then focus the majority of their efforts on "execution and implementation." The management system must be developed in a manner that people want to use it, not have to use it. The processes and examples I use are based on my large company experience, so pick and choose the concepts that are applicable to your company and adjust as appropriate.

World-class organizations and results focused leaders drive for consistency, reduce variation, and fine-tune the way work gets done. Good leaders build on the best practices that work and expect excellence in every detail. It makes no sense for people to continually "reinvent the wheel." Winston Churchill said it well, "Those who fail to learn from history are condemned to repeat it."

It doesn't matter if you have five people or 50,000 people in your organization, you need a management system. A management system documents best practices, provides clarity, and takes churn out of the organization. Your technology is key to your organization's success and needs to be documented and continually improved. A good management system gives people the confidence to know they are on the right track, the courage to drive harder, and the tools needed to win.

As an individual, you may not be responsible for the creation of documents in a management system, but you need to adhere to the requirements in your daily work. You have a responsibility to contact the appropriate person when a standard is too onerous, does not allow compliance to be reasonable, or if the document can be improved in any way. Work processes should be continually improved as new knowledge is gained. Everyone should play a role in the continual updating and improvement of management system documents.

When you have a good functioning management system, people will wonder how the organization ever functioned without one. Good management systems contain many elements, but some of the most important ones are expectations for the organization, clear accountability, required standards, technology, acquired knowledge, work processes, measurements, performance reporting, governance, and a regular cadence for overall management. Standardized ways of doing work drive efficiency, effectiveness, quality, and alignment and they add discipline to the organization. By standardizing the basics of work, people are free to be more creative and move faster on their areas of focus.

A strong management system along with a ZERO incident culture creates discipline and consistency that leads to improved performance in any organization. Without a management system, ways of working become entirely people-centric and can change every time the leaders or employees change. This creates enormous duplication of work, introduces variation in performance, adds to inefficiency, and increases risk since people continue to repeat the same old mistakes and don't build on best practices of how work should be done.

In this chapter, I'll describe various work processes and methods we found to be helpful in building a world-class, easy-to-use management system. I'll share many tips to assure the elements of the management system are effective and meet the needs of the organization.

EXCELLENCE NUGGET:
A management system documents best practices and enables focus on achieving excellence.

Management Systems

At the highest level in your organization, create the expectation for Operational Excellence in everything that people do. To align with this expectation, create one overarching Operational Excellence Management System. Avoid the use of multiple, competing systems such as a Quality Management System, Production Management System, and Process Safety Management System. These types of systems are commonly found in companies to align with corporate functions. This siloed approach creates redundancy and confusion in the organization. Rather, elevate the approach to a higher level and include each of these areas as sub-processes within the overall Operational Excellence Management System.

In many cases, an organization's so-called management system has become too complex over the years and provides a false sense of security. In other cases, documents exist but never get used. Leaders will claim they have a management system, but how well is the system followed in the organization? Can people find the information they need? Is there consistency across the organization?

Most organizations need to update their management system and improve the way information is organized. A few of the problems that organizations have with their management systems are:

- It's not easy for people to find the information they need in an efficient manner.
- Too many complex documents have been developed over the years.
- New documents continue to be created, but nothing ever seems to be deleted.
- The number of requirements in standards continues to increase.
- Information is not organized in a consistent manner.
- Confusion with requirement interpretation exists in the organization.
- It's difficult to institutionalize learnings from incidents to prevent recurrence.

- High priority items are mixed with low priority information.
- Too much knowledge resides in people's heads and is not captured for the organization.
- Repeat incidents occur because organizations fail to learn and remember from the past.
- No one is in charge of information management.

These issues have been apparent in almost every company I've dealt with. The advent of computers has proliferated the problem. It becomes easier for people to generate numerous documents and more difficult for users to find the prioritized information they need.

These problems can be prevented by applying proactive management to information overload. A management system has two primary stakeholder groups: subject matter experts for each topic and the users in the organization who are expected to utilize the system.

The subject matter experts want an organized way to store their information and documentation. Experts want to make information available for the users and build on what has already been developed.

The users in the field want "simplicity." Users want to be able to find the right information they need in an efficient manner. The users don't want to sift through considerable amounts of information to determine what is most important. Users believe that the subject matter experts should prioritize the information for them. Operations people often say, "Just tell me what I have to do, and I'll do it."

Meeting the needs of both stakeholders isn't difficult. Begin by developing guidance and expectations for how your management system is organized and maintained. A few examples of management system design requirements are:

- Consistent design and structure
- Easy to find information
- Prioritization of important information
- Very clear listing of requirements
- Work processes
- Examples of good practices

- Past incidents and learnings
- Training materials
- Access to subject matter experts
- User friendly software

Consistent terminology and vocabulary are critical to avoid confusion in the organization. Providing clarity and ease of understanding are important to the organization. A good functioning management system provides a consistent platform from which leaders can lead.

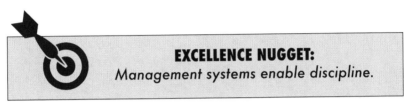

EXCELLENCE NUGGET:
Management systems enable discipline.

Getting Started

A management system and the associated documents should be designed and maintained such that the information is clear to understand. If the system is too complex and overbearing, it will be impossible for people to comply with the system, and, thus, you will have a culture of noncompliance.

If your company doesn't have a management system that describes consistent ways of doing work, get started today. The results will be well worth the effort. Divide the management system into reasonable components and get started.

How would you describe the perfect management system? A few of the key words that come to my mind are simplicity, crisp, intuitive, logical, fit for purpose, helpful, user-friendly, and up to date. Start with the end in mind and develop your system to fit the users' needs.

It's important for people in your organization to understand and align on the concept of a management system. A management system is often referred to as an operating model. My simple definition is that a management system is an organized, disciplined structure for documenting "how we want to do things around here." A management system should be clear to understand and serve as a useful reference for people in the organization.

It's always helpful to start with the end in mind. What would it be like if you truly had a robust, functioning management system? A good system is a terrific enabler for performance. Here are some of the many advantages of a good management system:

- Consistent, predictable performance
- Reliable operations
- Improved customer experience
- No surprises
- A culture of full compliance
- Minimization of confusion and complexity
- Improved employee engagement
- Effective communication and collaboration
- Utilization of best practices
- Efficient maintenance and operation of equipment
- Simple, effective work processes
- Documents readily available and easy to find
- Competent and dependable people
- Identification of defects and corrective actions to improve
- Metrics and key performance indicators

If you have a small company, organization of your documentation can be fairly easy. As your company gets larger with a high number of employees, the organization and availability of materials becomes much more important and requires a clear structure.

A good management system can help to accelerate improvement in an organization, but why do so many organizations have problems with their system? Most documents in systems are simply too long and complex. Most people won't read excessively long documents. Documents may have been written by many different authors through the years without a consistent format or style. The result is a system that has morphed over time without an overall structure. People have difficulty finding information they need with poorly maintained systems.

The key to the success of your management system is to create documents that people in the organization want to use rather than are forced to use. Users want to know why the documents are important, see the value, find information they need quickly, and get on with their work. The management system becomes an enabling tool for doing work. Make the system and sub-processes intuitive.

People shouldn't need any special training if you develop documents by working backwards from what users actually need. Employees will trust the system if the tools, processes, and information help them to work smarter.

Remember the saying, "The best time to plant an oak tree is 20 years ago. The second best time is today." The same is true for establishing and executing a good management system. It's never too late to do the right thing. Begin today.

Back to the Basics

Lessons don't come cheap in manufacturing industries with fires, explosions, environmental damage, injuries, and even fatalities. We often say there aren't many new types of root causes to incidents, just repeats of the same old mistakes. That's a sad statement of fact. The challenge is in how to capture these lessons and embed them into the everyday work practices and the culture of a company.

Many companies experience a series of problems or a major incident and you'll hear leadership say, "We need to get back to the basics." I've heard this phrase many times and I'll bet you have too.

Why do companies have to keep learning the same lessons over and over? You can be proactive by creating an effective management system that becomes the cornerstone for your company's operating culture. Once you have an effective system and execute with a Goal ZERO mentality, you'll never have to "get back to the basics" again.

Simplicity

Before discussing the creation of a management system, I want to emphasize the importance of simplicity. Simplicity is a prevailing theme throughout this book. Simplicity is the ability to make something easy to understand. Simplicity in a complex world is powerful. One of my favorite books is *Simplicity* by Bill Jensen. The book is a must-read. Bill Jensen looks at the human side of work focusing on what the organization needs. Many things are just too complex. He lays out an organized plan to cut through the mess or to completely eliminate it.

A few key points that are applicable to management systems and communication are:

- Information should be user centered.
- By making the complex clear, it helps people to **work smarter.** It's a lot easier to figure out what's important and ignore what isn't.
- The way to reduce work complexity is to make it easier for the average employee to adapt the tools, processes, and information in the system to the way he or she needs to use them.
- Just because you have access to everything, doesn't mean you need it. People feel better about not having to see everything. Being able to zoom in and out from the larger picture is important.
- Clutter stops you from breakthrough thinking. Anything that helps you organize your thinking is going to take you to a higher level.
- It's a lot easier to succeed when something is designed to help you get in, get what you need, and get out.
- Make it easier for people to find their own way and they'll be successful more often.
- Work backwards from what people need to work smarter. Most everyone is a lot smarter than we are letting them be.

The opposite of simplicity is complexity. An example of an overbearing management system was with Union Carbide. Union Carbide was a leading international chemical company that was formed in 1898. On December 3, 1984, a major gas release of methyl isocyanate occurred in Bhopal, India, resulting in the deaths of thousands of people. This began a downward spiral for Union Carbide, eventually ending when Dow Chemical purchased the company in 2000.

I met with the CEO of Union Carbide, Bill Joyce, during the transition process to becoming part of Dow. I asked about his concerns and any suggestions he may have had. He said that following the tragic Bhopal incident, the board of directors had directed the company to create an extensive management system of requirements and then insist on full compliance across the organization. The problem was that the system became overly complex and took requirements to a degree with which it was almost impossible to comply.

In addition, the company hired an external firm to conduct extensive audits of system compliance. It was the kiss of death for a plant manager to not pass a compliance audit of their facility. Mr. Joyce said the system had become so overbearing that the people spent considerable time focused on passing audits instead of running their facilities efficiently.

This poorly designed system of overbearing standards and severe consequences for noncompliance was one of the factors that led to the company's demise. A management system needs to be an enabler for the organization and increase efficiency, not one that creates unnecessary work and drags people down.

EXCELLENCE NUGGET:
*Making the complex seem
simple is powerful.*

Improving the Consistency of Work

Progressing through each company in my career, I increasingly understood the power of standardization and simplicity. We worked to reduce our number of requirements, improved clarity of each requirement, and increased the focus on full compliance. To provide some examples, and perhaps some similar to your current situation, I'll describe a few of my experiences.

At my summer job with Exxon in 1974, I was working at the huge gas processing plant on the famous King Ranch near Kingsville, Texas. Exxon had a series of company-wide operating manuals for gas processing. The manuals were written in a practical manner and were easy to understand. Every gas plant in Exxon relied on the knowledge and information in these manuals.

ExxonMobil was an early leader in the use of standardized management systems. The company's system is called the Operations Integrity Management System (OIMS) and is well known across the industry. I'm confident that OIMS is one of the primary enablers of ExxonMobil's long-term operational success.

At Dow Chemical, the company had a long history of a good management system. The system was called the Operating Discipline Management System (ODMS). In addition, the company had a concept of global expertise centers consisting of subject matter experts accountable for the rules, processes, and technology in their particular area. These expertise centers were charged with collecting and communicating best practices across the organization and were extremely effective.

When I became Vice President of EH&S at Dow, I began to understand how some of our global standards and requirements had become too complicated and detailed, making compliance very difficult. We soon began work to improve the clarity and understanding of the requirements in our management system, making them all as practical as we could.

When I arrived at Shell in 2004, I found that the company governance structure was quite different. Royal Dutch Shell was a joint venture with numerous independent subsidiaries and the organization was managed by a "Committee of Managing Directors." The company was known as the Royal Dutch Shell Group of Companies (the Group). The legal guidance was that the parent joint venture organization could not dictate requirements for the "independent" operating subsidiaries. Each of the operating companies had full autonomy—quite the opposite from my experience at Exxon and Dow.

The lack of a standardized approach and consistency across the organization resulted in significant problems. In 2003, a year before I joined Shell, the company had experienced a major setback when the Securities and Exchange Commission

(SEC) found that the company had been accounting for oil and gas reserves differently in various countries. Shell had to significantly restate its reserves, resulting in a 20% reduction, the company stock taking a major hit, and the termination of the Chairman of the Committee of Managing Directors and Executive Vice President of Upstream. There was significant value destruction.

The SEC determined that Shell could no longer operate with such global inconsistency and noncompliance with the rules. As a result, Shell began to hire global functional leaders, such as myself, to improve global functions and drive global consistency. In 2005, the joint venture was abolished, and Royal Dutch Shell became one company with a single CEO for the entire organization for the first time. The result was a green light for global consistency, and we wasted no time moving forward and driving standardization across the company.

One of the first examples was in preventing motor vehicle accidents, which had been a major cause of injuries. Motor vehicles included trucks delivering products as well as individual vehicles. Shell had over 20,000 trucks on the road daily delivering gasoline, jet fuel, and other products. Everything at Shell was huge. I commissioned a small team to develop a safe driving standard. The first draft the team presented to me was 67 pages. However, I wanted a much shorter document, one that every driver would actually read and remember.

I sent the team back a couple of times to tighten up the document. I said that no one would read a long document and the documents wouldn't change behavior. One of the team members finally said, "Sam, I think I've got it. You want the Ten Commandments, not the Bible!" I chuckled and said, "That's right. You have it."

The final document was simple and was only a handful of pages. The new document contained only the most important requirements that every driver could easily understand and follow. This new safe driving standard was the beginning of our simplification process for requirements at Shell.

By the time I was recruited to LyondellBasell in 2009, I had reached full stride in our approach to Operational Excellence. LyondellBasell had been created in early 2008 when Basell (a private Dutch company) purchased Lyondell (a publicly traded U.S. company). This transaction occurred just prior to the economic crisis of 2008 and the merger quickly failed. The company declared bankruptcy in early 2009. The two companies had never fully integrated and very little consistency in the management system and associated processes existed.

Legacy Lyondell had a complex set of overbearing documents with many requirements. Legacy Basell had a handful of optional guidelines. The performance results of the company were not up to expectations. A significant process safety incident was occurring every other week in which the primary cause was either noncompliance or not following a well-known requirement in another part of the company.

We knew that to truly achieve progress in overall performance, it would take a concerted multifunctional approach to simplify the management system, develop standards, implement work processes, eliminate variation, and drive performance improvement. In addition, by a focus on Operational Excellence and driving a Goal ZERO culture leading with safety, we knew we would achieve benefits in reliability, quality, cost control, and many other areas.

Leadership Alignment

The creation or enhancement of a management system requires alignment among leadership. This applies to company executives or leaders in departments. One of the first actions in my Global Vice President role at LyondellBasell was to form an Operational Excellence Leadership Team (OELT) consisting of the heads of manufacturing, human resources, legal, business, and myself. I led the team, and we had the full and complete support from the CEO. We wanted to break down the barriers between functions and align on our approach to Operational Excellence. The team discussed any new standards, rules, and processes that were developed. The OELT provided me with the perfect forum for bringing the key leaders along in the process and in proactively working through obstacles and issues.

Remember that with a Goal ZERO mentality, compliance is mandatory, and requirements typically have people, legal, and cost implications. Don't create a rule or requirement unless you expect full compliance—be reasonable. And, certainly, don't add new requirements every time an individual fails to conduct his or her work properly. Don't punish and bog down the entire organization because of the actions of one person.

Human resources representation was critical at the table since so much of Operational Excellence is based on human factors. Business representation on the team was vital because a cost was often associated with any new requirement, and it was important to have their understanding and support from the very beginning.

Strict prioritization, simplification, and clarification was emphasized at every step along the way as we updated and created management system documents. I personally reviewed and edited every line of every revised standard to make sure all content was fit for purpose. I worked hard to cull out lower priority items and reduce complexity. I used my years of plant management experience and always asked the question, "Would I be comfortable with this requirement if I were a plant manager?"

As our people began to develop our management system, we first created a list of Operational Excellence Expectations to guide the organization (Chapter 4). Then we developed an entirely new set of global standards, initiated new work processes, and began to empower the various functional groups. We created an approach in which the requirements were succinct and easy to understand.

All of this effort led to the creation of our management system, which we called Technology and Knowledge Management (TKM). We created a series of Excellence Models within each major category of work. I'll describe the Excellence Models later in this chapter. The Excellence Models contained the priority information associated with each topic: technology, mandatory standards, procedures, best practices, work processes, training information, and reference material. Once we established a good Management System, we were able to focus on flawless execution and driving rapid transformation of performance improvement.

Categories for a Management System

Organization of your management system is extremely important. Think of it as cleaning out a storage area and then putting things back in an orderly manner. Management systems can be organized in a variety of manners. The easiest way is to group items into "Management System Categories" that are intuitive and make sense for your organization. If your company is small, you might not have many categories. The number of categories can grow as the company grows. Each category can have several sections. An "Excellence Model" is then created for each section.

Here is an example for a manufacturing company. Remember, the documents within each category section describe how work should be done.

Management System Categories (Manufacturing Example)

1. **Technology**
   This category documents the technology for "how" to produce your particular product or provide your service. Excellence models might include:
   a. Polyethylene
   b. Epoxy
   c. Glycerine
2. **Operations and Support**
   This category of the management system includes standards and operating practices that are common across all of your various process technologies. Excellence Models include:
   a. Common operating practices
   b. Maintenance
   c. Reliability
   d. Turnarounds
   e. Capital projects
   f. Energy
   g. Utilities

3. **Asset Integrity**

   The Asset Integrity category includes standards, processes, and procedures for design, maintenance, inspection of your equipment and facilities. Excellence Models include:

   a. Stationary equipment
   b. Machinery
   c. Instruments and analyzers
   d. Electrical
   e. Utilities
   f. Engineering standards

4. **Health, Safety, Environment, Security and Quality**

   Functional activities are included in this category. Excellence Models include:

   a. Personal safety
   b. Process safety
   c. Product safety
   d. Quality
   e. Environmental
   f. Industrial hygiene
   g. Medical
   h. Security

5. **Talent Management**

   The management system is the perfect place to document work processes for the human resources function. The people component for achieving Operational Excellence is essential and full alignment is key. Example topics include recruiting, hiring, onboarding, training, talent development, succession planning, and leadership assessment.

6. **Include additional support functions** such as procurement, supply chain, etc., as appropriate.

Excellence Models

An Excellence Model is developed for each section within the management system categories. The Excellence Model includes prioritized documentation, information, and collective knowledge. The Excellence Models are organized in a consistent manner for ease of access and utilization. Each Excellence

Model looks and feels the same, so people in the organization become comfortable and competent at using the system and finding information.

Establish a Tier 1, Tier 2, and Tier 3 framework for organizing material in each Excellence Model. Include a section in each Excellence Model listing people with appropriate levels of expertise. A typical Excellence Model will have these components:

Tier 1 (Mandatory)
- Critical few documents and requirements
- Standards, policies, procedures, and mandatory processes

Tier 2 (Recommended)
- Highly encouraged work practices and processes
- Users have flexibility to deviate if they can meet the intent in other ways

Tier 3 (Reference)
- Tools, templates, examples, and lessons learned
- Educational material
- Support information
- Past incidents and learnings
- Metrics and key performance indicators

Excellence Model Resources
- Excellence Model owners
- Excellence Model teams
- Extended networks
- Individuals with expertise

Separating the mandatory from the recommended materials is extremely powerful. This separation provides clarity for the organization and helps to enable Goal ZERO performance. Excellence Models contain the information necessary to establish consistency across the organization. Local sites and departments follow the same format for their site-specific Tier 1, 2, and 3 documents. Detailed procedures, local rules, and processes are included in the site-specific section of the Excellence Models.

It's amazing how much a consistent framework and way of working can help the effectiveness of an organization. Once the Excellence Model framework is established, work becomes much more efficient. For the first time, document generators know how and where to store their documents. And, more importantly, users know how to find and use them.

Excellence Model Roles and Responsibilities

The power of the overall concept that I am describing is the *alignment and interaction of subject matter experts and users with the management system*. A clear owner must be assigned for each Excellence Model. In a large company, the owner can be assisted by an Excellence Model Team. The individuals on the team must be active and have very clear role responsibilities that include prioritizing, writing, maintaining, and updating the information in the Excellence Model.

The Excellence Model Owner and Team sort through all existing documentation, prioritize information, simplify each document, and insert the prioritized documents into the Excellence Model framework. The benefit is that you can begin utilizing the Excellence Model concept rather quickly. You probably already have more available documents than you need, but many may be too complex. Strict prioritization and simplification are essential steps in the process.

The following includes some important roles for a large company. For smaller organizations, the teams and networks may not be necessary. In almost all cases, these roles are part-time. Use caution to not create additional full-time functional overhead.

- **Management System Owner.** This person has overall responsibility for coordinating the development and maintenance of the management system.
- **Excellence Model Owner.** This individual has the sole ownership of the Excellence Model. If more than one person owns it, nobody owns it.
- **Excellence Model Team.** Each Excellence Model has a team to work with the owner to develop and maintain the Excellence Model. The members of the team are expected to "do work and contribute," not just attend meetings. Each person has specific assignments.

- **Excellence Model Extended Network.** This group of interested individuals for the topic is used for two-way communication and collaboration.
- **Site Excellence Model Focal Point.** This individual at each location is responsible and accountable for transferring the Excellence Model information within the site.

It's important to assign an overall owner for the company's management system. Every Excellence Model should be created with the same methodology and format. The owner is critical to keep progress moving in a consistent manner. Coaching the Excellence Model Owners and their teams is important so that these individuals continue to deliver products consistently and meet desired expectations.

With the advent of the new Excellence Model System and assigned owners, we fundamentally changed the way our subject matter experts worked. The subject matter experts became much more proactive. Each Excellence Model Owner and Excellence Model Team had the accountability to develop and update their Excellence Model. The owner and teams received and monitored company performance relative to their particular Excellence Model. No longer were these subject matter experts judged only for what they knew, but also for how well they contributed to the Excellence Model and how well the organization performed in their area of focus.

By tracking the progress of each Excellence Model Team and with assigned due dates for completion, technical organizations have a new sense of urgency for driving progress. Excellence Model Team agendas are proactively created to review and update the various documents in the Excellence Model. Each team member is expected to actively contribute and should be given a small percentage of time by his or her supervisor to work on the Excellence Model Team activities.

Work does not stop with the development of the Excellence Models. Utilize the Learning from Experience Process (Chapter 5) to capture learnings and continually improve the system. The Excellence Models make it easy and efficient to capture input from a variety of sources. The Excellence Model Owners review incident investigations and audits to determine areas for improvement within their section of the management system. In addition, anyone in the organization is encouraged to submit good ideas or learnings from various sources into the system which then are routed to the right Excellence Model Owner and associated team.

The Excellence Model design aligns the management system with the technical people in the organization. This structure provides career growth opportunities for technical professionals that should be integrated into your people management process.

If you are a person new to the organization, the employee value proposition becomes clear. As you gain expertise in a particular area, you can be assigned to a Site Excellence Model Focal Point position, and, in doing so, become a member of the Excellence Model Network. As you continue to grow, you can advance to become a member of the Excellence Model Team. Finally, you might even be chosen as the company Excellence Model Owner. Development opportunities and succession planning in the technical community become much easier and intuitive to manage.

The Excellence Model Owners have considerable responsibility and should be given visible recognition. The position should become one that others aspire to achieve. Depending on the size of your organization and the number of Excellence Models, you might be able to assign a different person as the owner for each model. In all cases, create clear expectations of responsibility and ownership. These responsibilities and expectations help raise the self-esteem of the professional community through their visible and proactive contributions to Operational Excellence. Every Excellence Model contributes to the overall success of the company.

Prioritize and Minimize the Number of Documents

The next few sections deal with making your management system as user friendly as possible. This requires the system and document owners to work with a culture of prioritization, simplification, and clarification.

An Excellence Model consists of Tier 1, 2, and 3 documents. For any topic, an endless number of documents are available from many sources, both internal and external to the organization. Anyone can cram existing documents into these tiers and overload the system, but this makes it difficult for the user. Lack of prioritization is a huge mistake; it's easy but ineffective. Rigorous prioritization and simplification of documents are key to effective utilization and execution.

The responsibility of the Excellence Model Owner and the Excellence Model Team is to strictly prioritize and limit the number of documents that are included in Tiers 1, 2, and 3 of the Excellence Model. These individuals should play a very strong gatekeeper role. Figure 5 is a graphical description for managing Tier 1, 2, and 3 information.

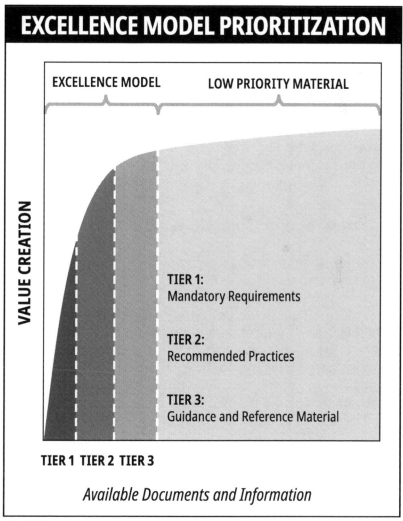

FIGURE 5: EXCELLENCE MODEL PRIORITIZATION

Note that only the most important, value creating documents are included in the Excellence Model. The potential documents for an excellence model should be ranked from left to right by their value creation. Think of the 80/20 model in which 20% of the information yields 80% of the results. Be selective and use strict prioritization for the material that gets added to the Excellence Model.

Failure to prioritize leads to inefficiency with the people using the system. A corollary is when you conduct an internet search for information. When you conduct the search, you'll get a large number of results. However, you must then sort through the documents to determine the ones that are accurate, important, and relevant. Sorting the important information from the less important is time consuming.

Utilizing Excellence Models should be different. The Excellence Model Owner and the Excellence Model Team should perform the prioritization work for the people in the organization. The owners and teams prioritize the most important documents and then insert them into the appropriate Tier 1, 2, or 3 section of the Excellence Model. Their prioritization work has a multiplying effect on productivity, accuracy, and effectiveness.

Prioritize and Minimize Document Content

In addition to minimizing the number of documents in an Excellence Model, it's important to minimize the length and amount of information in each document, especially for Tier 1 documents. Some authors of documents ramble on, adding additional information with not much effort put into prioritization and document structure to help the reader.

These authors believe that including everything possible is good when all of this material actually confuses the organization. The old quote applies perfectly, "I didn't have time to write you a short letter, so I wrote a long one instead."

Here are a few contrasting examples of document length:

1. The Lord's Prayer: 66 words
2. The 10 Commandments: 179 words
3. The Gettysburg Address: 286 words

4. The Declaration of Independence: 1,300 words
5. U.S. Government regulation on the sale of cabbage: 26,911 words

When creating mandatory standards, success lies in prioritizing and including only the critical few items that are most important and that people can understand and remember. Culling out lower priority potential requirements is difficult to do, but extremely important. Too many requirements in standards makes it almost impossible for people to comply with all of them. Employees inherently begin to decide for themselves which requirements in the standard are really important. Energy is spent on low priority items and the most critical requirements might end up with a low level of compliance. Lower priority items are better placed in Tier 2 recommended practice documents.

Shorter is always better and more effective. The challenge is getting everyone aligned on the same concepts. Provide a clear answer to the question, "What does good look like?" The authors and the users often have widely different concepts of a good and effective document.

- Technical authors typically want to be complete and not omit anything. Technical authors do their research, gather all the data they can, and believe it's all important.
- The users want documents to be short, clear, and concise. Users don't want someone else to explain what is intended or to interpret the definition of a particular requirement.

Figure 6 illustrates the point I am making when creating Tier 1 corporate mandatory standards.

Let's assume that this chart represents the potential requirements that could be included in an individual Tier 1 companywide standard. One hundred potential requirements are available to include in the standard and each item has been prioritized by value creation from left to right.

With no corporate standardization at all (left-hand side of the chart) and every location developing its own ways of doing work, the result is tremendous duplication of effort and considerable

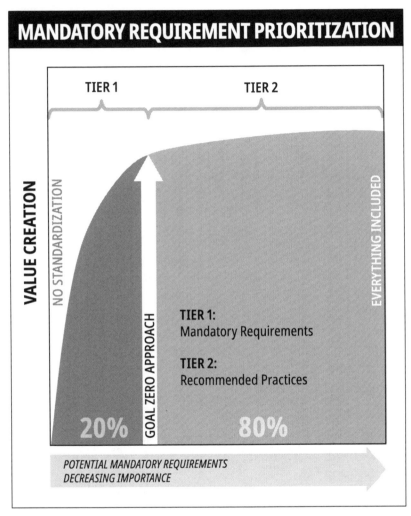

FIGURE 6: TIER 1 DOCUMENT CREATION (MANDATORY STANDARD)

variation in performance across the organization. People in these organizations spend more time determining "how" to do work at their particular location rather than focusing on delivering the product or service of the company.

On the other extreme, if the author includes all 100 potential requirements, which is commonly done in corporate standards, the document becomes onerous to read and impossible to comply with, destroying value. The user spends valuable time complying with low priority items on the right side of the chart and is likely to miss compliance with one of the higher priority ones. Technical individuals are often guilty of overloading the requirements in standards; they don't want to leave anything out.

The secret for a Goal ZERO organization is to be very disciplined in limiting the number of requirements that make it into a Tier 1 document. I would rather have 10 critical items in a standard that are 100% followed than 100 items with considerable noncompliance. Save the extra 90 items for recommended practices (Tier 2) and insist on full compliance of the 10 highest priority items for a Goal ZERO approach. Deliver a product the users want and will use, rather than everything the technical expert thinks is important.

As time goes on, resist the urge to add a new requirement in a Tier 1 document every time an incident occurs or someone creates an error. Don't punish the entire organization based on an individual's mistake. Be disciplined in regard to adding additional lower value requirements.

The people in your organization are smart and trust is important. Individuals can take the Tier 2 recommended practices and adopt them as requirements in their site management system or deviate depending on their particular situation. Once an item is written as a requirement, the requirement must be complied with at all times—Goal ZERO performance.

Finally, you don't need the commonly used legal phrase in every document, "Failure to comply will lead to discipline, up to and including discharge." The phrase may appear once in an overarching document and be omitted from the rest. Lawyers generally like the phrase, but the wording comes across as negative and a threat to people.

EXCELLENCE NUGGET:
Reduce complexity through disciplined prioritization.

Legal Implications

Managing risk and preventing legal liability is an important activity within each company. A Goal ZERO approach to eliminating incidents and defects is the best measure you can take to reduce liability.

It's also crucial to do what you say you are going to do. If you have a company standard of requirements, your people better be following all of the requirements. That's why strict prioritization of the requirements you include in standards and then 100% compliance is so important. You are creating legal liability for your company if there are excessive requirements that aren't followed across the organization.

An essential part of OSHA's process safety management standard is called "Recognized and Generally Accepted Good Engineering Practices" (RAGAGEP). Employers may select the RAGAGEP that applies to their operations. Widely accepted industry "standards" also serve as RAGAGEP. However, industry "guidance documents" can be problematic and be considered RAGAGEP if your company does not have its own company standard for a particular topic. A good practice is to review industry recommended practices and create your internal standard requirements based on the elements with which you expect full compliance.

Digitization of the System

Throughout this book, I describe methods for creating business value, improving quality, reducing customer incidents, enhancing safety performance, assuring compliance, and inspiring your workforce. A well-functioning Operational Excellence software system is essential to enhance and enable the efficiency, effectiveness, and execution of your management system. A good software system provides a digitized structure for aligning corporate and local information in an easy-to-use format. There is an avalanche of new technology on the market. Today's software technology can become a differentiating factor in your operations, with your employees, and with your customers.

Your organization, like all others, has a significant amount of information organized in many different ways. The key to a good functioning management system is to organize your documentation in a way that makes the information accessible by the people when they need it.

Bill Gates wrote a book entitled *Business @ the Speed of Thought*. I've always thought it's the perfect title for how we should conduct our business efficiently through the utilization of a good management system and excellent software technology. The technology exists such that people should always be able to access the prioritized information they need and then quickly execute their work. There should be one "source of truth" for data and information. People shouldn't waste time looking for information and trying to interpret it or determine what is most important. People shouldn't repeat the same mistakes of others or fail to capture value creating opportunities that others have identified.

Most companies have software systems that store documents, collect data, and manage information. Each one of these software systems serves its particular purpose, but has the overall system been developed from the users' perspective? Is the software easy to use and intuitive for the users to find the information they need quickly? Does the software serve as an enabler for your management system and provide real time feedback?

As we worked through our journey of achieving Operational Excellence, we realized that to achieve "Business @ the Speed of Thought," we needed to have an aligned set of software systems. It is essential to make information and data accessible and work across functions.

We wanted a system that would digitize and enhance our management system to drive performance improvement. Automated workflow for critical processes is much more effective than the use of email and spreadsheets. We brainstormed the characteristics for "the perfect software system" to aid in achieving Operational Excellence.

We evaluated the most popular public internet sites such as Google, Amazon, Facebook, and Twitter to determine why these software systems were successful. These sites don't require special training and are intuitive for the users, which is why they are so widely used. Software systems for industry should have the same characteristics.

Some important elements of a perfect Operational Excellence software system are:

- Provides a portal for all information
- Is intuitive and user friendly
- Is searchable

- Is cost effective
- Integrates with other systems
- Is fit for purpose: corporate level, site, or department level
- Breaks down barriers between functions: operations, EH&S, quality, human resources, etc.
- Connects people with other people
- Enhances compliance assurance
- Provides data analytics
- Utilizes artificial intelligence to speed progress
- Utilizes statistics to help drive desired behaviors
- Enables continuous updating and approval of the management system
- Generates management reports
- Increases accountability of subject matter experts and users
- Prioritizes information for the user
- Creates effective document control and records management
- Allows alignment of local and corporate requirements, preferred practices, and guidance documents

A good software system must be designed with the users in mind and the information each person in the organization needs to do his or her job. Document creators and Excellence Model Owners have a single place for receiving new information and documenting their work product. Users in the field have a single source of truth for information they need and can find information they need quickly.

The system serves as a portal for other existing software tools that store information. A good software system integrates management system documentation, previous incident and audit reports, performance data, chat functions, and employee information in an easy-to-use manner. People are incorporated in the system by aligning and connecting owners, teams, subject matter experts, and interested users associated with a particular Excellence Model. Everyone in the organization has the capability to submit ideas, suggestions, and new information into the system directed at the right individuals. This type of software system proves immensely valuable in keeping the management system continually updated.

Realtime statistical and benchmark data on specific behavioral aspects and their relationship on performance help drive the right behaviors in leaders and people across the organization. Statistics help identify the specific behaviors that drive performance improvement. Online evaluations by users of management system documents keep document writers linked to user demands and feedback.

An integrated Operational Excellence software tool that matches and enables the execution of your management system is powerful. By digitizing the elements of leadership, people, systems, and culture, a good functioning software system enhances the ability of people to conduct "Business @ the Speed of Thought" and drive rapid transformation.

EXCELLENCE NUGGET:
*Digitization technology can be
a significant process enabler.*

The Integrated Approach to a Management System

The bottom line of this chapter is to seamlessly integrate the management system with everyday work. The power is in the combination of the structure of each Excellence Model, the enabling Operational Excellence software system, a ZERO defect culture, and the right people with the proper skills and guidance. This combination provides an integrated platform for organizing documents, creating ease of access, improving contribution from experts, and continual use and updating of the system.

Begin by creating the framework for your management system. Determine the appropriate management system categories and the associated Excellence Models that should be developed. Focus on a few categories and Excellence Models to get started; you can add more as the process gains momentum. An Excellence Model should be developed for the sub processes of each global category in which all documentation, information, and collective knowledge is stored and maintained. The Excellence Models are organized in a consistent manner for ease of access and utilization. Each Excellence Model looks and feels the same so people in the organization become comfortable and competent in using the system.

A good functioning management system provides a consistent platform for leaders to lead and focus on execution. The system gets everyone on the same page regarding requirements and procedures. Consistent terminology and vocabulary are critical to avoid confusion in the organization, especially if you conduct business in countries with different native languages. Providing clarity and ease of understanding are motivational to the organization.

Once the companywide system is in place, locations can build on the framework and add details for how work should be done locally. The end result for the user in the field is a system that includes corporate and local requirements in an easy to use, aligned manner.

Finally, it's crucial to keep your management system up to date on a continuous basis. The Excellence Model owners and teams have this ongoing responsibility but everyone in the organization should provide input and suggestions for improvement. Make sure the documents in the system continually provide the guidance needed to help maintain the desired culture in the organization as well as enable leaders and people to do their very best. The management system should be alive and continually receive input from leaders and people through the Learning from Experience process.

Pulling It All Together in a Management System
A SUMMARY

- A management system is a documented collection of knowledge, lessons learned, best practices, processes, procedures, and key information. The system determines how work should be done and builds on past experience.

- The management system contains clear expectations for the organization which provides the foundation for establishing a culture of excellence.

- Remember simplicity when developing a management system. The system must be practical, fit for purpose, and fully endorsed by the people. Utilize strict prioritization for the items that get included in the system.

- A clear structure for the system and consistent Excellence Model design helps people to get information quickly.

- Roles and responsibilities for the management system must be clearly identified.

- A well designed Operational Excellence Software System will enable you to conduct business at the speed of thought.

CHAPTER 7

Summary—The Daily Pursuit of Excellence

"Perhaps the best test of a man's intelligence
is his capacity for making a summary."
– Lytton Strachey

I've captured many of the key learnings from my 50+ year career in this book. I wrote the book to help you learn from my experiences and to be successful throughout your career. You can be a leader and influence others at any level in the organization. Use the book as an ongoing reference, referring back to it often. Secure a copy for each of your team members.

The book is a compilation of successful practices combined in a comprehensive approach to driving improvement. The applicable audience is very broad—from new people on up to CEOs. Throughout the writing process, I performed deeper research into several of the topics and learned additional information that would have been extremely helpful earlier in my career. I've captured those new learnings throughout the book. Good people never stop learning.

I've always felt that if I could take away one or two learnings from a book, then buying and reading the book was worthwhile. My wish is that you will have gathered at least a few tips in this book that will help you in your career and make your company better. You should be able to achieve improved reliability, quality, cost control, environmental performance, enhanced customer satisfaction, and safety.

I was blessed to have a unique career: leading manufacturing operations for the first half and leading global EH&S and Operational Excellence during the second half. We found that the actions required for good safety performance applied to everything else: product quality, reliability, cost control, people leadership, and on and on. Leading with a focus on safety makes sense to everyone and drives Operational Excellence progress which in turn leads to business value creation.

I've explained how everything falls under the leadership, people, systems, and culture aspects of the Operational Excellence Model. People can understand this model which provides a balanced approach for improvement. Any organization can have assets, management systems, and a good strategy, but the differentiator is how well people execute and deliver excellence.

Everything begins with strong leadership. Superior leaders know and understand how to attract, develop, inspire, and motivate the people around them. Creating pride in the organization and an attitude of winning will deliver best-in-class results. Leaders must communicate a compelling vision, create a winning culture, provide the resources needed for success, and drive progress through a well-established management system.

Leaders who are highly visible in the workplace are the most effective; talking with and listening to their people. People appreciate knowing that you care about them, their welfare, and what they do each day. People are most motivated when they are future focused and fully understand the direction of the company and its objectives.

Communication is such an important part of being an outstanding leader. People in an organization and other stakeholders want to know what's going on and must be kept updated. Fine-tune your communication skills in the various communication modes such as person to person, group settings, email, social media, newsletters, videos, etc. Never leave people in the dark, especially during challenging times.

A Goal ZERO culture is simple and yet so powerful. Goal ZERO establishes a very clear expectation for the kind of performance that is expected. Goal ZERO applies to all areas of an organization as well as to each individual. Goal ZERO is a concept that says we expect zero defects, zero incidents, zero rule breaking, zero noncompliance, zero quality incidents, zero injuries, and zero missed opportunities that create significant value. In other words, employees should strive for perfection recognizing they will hit excellence along the way.

I discussed the importance that results focused leaders place on a robust management system. The management system is equivalent to the bare wood when you are doing a home remodeling job; you need something foundational upon which to build. A good functioning management system that is updated continually and followed consistently will assure that you never have to "go back to the basics" again.

I covered the importance of developing Excellence Models. Excellence Models contain documented best practices for a particular topic that are continually updated. A good Operational Excellence software system enables the continuous improvement process and the ability to conduct your business "at the speed of thought."

Excellence Model owners should be carefully selected, and their performance monitored. No longer are these roles just filled with subject matter experts who respond to problems. These individuals must have the skills and abilities to document and communicate their information in a clear and concise manner understandable to others. The Global Excellence Model framework provides excellent growth opportunities for technical professional individuals.

I hope you understand by now that I'm a strong advocate of consistent terminology and consistency of purpose. It's effective to choose consistent terminology and "elevator speech" messaging, and then repeat the messages over and over. It takes time in an organization for people to understand new information. Stay away from programs of the month and be consistent over the long haul. That's the way to build a culture of excellence.

Simplicity is a prevailing theme throughout the book. Most things are too complicated and need to be simplified. Take the time to write documents the right way and use the Flesch Reading Ease Score method to measure results. Simplicity applies to work processes, procedures, standards, guidance documents, and so many other concepts. Remember, if you can't explain your message simply, then you don't understand it well enough.

Many people have asked me what I would do if I was to join a new company needing improvement. My first actions would be to meet the people, learn all I could about the company, and then work with the team to determine what is working well and what needs improvement. Beyond these initial actions, I've developed a roadmap below that I would follow, using the change management process described earlier. This book includes details on each of the steps. I would follow this roadmap and close gaps as necessary. Effective communication and interaction at every step along the way would be critical. I hope this roadmap will be useful for you.

The Roadmap for Achieving Excellence

1. Define the **Case for Change and a Clear Vision for the Future.**
2. Develop a **Communications Strategy** for the concepts of the Operational Excellence Model—Leadership, People, Systems, and Culture
3. Establish a **ZERO Defect Mentality and Culture.**
4. Develop a set of **Operational Excellence Expectations.**
5. Create the framework for the **Management System.**
6. **Digitize the System** to connect people and the system to accelerate improvement.
7. **Assign the Right People** for ownership of the Excellence Models. Establish clear roles and responsibilities for developing, updating, and utilizing the Excellence Models.
8. **Simplify Documentation and Build the Excellence Models.**
9. **Routinely Roll Out New Documents to the Organization** and close gaps at each location.
10. **Execute, Continually Update the System, and Celebrate Success.**

Throughout this book I talked about the importance of humility. Many of you could have written a similar book. I have suggested ways to achieve Operational Excellence, but absolutely there is more than one way. You may disagree with some of the concepts I've described and that's okay; diversity of thought is good. Work hard, do your best, be proud of your progress, but never be satisfied with how well you are doing.

Take your work seriously, but not yourself. Enjoy your life and remain balanced; remember the Seven Fs. If you have a good succession planning process in your company, the company will be just fine after you leave. You only live once, but if you do it right, once is enough.

As I end this book, I'd like to share a poem I enjoy that puts everything into perspective.

"Indispensable Man"
by Saxon White Kessinger

Sometime when you're feeling important;
Sometime when your ego's in bloom
Sometime when you take it for granted
You're the best qualified in the room,

Sometime when you feel that your going
Would leave an unfillable hole,
Just follow these simple instructions
And see how they humble your soul;

Take a bucket and fill it with water,
Put your hand in it up to the wrist,
Pull it out and the hole that's remaining
Is a measure of how you'll be missed.

You can splash all you wish when you enter,
You may stir up the water galore,
But stop and you'll find that in no time
It looks quite the same as before.

The moral of this quaint example
Is to just be the best that you can,
Be proud of yourself but remember,
There's no indispensable man.

In closing, I have enjoyed writing this book more than I ever imagined. Like they say, writing the book was a labor of love and it took many, many hours to write—but it's been rewarding. All the best to you in your Goal ZERO journey and your daily pursuit of excellence, superior performance, and protecting people! **Thanks for your attention.**

EXCELLENCE NUGGETS

Sam's Favorite Quotes

*"A journey of a thousand miles
must begin with a single step."*
– Lao Tzu 600BC

*"You cannot be disciplined in great things
and undisciplined in small things."*
– General George Patton

"Autograph your work with Excellence."
– Linda Wallace

*"If you don't execute well,
it doesn't matter what your strategy is."*
– Tom Peters

*"The bitterness of poor quality remains long after
the sweetness of low price is forgotten."*
– Benjamin Franklin

*"Great leaders are almost always great simplifiers,
who can cut through argument, debate and doubt,
to offer a solution everybody can understand."*
– Colin Powell

*"The person who says it cannot be done
should not interrupt the person doing it."*
– Chinese proverb

"Fall seven times, get up eight."
– Japanese proverb

*"It's better to be safe 100 times
rather than get killed once."*
– Mark Twain

"When I go into a situation,
I take the attitude that "I don't know."
If I go in thinking "I know," then I don't learn anything."
– Albert Einstein

"The day soldiers stop bringing you their problems
is the day you have stopped leading them."
– Colin Powell

"Treat every man as he is, and he will remain as he is.
Treat a man as he can and should be
and he will become what he can and should be."
– Goethe

"If it goes good as a team, they did it.
If it goes okay as a team, we did it.
If it goes bad as a team, I did it."
– Coach Paul "Bear" Bryant

"Most people are about as happy as
they make up their mind to be."
– Abraham Lincoln

"Luck is a dividend of sweat.
The more you sweat, the luckier you get."
– Ray Kroc

"Enjoy life—it has an expiration date."
– Zayn Malik

"Experience is a hard teacher because
she gives the test first, the lesson afterward."
– Vernon Law

"Never miss a good chance to shut up."
– Will Rogers

"Life is tough,
but it's tougher when you're stupid."
– John Wayne

Bibliography

1. Ayub, Mohammad. "Investigation of the March 15, 2008, Fatal Tower Crane Collapse at 303 East 51st Street, New York, NY." US Department of Labor, Occupational Health and Safety Administration, Directorate of Construction, September 2008.

2. Belitz, Justin. *Success: Full Living. Knowledge Systems,* 1991.

3. Csikszentmihalyi, Mihaly. *Flow - The Psychology of Optimal Experience.* New York: Harper & Row Publishers, 1990.

4. Daniels, Aubrey C. *Bringing Out the Best in People: How to Apply the Astonishing Power of Positive Reinforcement.* New York: McGraw Hill, 1994.

5. Deming, W. Edwards. *Out of the Crisis.* Cambridge, Massachusetts: Massachusetts Institute of Technology, Center for Advanced Engineering Study, 1982.

6. Denny, Richard. *Motivate to Win: How to Motivate Yourself and Others to Really Get Results.* Kogan Page, 2009.

7. Flesch, Rudolph F. *How to Write in Plain English: A Book for Lawyers and Consumers.* New York: Barnes and Noble Books, 1979.

8. Gray, William S. and Leary, Bernice E. *What Makes a Book Readable?* Chicago: The University of Chicago Press, 1935.

9. Jensen, Bill. *Simplicity: The New Competitive Advantage in a World of More, Better, Faster.* Cambridge, Massachusetts: Perseus Publishing, 2000.

10. Klare, George R. and Buck, Byron. *Know Your Reader: The Scientific Approach to Readability.* New York: Hermitage House, 1954.

11. Kincaid, J.P., Fishburne, R.P., Rogers, R.L., & Chissom, B.S. "Derivation of new readability formulas (automated readability index, fog count, and Flesch reading ease formula) for Navy enlisted personnel." Research Branch Report 8-75. Chief of Naval Technical Training: Naval Air Station Memphis. 1975.

12. LyondellBasell. "Operational Excellence Management System Expectations." March 2015.
13. Martin, Roger L. "M&A: The One Thing You Need to Get Right." Harvard Business Review, June 2016.
14. Maslow, Abraham H. "A Theory of Human Motivation." Psychological Review, 1943.
15. Michaels, Dr. David. "7 Ways to Improve Operations Without Sacrificing Safety." Harvard Business Review, March 21, 2018.
16. Piasecki, Bruce. *Doing More with Teams: The New Way to Winning.* New York: Square One Publishers, 2016.
17. Spear, Steven J. *The High Velocity Edge: How Market Leaders Leverage Operational Experience to Beat the Competition.* New York: McGraw Hill Education, 2009.

About the Author

As I look back, my values were heavily shaped by my parents, my faith, the Boy Scouts, and my competitive spirit from playing sports. Values are embedded in each of us at a very early stage in our lives.

Our childhood shapes who we become. I grew up in the very small town of Newgulf, Texas. Newgulf was a company town of around 1,000 people with all of the white houses on blocks owned by the company, Texasgulf Sulphur Company. The Newgulf site was the largest sulphur-producing dome in the world with up to 15,000 tons of sulphur produced and shipped each day.

We had six children in our family; I was the oldest and had five younger, wonderful sisters—Lou Ann, Gayle, Jackie, Gina, and Lisa. I believe being the oldest of six children taught me a sense of responsibility that lasted my entire life. We had, and still have, a loving and close family and growing up in Newgulf was wonderful.

We had enough money for the basics, but that was about it. The town was loaded with pecan trees, so we picked pecans every fall to earn spending money. We looked for discarded soft drink bottles to cash them in for 2 cents each. I looked for work at every opportunity—putting circulars on doors from the local grocery store, mowing yards, washing cars, preparing the Little League baseball field prior to games, and hauling thousands of bales of hay each summer as I got older.

My dad was an athlete. He was fast; in fact, he won the Texas State Championship in hurdles in high school and went on to star as a running back at Wharton County Junior College and North Texas State, now called University of North Texas. In adult life, his entire focus was on raising his family. He and I spent a lot of time hunting and fishing. This time together developed my great love for conservation and the outdoors. He also devoted his time to coaching our Little League baseball teams and as a Boy Scout leader. He was highly competitive and expected us to be the best at all times and to win.

My mother was loving and instilled unconditional love in each of us. She was smart and was always there with a smiling face, helping and encouraging us. I miss them both and will forever be grateful for their guidance and support throughout my life.

I believe parents have the most influence over their children until around 12 years of age. Children's values, attitudes, and behaviors are largely established by then and parenting becomes more of coaching and persuasion after that. So, parents, begin from day one and make the most of those first 12 years.

My parents encouraged us to participate in as many activities as we could manage. Participation in multiple activities was easier back in those days growing up in a small town and attending a small school. Our parents expected us to make top grades in school and to always do our best. One incentive was free baseball tickets provided by the Houston Astros if you made straight A's the entire school year.

We were fortunate in Newgulf to have a youth golf organization with the clever name, "Divot Diggers." One of the local men, Harry Norrell, had a passion for youth and ran the club. Mr. Norrell spent a lot of personal time and energy helping us to learn the finer aspects of golf. One principle he instilled was attention to detail even when practicing—make every swing count. Treat each putt during practice as just important as the final putt of a tournament. My claim to fame in golf was playing in the same Texas High School State Championship Tournament as Ben Crenshaw (although we never met each other).

Another principle Mr. Norrell taught was being able to remain calm during competition and adversity. He taught this lesson by constantly creating a competitive environment. After school, we would have small contests for putting, chipping, driving, or any aspect of the game. The prize was typically a hamburger or a milkshake at the local cafe which was a real treat for us. His real objective was to treat practice the same as a competitive event and this experience served us well for the many tournaments in which we participated.

I loved my Boy Scout Days and proudly earned the rank of Eagle Scout. I progressed into leadership positions from a very early age. In Boy Scouts, I achieved Patrol Leader and then Senior Patrol Leader of the troop. I was pitcher on our baseball teams, played quarterback on our high school football team, played in a dance band, and held numerous officer positions in high school and college organizations. I became fascinated with the concepts of leadership, excellence, and how to get the best out of people. This fascination has remained with me throughout my life.

I paid my own way through college by earning scholarships, working summer and part-time jobs, and taking out a modest student loan which I paid back over the next 10 years. I received a Bachelor of Science degree in Chemical Engineering at The University of Texas. I had terrific friends in college, and we were all in a similar situation, with not much extra spending money. On spring break, for example, we never even thought about going to Cancun or any other hot spot. We were out hustling some work to make a little extra spending money. In the long run, we all look back and know that needing money didn't hurt us. In fact, this experience helped shape our behaviors and work ethics for the rest of our lives.

I've always had a strong sense of curiosity in a wide variety of topics. I enjoy learning about techniques that motivate people and how to make things better. I tend to face problems in a positive manner, not only addressing the problem at hand but naturally focusing on how to make improvements. In a strange way, I see difficulties as an opportunity to get better.

My colleagues have described me as being extremely persistent. It's true—I don't give up easily. Driving change takes persistence since most people are resistant to change. If you believe strongly in something or have a clear vision of what needs to be done, never give up.

I loved the people I worked with and always tried to show the same respect for our cleaning staff as I would for any top-level executive (the cleaning staff employees were actually a lot more fun). Every person tried to do his or her best and I always appreciated that fact. Although I relocated a few times, I still remember the people I worked with at each location and the contributions they made to our success. I have long lasting friends in many countries around the world that I can call tomorrow for help or just to have a friendly conversation.

I had a relatively unique career. The first half consisted of research and manufacturing plant leadership roles. I was able to obtain one United States patent. I had a reputation for improving a plant's operation and the morale of the workforce. As a result, I was "rewarded" by being sent to a number of manufacturing plants with significant problems. These plants required a lot of hard work, but, in the end, these experiences prepared me well.

During the last 20 years of my career, I was given the opportunity by the three companies I worked for to lead the global Environment, Safety, Health, Security, Operational Excellence, and Sustainable Development functions. Leading these global functions was a major change for me.

On the one hand, driving performance improvement for tens of thousands of individuals in countries all over the world was a huge challenge. On the other hand, I found it easy since I had been in the shoes of the many people that I was now expected to influence. Leading the global function was the first opportunity in which I had the time to focus on the finer aspects of human behavior, organizational efficiency, culture, the power of management systems, and working through influence of others to drive improvement. I found it extremely rewarding to set ambitious goals, provide leadership, create the system, and observe a paradigm shift in performance that we expected from our people around the world. The most gratifying aspect was the number of injuries we prevented around the world and the lives we potentially saved.

During each of my assignments, I had a passion for learning and for leadership. Throughout the years, I worked to capture these learnings and build on them with each successive assignment. The companies that I worked for included:

- **Summer jobs with Texasgulf Sulphur Company, Atlantic Richfield (ARCO) and Exxon**
- **The Dow Chemical Company**
  - Research, Manufacturing, and Global Vice President— Environment, Health, Safety, Security, and Sustainable Development
- **Shell**
  - Global Vice President—Downstream Environment, Health, Safety, and Sustainable Development

- **LyondellBasell Industries**
  - Senior Vice President—Americas Manufacturing and Global Vice President—Environment, Health, Safety, Security, and Operational Excellence

Since my retirement, I have remained active in the industry and serve on one public and one private company board of directors. I provide a small amount of consulting associated with the materials in my books. I stay technically stimulated by serving as a member of the Dean's Engineering Advisory Board at The University of Texas.

I have chosen to spend the majority of my volunteer efforts with Ducks Unlimited, the world's leader in wetlands and waterfowl conservation. I serve on the board of directors and numerous sub committees. Wetlands and associated habitats are rapidly vanishing due to population growth, storms, and many other factors. My children and grandchildren share my passion for the outdoors and I want to do whatever I can to help protect these precious resources for them and future generations. Wetlands provide needed habitat for migratory birds and provide many public sustainability and ESG (Environment, Social, and Governance) benefits such as water purification, ground water recharge, flood control, and carbon capture. Ducks Unlimited is an outstanding organization and I was proud to receive the Ducks Unlimited Conservation Stewardship Award in 2021.

I remain as busy as ever enjoying life and creating Flow. I'm a firm believer that people who retire to the rocking chair don't rock very long. I remain faithful to God and am ready for what comes next. I love hanging out with my family and friends and spending a lot of time outdoors. Staying in good shape is a priority. Having fun is always high on the list. Balance is key.

Made in the USA
Columbia, SC
11 September 2022

66813878R20150